Peacemakers

CRITICAL HISTORICAL ENCOUNTERS

Series Editors
James Kirby Martin
David M. Oshinsky
Randy W. Roberts

Peacemakers

....

The Iroquois, the United States,
and the Treaty of Canandaigua, 1794

MICHAEL LEROY OBERG

State University of New York at Geneseo

New York   Oxford

OXFORD UNIVERSITY PRESS

Oxford University Press is a department of the University of Oxford.
It furthers the University's objective of excellence in research,
scholarship, and education by publishing worldwide.

Oxford   New York
Auckland   Cape Town   Dar es Salaam   Hong Kong   Karachi
Kuala Lumpur   Madrid   Melbourne   Mexico City   Nairobi
New Delhi   Shanghai   Taipei   Toronto

With offices in
Argentina   Austria   Brazil   Chile   Czech Republic   France   Greece
Guatemala   Hungary   Italy   Japan   Poland   Portugal   Singapore
South Korea   Switzerland   Thailand   Turkey   Ukraine   Vietnam

Copyright © 2016 by Oxford University Press

For titles covered by Section 112 of the US Higher Education
Opportunity Act, please visit www.oup.com/us/he for the
latest information about pricing and alternate formats.

Published by Oxford University Press
198 Madison Avenue, New York, New York 10016
http://www.oup.com

Oxford is a registered trademark of Oxford University Press

The CIP Data is On-File at the Library of Congress.
ISBN: 978-0-19-991380-0

Printing number: 9 8 7 6 5 4 3 2 1

Printed in the United States of America
on acid-free paper

CONTENTS

....

The volumes in this Oxford University Press book series focus on major critical encounters in the American experience. The word *critical* refers to formative, vital, transforming events and actions that have had a major impact in shaping the ever-changing contours of life in the United States. *Encounter* indicates a confrontation or clash, often but not always contentious in character, but always full of profound historical meaning and consequence.

In this framework, the United States, it can be said, has evolved on contested ground. Conflict and debate, the clash of peoples and ideas, have marked and shaped American history. The first Europeans transported with them cultural assumptions that collided with Native American values and ideas. Africans forced into bondage and carried to America added another set of cultural beliefs that often were at odds with those of Native Americans and Europeans. Over the centuries America's diverse peoples differed on many issues, often resulting in formative conflict that in turn gave form and meaning to the American experience.

The Critical Historical Encounters series emphasizes formative episodes in America's contested history. Each volume contains two fundamental ingredients: a carefully written narrative of the encounter and the consequences, both immediate and long term, of that moment of conflict in America's contested history.

When the United States and the Six Nations of the Iroquois gathered in Canandaigua, New York, in the autumn of 1794, a great deal seemed to be at stake. Native American warriors in the Ohio Country—Shawnees, Delawares, and many others—had destroyed the American armies sent to subdue them in 1790 and 1791. Creeks and militant Chickamauga Cherokees held their own against aggressive frontier settlers and violent militias in the southern states. The British, meanwhile, continued to maintain forts on American soil, raising the daunting prospect that they might assist aggrieved Indians against the United States. The Iroquois shared the grievances of their native neighbors. They complained of coerced and fraudulent land cessions, of the relentless encroachment on their remaining territory by frontier settlers, and of a string of murders committed in southern New York and northwestern Pennsylvania. Should the Iroquois join this native resistance movement, the entire American frontier would be exposed.

The Treaty of Canandaigua, the resulting agreement, brought peace to the New York frontier, ended the threat that the Six Nations might align with the native nations in the Ohio Country, and helped to isolate the British posts. The treaty also recognized the Six Nations' right to the "free use and enjoyment" of their remaining lands. Of course, upholding these terms has not been easy, and the treaty has left an ambivalent legacy. Yet Iroquois people continue to live upon their homelands in New York state, and they invoke the Treaty of Canandaigua in defense of their rights and their autonomy as recognized nations in the modern United States.

ACKNOWLEDGMENTS

....

James Kirby Martin, my colleague during the brief year I spent beginning in 2009 at the University of Houston, invited me to contribute a volume relating to the history of the Haudenosaunee for his "Critical Historical Encounters" series at Oxford University Press. I did not stay in Houston, but I did stick with this project, and I am grateful to him for the opportunity. Jim offered important support and advice, but so did many other colleagues. My friends in the Department of History at SUNY Geneseo have always offered encouragement for my work, and the administration allowed me a sabbatical in the spring of 2014 that made it possible to complete a solid first draft. My talented students at SUNY Geneseo always have been ready and willing to debate the significance and insignificance of American Indian treaties, and from my conversations and discussions with them, I have learned a great deal indeed. David Silverman, Jon Parmenter, and James Rice read the manuscript, as did Nancy Shoemaker, Ronald Angelo Johnson, Chris Friday and Shawn Grant Weimann. Their comments, criticisms, and suggestions made this a stronger book, I'm sure. All of them set aside their own important work to look at mine. I am also grateful to Larry Hauptman, Steve Webb, Alyssa Mt. Pleasant, Paul Otto, Angela Workoff, Tom Callahan, and many others for conversations in person and online that helped me work through the issues that writing this book presented. Archivists and staff at the New York State Archives, the Holland Land Company collection at SUNY Fredonia, and the New York

Historical Society provided access to documents and illustrations. Ed Varno and Ray Shedrick at the Ontario County Historical Society in Canandaigua offered especially important assistance. Robert Odawi Porter, past president of the Seneca Nation of Indians, asked some of the questions, and provided the opportunities, that long ago first provoked my interest in the Treaty of Canandaigua and my belief that the subject was worthy of a book-length treatment.

At Oxford University Press, Brian Wheel and Gina Bocchetta helped steer the manuscript through the process toward publication, and they promptly replied to my emails. I appreciate all of their work in seeing this through to the end. My family tolerated the organized chaos that sometimes accompanies the process of researching and writing and revising a book. To them, as always, something much more is due than a mere "Thank you."

And a final note: Haudenosaunee people not only meet every November to commemorate the Treaty of Canandaigua but continue to act on its principles, including the recognition on the part of the United States of their preexisting right to the "free use and enjoyment" of their lands. It owes to the work of Haudenosaunee people over many decades that the Treaty of Canandaigua has not become yet another forgotten and ignored American Indian treaty. It is this important work, more than anything else, that made this book possible.

Michael Leroy Oberg
Rochester, New York

INTRODUCTION

·····················

Sixteen hundred Iroquois Indians, members of the Haudeno-saunee, or the Six Nations, came in the fall of 1794 to the recently settled frontier town of Canandaigua, in Ontario County, New York. They traveled there to meet with the commissioner appointed by the United States, Timothy Pickering, by now a man with some experience in conducting diplomacy with the Iroquois. Four Quakers from the Philadelphia Yearly Meeting of the Society of Friends attended the treaty as well, witnesses welcomed both by the United States and the Iroquois. Many others gathered there too, a motley collection of townspeople and traders, spies and mystics, to attend the council and observe a meeting where much indeed seemed to be at stake.

It was serious business. At the time the call went out from the American government to invite the Six Nations to a council, the United States feared that Iroquois warriors might join a powerful Indian confederacy north of the Ohio River that already had defeated two American armies. President George Washington and his advisers worried that the British, who still held forts on American soil, and whose own relationship with the new nation teetered on the edge of war, might ally with the Indians to set the American borderlands ablaze. With Creek and Cherokee warriors already attacking settlements in Georgia, the Carolinas, and Virginia, Washington feared that if the Iroquois joined with the Shawnees, Delawares, Miamis,

1

and others in the recently defined "Northwest Territory," the entire frontier, from the Great Lakes to the Gulf of Mexico, might come under attack.

The Iroquois shared many of the grievances of their Indian neighbors. Although the American Continental Army invaded the heart of their homeland in 1779 during the Revolution, and the forces led by Major General John Sullivan burned many villages to the ground, their warriors had not been defeated in battle. They had participated during the 1780s in the intertribal diplomacy and coalition building that linked Indian communities throughout the northeastern woodlands. They still smarted from treaties that they felt had been coerced or fraudulent. They came to Canandaigua looking for relief from aggressive encroachment on their lands, limits on their ability to move through their homelands, and a series of murders committed by white frontier settlers on their people.[1]

The Iroquois League, or the Haudenosaunee, originally consisted from east to west of the Mohawks, Oneidas, Onondagas, Cayugas, and Senecas. In the 1720s the Tuscaroras arrived in southern New York to become the last of the Six Nations. Once the League had stretched across today's upstate New York, much like the metaphorical longhouse upon which it was patterned, from the Hudson to the Genesee and beyond. But by the 1790s, things had changed. Despite their deserved reputation as formidable warriors, the Iroquois did not have the power to achieve their goals unilaterally—not anymore. Clusters of Iroquois people remained in their homelands, but many lived after the Revolutionary War in a line of refugee settlements along the Niagara River. Others had crossed that river, relocating to the Grand River in Ontario. The war drove the Mohawks from their homelands, and those not settled at Grand River moved to settlements in the north along the St. Lawrence River. The Mohawks were barely represented at Canandaigua at all, and significant divisions ran rife through the other five nations as well. Disease took its toll during the war years, as did hunger. To fight any longer was likely a losing proposition. But the Iroquois possessed a reputation for skilled diplomacy as well as war, and the strength of their commitment to cultural protocols that emphasized the importance of peace remained strong. The Canandaigua council must have seemed to the gathered members of the Iroquois

League as an important, and perhaps a critical, opportunity to protect their communities' interests in New York's borderlands.[2]

American Indian treaties, like that negotiated at Canandaigua in November 1794, occupy a central place in Native American history, of course, but also in the larger history of the United States. Under the U.S. Constitution, written in 1787, ratified in 1788, and implemented in March 1789, treaties along with acts of Congress are "the supreme law of the land." Formal agreements between the United States and Indian nations, ratified by the president with the advice and consent of the Senate, treaties rest at heart upon a recognition of American Indian tribal sovereignty, even if the nature and limits of that sovereignty have been fiercely contested throughout the nation's history and eroded significantly by the federal courts and Congress.[3]

The 370 ratified Indian treaties negotiated between the United States and Indian tribes, from the beginning of the nation's history until 1871 (when Congress unilaterally ended the practice), served a variety of functions. Some secured peace after periods of war. Others defined the limits of those lands a tribe possessed or the bounds of the lands it ceded to the United States. Many treaties included provisions establishing programs to transform the culture of native peoples, to compel them to live more like their growing numbers of white neighbors. Plows and livestock and spinning wheels, or salaries for schoolteachers or blacksmiths or model farmers—all might be provided through the terms of a treaty. And if treaties rested upon an assumption that American Indian tribes possessed some degree of sovereignty, and at least some of the qualities associated with independent nations, they also could serve as instruments of colonialism and control, the legal arm of dispossession. Through treaties, for instance, the United States at times acquired rights on paper to regulate the trade and commerce of a tribe, and a sole and exclusive right to purchase their lands, what lawyers call a right of pre-emption, that reduced their value significantly by excluding other potential buyers. It was through the instrument of treaties that many millions of acres of Indian land became part of the United States.[4]

Some of these treaties were fraudulent or deceptive, others coerced. Many extended the power of the United States over native peoples who, the Supreme Court ruled in 1831, were best viewed not as independent and entirely sovereign governing entities but as "domestic dependent nations" whose relationship to the United States resembled that of "a ward to its guardian." Subsequent Supreme Court cases, asserting the "plenary" power of the federal government over Indian affairs, held that the United States possessed the right to alter or abolish these treaties unilaterally through congressional enactment.[5]

Still, throughout the treaty period, councils remained significant events. Treaty councils brought together large numbers of Indians and other Americans. They were cultural encounters. The Iroquois, who negotiated with the United States at Canandaigua, possessed enough power still to influence the shape of the proceedings. American officials had to conform to Iroquois diplomatic protocol, to the pursuit of peace and a "good mind." American officials exchanged strings of wampum, beads produced from shell imbued with symbolic and spiritual meaning. These beads served to make tangible abstract words and, when woven into belts of wampum, served as records of a council's proceedings. American officials spoke of clearing paths, burying hatchets, and offering condolence to those who grieved. They spoke of opening ears, unstopping throats, and drying eyes. They struggled to find reliable interpreters, individuals upon whom they might rely to communicate in an idiom understood by Iroquois diplomats and orators whose people had conducted their relations with natives and newcomers according to these forms for longer than the American colonies had existed. Native diplomats at these councils, to be sure, could be deceived or misled. The councils nearly always resulted in a written and signed document that native peoples could not read without the assistance of interpreters who did not always have their interests at heart. But the power of the Indians over the conduct of the proceedings should not be underestimated. Talented native leaders maneuvered on difficult ground as they worked to protect the interests of their communities. That is what happened at Canandaigua in the fall of 1794. They argued with their would-be overlords. They shaped the outcome of the negotiations. They attempted to hold a nation accountable, to compel it to honor its past agreements, obey its own laws, and renounce its aggressions. They used the treaty process to protect their nationhood. At Canandaigua, they succeeded, although not without cost.

The history of native peoples in the United States is all too often told as a tale of defeat and dispossession. The Treaty of Canandaigua allows for an alternative narrative, a different outcome, in the form of a comparatively brief treaty that recognized the right of the Six Nations to the possession and the "free use and enjoyment" of their lands for as long as they chose to hold them. It was not easy, but Iroquois people today, many of whom continue to live upon ancestral homelands in New York state, invoke the Treaty of Canandaigua in defense of their rights and their autonomy. They continue to assert, in the face of many efforts to drive them out, that they remain committed to living as they choose on lands that remain their own.

CHAPTER 1

·······················

Guswenta

The League of the Iroquois is very old. It stretched geographically across today's upstate New York in the form of a metaphorical longhouse, with the Mohawks serving as the keepers of the Eastern Door, the Senecas keeping the Western Door, and the Onondagas tending the League's central council fire. The Oneidas lived between the Mohawks and Onondagas, while the Cayugas lived roughly between the Onondagas and Senecas. In the 1720s the Tuscaroras migrated from North Carolina to become the sixth nation. Some scholars, resting their arguments on a quite literal reading of Iroquois history and myth, suggest that the League originated more than a thousand years ago, in the distant mists of time immemorial, on the shore of Onondaga Lake in central New York. Others, relying upon the historical and archaeological record, suggest a later date, and a long process, completed sometime near the end of the sixteenth century. Wherever one stands on the antiquity of the Iroquois League, no serious scholar disputes the assertion that it predated the establishment of permanent European colonies in the American Northeast, and that it has endured through many trials and ordeals. Indeed, although much has changed, the League still exists. The Longhouse still stands.[1]

Artifacts excavated from Iroquois sites provide the proof of increasing contact between the Iroquoian communities of upstate New York beginning in the fourteenth century, and evidence of an emerging Iroquois League. Onondaga chert, for instance, the stone used to fashion arrowheads and other tools, appears far removed from quarry sites, indicating the existence of networks of trade and exchange

THE IROQUOIS HOMELANDS ON THE EVE OF THE CANANDAIGUA TREATY

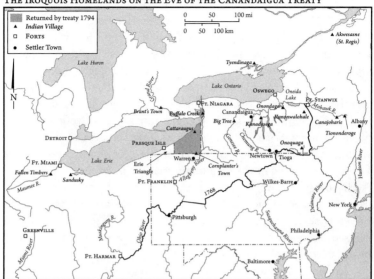

The Iroquois and their neighbors.

among Iroquois peoples. Pottery observed in early Onondaga sites shows signs of having been fabricated by Iroquoian women from the St. Lawrence River Valley and the Huron country north of Lake Ontario. Two possible explanations account for the presence of these exotic ceramics at Onondaga. The first relates to the warfare that ravaged Iroquoia in the sixteenth century. Women captured and adopted into Haudenosaunee communities by Onondaga raiders, in this view, may have continued to make pottery that bore the marks of their natal communities. But exchange networks might offer a better explanation. Women who visited their neighbors to trade learned new ceramic manufacturing techniques from their partners. When they returned home, these travelers and traders incorporated new ideas into their community's ceramic traditions.[2]

Copper also entered Iroquoia via indigenous trade networks and moved throughout the Iroquois Longhouse. In the early seventeenth century, powerful native communities isolated the Haudenosaunee from nascent colonial outposts in the St. Lawrence, in the Hudson, in New England, and in the Chesapeake. They could not trade directly with Europeans for copper. Canadian Algonquians stood between the Five Nations and the early French settlements to their north; the Hudson Valley Mahicans stood between the Mohawks and the Dutch at Fort Orange (present-day Albany, New York) and English settlements farther east until 1628; and the Susquehannocks stood as a powerful barrier between the English settlements in Virginia and the western Iroquois. The European trade goods that originated in those settlements, as a result, could only arrive in Iroquoia via indigenous networks of exchange. Copper artifacts began to arrive in significant quantities at Onondaga, at the geographic center of the League, beginning in the second quarter of the seventeenth century. Archaeologists have found European metal objects—copper and iron—in Seneca, Onondaga, and Mohawk sites as early as 1540. By the early seventeenth century the quantity of these trade goods increased. Iroquois artisans cut apart copper kettles to make arrowheads, cutting tools, and decorations.[3]

Iroquois men and women also exchanged tobacco and tobacco pipes. They grew the plant in fields apart from the "Three Sisters," maize, beans, and squash, the foundation of their subsistence, because tobacco possessed enormous ritual significance for the Haudenosaunee. Tobacco had the power to place one in a spiritually exalted state. "They never attend a council," wrote the French Jesuit father Jean de Brebeuf in 1636 of the culturally similar Hurons, "without a pipe or calumet in their mouths. The smoke, they say, gives them intelligence, and enables them to see clearly through the most intricate matters." Lewis Henry Morgan, the nineteenth-century anthropologist, wrote that the Iroquois believed that powerful spiritual forces provided them with tobacco to facilitate communication with the spirit world: "By burning tobacco they could send up their petitions with its ascending incense."[4]

Haudenosaunee peoples produced an enormous number of smoking implements that archaeologists call effigy pipes. Some they carved from stone. More commonly, they molded them from clay. These effigy pipes present a number of common motifs across Iroquoia, and their distribution sheds light on the formation of the League. As men traveled to conduct diplomacy and trade, they carried with them their pipes. Effigy pipes, which first appeared in the St. Lawrence Valley and along the eastern shore of Lake Ontario, began to appear in smaller numbers in eastern Iroquois towns belonging to the Mohawks, Oneidas, and Onondagas, evidence of the peaceful interaction of pipe-smoking men from a number of communities.[5] Archaeologists have shown that pipes produced in Mohawk country (the easternmost of the Iroquois nations) did not arrive at Seneca sites (at the western door of what became the Iroquois Longhouse) until some point between 1590 and 1605, suggesting that the Iroquois League was fully formed sometime toward the very end of the sixteenth century or very early in the seventeenth century.[6]

Pottery, copper, tobacco, and stone all moved about Iroquoia, carried by people who traveled widely. Marine shell also entered the Longhouse through networks of aboriginal exchange. Much of this shell came from whelks found along the coast of the Chesapeake Bay. Oyster and quahog from the coast of Long Island Sound also found its way into Iroquoia. The former would have arrived in Iroquoia via Susquehannock middlemen, who carried it north through the Susquehanna and Delaware river systems. Shell from the Long Island Sound entered the Longhouse via New England Algonquians and moved westward through Iroquoia.[7]

Shell beads entered the Haudenosaunee Longhouse at nearly the same time as European-manufactured beads began to appear, in the middle decades of the sixteenth century. Marine beads were of great significance in the conduct of Iroquois culture and diplomacy. They rested at the heart of the founding legends of the Iroquois League. That story, recorded in numerous versions over time, focused upon a man named Hiawatha. His story takes place in a world ravaged by warfare. Violence destroyed Hiawatha, drove him to cannibalism, and left him deranged from the grief caused by the death of his daughters. Mourning and grieving, Hiawatha wandered off into the woods, where he ultimately encountered Deganawidah, the Peacemaker, a transcendent bearer of the Good News of Peace and Power. He came from Ontario and crossed the Great Lakes aboard his magical white stone canoe. Deganawidah gave to Hiawatha strings of wampum as he spoke the words of condolence. The first dried Hiawatha's weeping eyes. The second opened his ears so that he could hear reason. The last opened his throat so that he could speak. Deganawidah restored Hiawatha to a good mind.[8]

The Deganawidah epic taught villagers the importance of maintaining balance, of alliance and exchange among the peoples of the

Iroquois Longhouse. It taught Iroquois people who they were and how they came to be. It is a story of travel and travail. The rituals of condolence became an Iroquois gospel, a message carried by Hiawatha and the Peacemaker to all the peoples of Iroquoia and beyond. The pair traveled through the war-haunted lands of the Haudenosaunee. They faced no challenge greater than that posed by the Onondaga sorcerer Thadodaho, whose misshapen body and hair made of a tangle of writhing snakes symbolized the disorder of his mind. If Hiawatha had been deranged by violence as a victim, a man whose grief had rendered him senseless, Thadodaho represented the opposite extreme. His own violence and wickedness had damaged him. A killer and a sadist, Thadodaho resisted joining the League. Over time, Hiawatha restored him to reason. Hiawatha combed the snakes from his hair and straightened out his crooked and deformed body. Thadodaho became the Firekeeper of the metaphorical Iroquois longhouse, and his home at Onondaga became the ceremonial center of the Haudenosaunee. It remains so today.[9]

Wampum beads, acquired by the Haudenosaunee through native networks of exchange, rested at the heart of Iroquois culture. Shell beads became the symbol of League activity, a vital part of the protocol of League diplomacy. Trade and exchange with peoples over a broad geographic expanse of the Northeast rested at the heart of the formation and function of the Iroquois League. And if the League was about preserving peace, power, and righteousness; protecting the Haudenosaunee from the constant warfare that cut gaping holes in the fabric of their world; and restoring the grieving to a good mind, the escape from this constant mourning came with marine shells turned into beads by distant native trading partners living along the coast, who with the help of metal tools obtained from Europeans traded them to the Haudenosaunee. Movement, trade, and exchange were all essential to the Iroquois.[10]

As Iroquois traders, hunters, and warriors acquired items from their trading partners and, indirectly, from the first Europeans, they did so on their own terms. Commerce and exchange were important to the Five Nations, but not necessarily in the way that Europeans imagined. The Haudenosaunee saw commerce not simply as a business transaction but as part of a relationship based on reciprocity, respect, and kinship. Mohawk orators later would lecture the Dutch at Fort Orange on the behavior they expected from their "Brothers." They provided the Dutch with etiquette lessons, rules for behaving in a relationship that had obvious economic elements but that was also emotional and spiritual. Their native trading partners would have understood this, but Europeans struggled as they listened to Iroquois orators speak of drying tears, of clearing throats, and of setting minds aright and removing obstructions from the path to the Dutch post. The Iroquois tried to teach the Dutch how they conducted business.[11]

After Deganawidah and Hiawatha reformed Thadodaho, Hiawatha raised up a string of white wampum and proclaimed, "These are the words of the Great Law. On these Words we shall build the house of Peace, the Longhouse, with the five fires that is yet one household. These are the Words of Righteousness and Health and Power."[12] The Mohawks, Oneidas, Onondagas, Cayugas, and Senecas joined together in a union or league housed metaphorically in one extended lodge that united them, while allowing each the continued autonomy of its own fire. Deganawidah and the fifty chiefs of the League planted the Great Tree of Peace at Onondaga, the home of Thadodaho. The evergreen Tree of Peace, a massive white pine, sheltered the League. Its roots spread out in four directions. All peoples might follow the roots back to Onondaga to join the Great League of Peace and Power. The chiefs then uprooted a massive pine tree, exposed the canyon beneath it, and threw in their weapons, which the river beneath carried away. They replanted the tree and proclaimed, "We bury all the weapons of war out of sight, and establish the 'Great Peace.' Hostilities shall not be seen or heard any more among you, but 'Peace' shall be preserved among the Confederated Nations."[13]

The Iroquois League was not a government in the way that Europeans understood that term. Rather, it was a gathering of chosen leaders—fifty League sachems who were selected by clan mothers and who fulfilled the role and took the names of the original League sachems—who came together to discuss common problems, perform the rituals of condolence, and preserve the Great Peace and avoid the ravages of war. The same rituals that governed relations between the Iroquois, and between the Iroquois and other Indians, were extended by the Haudenosaunee people to the first European voyagers, sometimes through the work of League sachems and sometimes through leaders who earned their status owing to their skills in warfare or diplomacy.

Europeans, for their part, learned that their colonial ventures would struggle without the assistance of native peoples. Europeans wanted to profit from their colonial ventures, through trade or by harvesting the New World's riches. They hoped to establish American footholds secure from enemies native and European. And they wanted to extend the reach of what they considered the one and only true religion. Indian allies would trade with them; Indian friends might teach them about American commodities. Hostile Indians might menace their outposts, or team up with one of their European rivals in an attack. And Europeans could not convert to Christianity the same Indians they might try to kill. European imperial promoters recognized that they might achieve their objectives of profit, security, and conversion, or their economic, military, and religious goals, more easily and with less expense with the assistance of native peoples. They also learned that to Iroquois people alliances were dynamic, ongoing relationships that took effort and attention to detail to maintain. Iroquois people constantly "reevaluated, refined, renewed and kept alive in ritual form" their connections to others. Reciprocal exchanges of gifts, or wampum at councils, or things such as aid supplied in times of need expressed mutual commitment and allegiance.[14]

In their early encounters with Europeans Iroquois people instructed the newcomers on how alliances should operate. Throughout their very long history, the Haudenosaunee consistently stressed the importance of autonomy and independence, both for their individual nations and for the Iroquois League as a whole. Today, Haudenosaunee people see this autonomy resting at the heart of a principle they call *guswenta*. Originally, *guswenta* was the general term used to designate a wampum belt.[15] Over time, it has taken on a more particular meaning and has come to be associated with the "Two Row" wampum, a belt consisting of parallel rows of dark wampum beads on a field of white. The two rows, Haudenosaunee people assert, represent two vessels traveling the same stream, one representing the Iroquois and the other the Dutch. They move together in peace and friendship, but they remain separate and pledged to noninterference in the affairs of the other. Whether the "Two Row" belt represents precisely what many Haudenosaunee claim, and although the meaning of the belt clearly has evolved over time, there is powerful evidence that the Haudenosaunee conducted their relations with their neighbors in accord with the contemporary understanding of the principle of *guswenta*.[16]

In 1613, Mohawks might have entered into an agreement with a shadowy Dutch trader named Jacques Eelkens. No credible written copy of this agreement exists, but Iroquois orators did on a number of occasions in the colonial period make reference to some sort of understanding at some point in their relationship with the Dutch. It is this agreement, some Haudenosaunee scholars assert, that provides the foundation for the *guswenta* principle. Neither would attempt to steer the other's canoe or interfere in the affairs of the other.[17] Travel and mobility always were important, and the Great Law of Peace allowed Haudenosaunee people to move in peace through the Iroquois Longhouse. When Harmen Van den Bogaert journeyed along the Mohawk River in December 1634, for instance, he came to a Mohawk village of thirty-six longhouses. These houses, he wrote, "had some interior doors made of splint planks furnished with iron hinges," a melding of Iroquois and colonial material culture. In other houses he saw ironwork, including "Iron chains, bolts, harrow teeth, iron hoops, spikes, which they steal when they are away from here." Five days later, "Three women came here from the Sinnekens [Senecas] with some dried and fresh salmon, but they smelled very bad." Although the Dutch used the phrase "Sinnekens" to describe any Iroquois west of Mohawk country, the fact that women traveled unaccompanied to trade showed the ability of ordinary Iroquoians to move safely through Iroquoia. The women "sold each salmon for one guilder or two hands of sewant [wampum]," an economic flexibility that testifies to their familiarity with intercultural trade and the travel required to make it happen. The women "also brought much green tobacco to sell, and had been six days underway." When they could not sell all their tobacco they carried on eastward to the next Mohawk town.[18]

To obtain the furs upon which the Dutch West India Company relied, its settlers needed the Mohawks. To obtain furs from tribes farther west, the Mohawks needed Dutch weaponry. Out of mutual necessity, the area around Fort Orange became a pragmatic meeting place, a middle ground where interdependence spawned by the fur trade forced newcomers to accommodate their Mohawk neighbors.

Maintaining these relationships could be challenging. New Netherland had a weak government, with little capacity to control the activity of its settlers who engaged in trade with native peoples. Traders rejected calls that they refrain from selling Indians alcohol, for instance, or employing brokers who moved through the woods and lured Indians to a trader's particular station at Fort Orange. As the French Jesuit Isaac Jogues, who spent some time with the Dutch in 1643, reported, "the trade is free to all; this gives the Indians all things cheap, each of the Hollanders outbidding his neighbor, and being satisfied provided he can gain some little profit." During the trading season, which lasted from May until October, large numbers of Dutch colonists swarmed into Fort Orange hoping to profit from the fur trade. The Mohawks complained that Dutch brokers "when they are in the woods to fetch Indians beat them severely with fists and drive them out of the woods." The Mohawks asked that "no Dutchman with horses or otherwise . . . be allowed to roam in the woods to fetch Indians with beavers, because they maltreat them greatly and presently ten or twelve of them surround an Indian and drag him along saying, 'Come with us, so and so has no goods,' thus interfering with one another, which they fear will end badly." Dutch authorities recognized that the rough handling of Mohawk traders was "contrary to the welfare and peace of this place," and they decided "to forbid all inhabitants . . . to go roaming the woods as brokers to attract Indians."[19]

The Dutch never succeeded in reining in the most aggressive traders. When the English conquered New Netherland in 1664, they saw the importance of the relationship with the Haudenosaunee, and they tried themselves to set their relations on a firm footing. In September of that year, English authorities met with "Ohgehando, Shamarage, Soachoenighta, Sachamackas of ye Maques" and four "Senecas." In the resulting "Articles" of agreement, the new English regime pledged that "the Indian Princes above named and their subjects, shall have such wares and commodities from the English for the future, as heretofore they had from the Dutch." The remaining articles dealt with reciprocal justice: Both the English and the Haudenosaunee pledged to catch malefactors whose violence threatened to disrupt the trade. The agreement included as well, after the signatures and marks, a set of additional articles that "wer likewise proposed by the same

Indian princes & consented to" by the English leaders. Here were the demands the Haudenosaunee ambassadors placed upon the new occupants of Fort Orange. The Haudenosaunee requested, and the English agreed, that hunters from the Five Nations "may have free trade as formerly."[20]

This early Anglo-Iroquoian treaty should not be read apart from a body of laws implemented by the English conquerors in 1664. Known as the "Duke's Laws," after the king's brother, James, duke of York, they empowered the governor of New York to grant licenses for the trade in fur, weapons, and alcohol. Only certain types of people should engage in trade, the thinking went, and the English hoped that a licensing system would give them some measure of control over intercultural exchange. The laws, furthermore, prohibited the purchase of land from Indians without the permission of the governor, an attempt to prevent avaricious settlers from coercing Indians into signing deeds of cession. The laws specified that "all injuryes done to the Indians of what nature soever shall upon their complaint and proofe thereof have speed redress gratis, against any Christian in as full and Ample manner . . . as if the case had been betwixt Christian and Christian." Through the Duke's Laws the English hoped to regulate those instances where native peoples came into contact with Indians, and to preserve peace and order along the frontier.[21]

While the English worked to establish a solid relationship with the Five Nations that benefited the empire, Iroquois people began moving north to the St. Lawrence beginning in the middle of the seventeenth century. There they interacted with increasing frequency with Jesuit priests set on Christianizing the native peoples of "New France." Founded in 1667, the mission settlement at Kahnawake blended French, Catholic, and Iroquois influences into something new. Some of the converts, Oneidas at first, followed by significant numbers of Mohawks, migrated to the St. Lawrence Valley hoping to avoid tension between Christians and non-Christians and the turmoil and disorder caused by French and Dutch traders who poured alcohol into the Mohawk Valley settlements.[22]

Kahnawake was one of a number of settlements planted outside of the territorial boundaries of the traditional Iroquois Longhouse. Onondagas and Cayugas settled at a site called Oswegatchie in northern New York, near present-day Ogdensburg. Senecas moved westward in the eighteenth century to a number of sites in the Genesee Valley. And migrants from Kahnawake moved roughly sixty miles up the St. Lawrence in the 1750s to Akwesasne, a site chosen most likely for its soil and superior access to water and timber.[23]

In 1677 Haudenosaunee diplomats and the English governor in New York, Sir Edmund Andros, negotiated an intercultural accord that came to be known as the Covenant Chain alliance. During the course of the seventeenth century, the years when Iroquois warfare reached its violent peak, Haudenosaunee warriors struck enemies far to their south, north of Lake Ontario, and in the western Great Lakes. This warfare emerged from powerful cultural assumptions about the nature of mourning and the dangers that grief unassuaged could pose for a community. The Deganawidah epic, in fact, emphasized the danger and the instability that grief could bring. Haudenosaunee warriors, launching "mourning wars" against people they defined as enemies, sought captives. Some they tortured in horrific displays of ritualized violence. Some they consumed. Others they adopted to take the place of those who had died in warfare or who had succumbed to disease.[24]

By the last quarter of the seventeenth century, the system had begun to collapse. Epidemic disease produced more deaths, requiring more raids for captives to assuage the grief of survivors or take the place of those who had died. These raids required attacks against native peoples increasingly armed with the same muskets Iroquois warriors carried, making the avoidance of casualties less likely. Additional casualties required additional raids. And to acquire the arms and ammunition they needed, Iroquois warriors had to obtain the furs their European trading partners desired. This required even more raids, and the risk of more casualties. The mourning war complex was no longer fulfilling its central function.[25]

Negotiated at a period, then, when the mourning war complex had produced heavy losses, the Covenant Chain alliance secured peace on the northern and eastern flanks of Iroquoia and set the stage for Iroquois raids to the west, strengthening their ability to move through territories they had traditionally traveled to conduct war, diplomacy, and trade. An important part of the agreement involved settling on the margins of Iroquoia New England Algonquians and Susquehannocks, both peoples battered during colonial uprisings of the mid-1670s (King Philip's War in New England and Bacon's Rebellion in the Chesapeake), for it expanded the geographic range of the Haudenosaunee as well, allowing them to move more easily into and through their now subject peoples' lands. And the Covenant Chain alliance was always conditional. When the alliance did not serve Iroquois interests, for instance, they ignored it. They always mediated between the French and the English. For them the Covenant Chain was an alliance without allegiance. They would hold the chain so long as the English fulfilled their responsibilities as allies. During the negotiations, furthermore, the Mohawks told New York Governor Andros that "if any difference should aryse betwixt you or your Indians, and our Indians, wee desyr that thar may not Immediately a Warre aryse upon the Same bot that the matter may be moderat & composed betwixt us, and wee do Inngage for our parts to give Satisfaction to you for any Eveill that our Indians might happen to doe." Satisfaction meant the exchange of goods to wipe away tears and restore those who grieved to a good mind. Alliances had to be refreshed and kept clean with the exchange of gifts.[26]

Trade preserved the Covenant Chain. In August 1684, for instance, Onondaga and Cayuga sachems, after informing the English pointedly that "we are a free people uniting ourselves to what sachem we please," requested that the governors of Virginia and New York "protect us from the French, which if you do not, we shall lose all our hunting and Bevers, the French will have all the Bevers, and are angry with us for bringing any to you."[27] Nine years later, New York Governor Benjamin Fletcher presented the Five Nations with gifts for holding fast the Covenant Chain. Fletcher gave them 86 guns, 36 rolls of tobacco, 146 bags of gunpowder, 800 bars of lead for casting bullets, 1,000 gunflints, and hatchets, knives, and a variety of trade cloths and finished clothing.[28]

When the English and the French both showed a willingness to enlist Haudenosaunee warriors in their fights but less inclination to treat them as allies, the Five Nations embarked upon a neutrality policy beginning in 1701. Neutrality helped cement the strategic position of the Five Nations and secure their ability to move throughout a Greater Iroquoia. Neutrality also allowed the Haudenosaunee to receive military assistance and trade goods from both the French and the English. They received gifts and presents, even if neither

European power could completely control the unscrupulous traders who so vexed the Haudenosaunee. The Haudenosaunee frequently received gifts of weapons, powder, lead, tobacco, alcohol, cloth, and metal from both the English and the French. The Onondaga sachem Teganissorens told New York Governor Robert Hunter in 1713 that he would "not hinder any nations of Indians who would pass through our country to trade with you." He was more than willing to pledge Haudenosaunee assistance to the English, but he also complained when he felt that the English had not conducted the trade fairly or in a manner that served Haudenosaunee interests. In 1715 he explained to Hunter that the Onondagas had "been obedient to all your commands." His patience wearing thin, he told Hunter that "we have often desir'd that the goods should be sold cheaper, which has not been comply'd with al, and we insist that goods may be sold at a more easy rate. It would be a great satisfaction to all our people." Hunter's response—an explanation of the laws of supply and demand—did not satisfy Teganissorens. Four days after his initial speech, he responded to Hunter once again. "Brother Corlaer," he said, "We must own that we have desire'd from time to time that goods should be sold cheaper which is the most materiall matter to us."[29]

Teganissorens' complaints reveal the difficulties Haudenosaunee diplomats and orators sometimes faced when they struggled to persuade their colonial trading partners to behave in a manner they thought consistent with allies. Both the British and French, of course, intended their alliance with the Haudenosaunee to serve the ends of empire. Both European powers wanted to control the west, and began to plan for the construction of forts in the homeland of the Iroquois. The French began construction of Fort Niagara in 1720, an attempt to stop the diversion of furs from western Indians through Iroquoia to the better prices and more abundant goods at the British posts on the Hudson River. By the middle of the 1720s, the British began construction of Fort Oswego, on the southern shore of Lake Ontario. The post, British imperial officials hoped, would draw in furs otherwise headed toward Montreal. Constructing Oswego may have rendered the position of the eastern Iroquois nations less important to the conduct of the fur trade, since traders could travel to a British post without passing directly through their territories.[30]

But the Iroquois by this point were hardly defeated and degraded peoples once their role in the fur trade was reduced. Before the construction of the forts at Niagara and Oswego, western Indians traveling to Montreal or Albany had to pass through Iroquois territory, and doing that required the formation and maintenance of alliances, the regular exchange of gifts, and the establishment of peace. Both the French and English presented the Senecas with gifts, for instance, to persuade them to direct their western allies toward Montreal or Albany. But even after the construction of Oswego, western Indians traveling to the English posts stopped along the shore of Lake Ontario in Seneca territory. The archaeological evidence suggests that Indians making this voyage still visited the Senecas and renewed the ties of kinship and exchange that they had forged since 1701. During these years, the Senecas altered their settlement patterns. They abandoned the western "Seneca Castle" near Canandaigua Lake at some point in the 1740s and moved westward toward the Genesee River. They did not move toward Lake Ontario to intercept western Indians but greeted those travelers at home, an indication that the alliances they had forged remained strong, and that their role in the western fur trade remained viable.[31]

As they relocated, the Senecas also abandoned life in multifamily longhouses packed tightly behind defensive palisades. Benefiting economically from the passage of western nations through their lands, and enjoying a period of unprecedented peace at home, Seneca families dispersed across the countryside in single-family farmsteads that preserved an open, central hearth. Women, the performers of agricultural labor, chose to live closer to their fields and to supplies of water. There were challenges during these years, to be sure.[32] Alcohol acquired from traders caused problems, and Iroquois leaders complained to the English at Albany about the effects of the rum trade on their communities. But the Senecas were far from powerless. They occupied a strategically critical territory and enjoyed an era of peace in their homeland after 1701. They possessed abundant lands in New York and asserted control over the lands of other nations. Because doing so made their lives easier, many colonists recognized these claims. This, coupled with the still-considerable military power of the Six Nations, and the enormous respect with which Europeans viewed their warriors, ensured the Six Nations a fundamental role in the fate of these empires in America. The Six Nations remained a force with which Europeans must reckon.[33]

By the middle of the eighteenth century, Haudenosaunee economies had become increasingly diverse. The Mohawk Valley town of Canajoharie, for instance, looked almost indistinguishable to many observers from the European settlements nearby. Warren Johnson, the brother of Sir William, observed that Mohawks could still make a living from hunting but that they also made ends meet by selling their labor and working for wages. These observers remarked upon the Mohawks' agricultural prosperity. According to Peter Gansevoort, one of the American soldiers who observed at first hand the prosperity of Haudenosaunee settlements in the 1770s, Canajoharie was "abounding with every Necessary so that it is remarked that the Indians live much better than most of the Mohawk River farmers their Houses very well furnished with all necessary Household utensils, great plenty of grain, several horses, cows and wagons."[34]

Haudenosaunee people became increasingly discriminating consumers of European material culture. Mohawks ate from a variety of native and colonial ceramics, pewter ware acquired from their nonnative neighbors, copper kettles, and expensive china sets. Warren Johnson encountered Indians wearing wigs and playing fiddles. Class differences began to manifest themselves in terms of how Haudenosaunee dressed themselves and equipped their homes. One observer noted that most Iroquois "use but little" clothing, "sometimes a shirt or shift with a blanket or Coat, a half-gown and Petticoat, and sometimes the latter only without linen." The wealthiest men, however, "imitate the English mode and Joseph Brant," perhaps the wealthiest of all, "was dressed in a suit of blue Broad cloth and his wife was in a callicoe or Chintz gown." Brant brewed his tea in imported Jackfield teapots, drank his tea from white salt-glaze stoneware teacups, and ate from Wedgewood china with bone-handled forks and knives.[35] Mohawks at Canajoharie maintained herds of livestock, and some of them owned sleighs to facilitate winter travel and the transport of wood, trade goods, and pelts to exchange points in colonial trade networks. The homes of the wealthiest Mohawks at Canajoharie had limestone foundations, glass windows, wooden floors, curtains, and a variety of outbuildings.[36]

Mohawks and Oneidas residing in the Mohawk Valley in the middle of the eighteenth century had changed certain elements of their ways of life as a result of living in close contact with European settlers. They made their living, increasingly, in the same way that European farmers did, by selling their produce in local markets. This exchange produced some extremes of wealth, but the bulk of the Mohawks in the Valley lived no worse than the poorer European farmers, and often they had access to trade goods that the settlers did not. Indeed, there is some evidence that the European settler communities in the Valley relied upon Haudenosaunee peoples as an outlet for their surplus crops and goods. Eighteenth-century account books show that settlers commonly acquired trade goods that they later sold or bartered to local natives: rum, vermillion, wampum, blankets, powder, shot, strouds, and linen. Haudenosaunee people occupied an important part in an intercultural colonial economy.[37]

Mohawks and Oneidas traded furs, agricultural produce, and ginseng and ginger roots in return for what they wanted. Between 1751 and 1753 something of a ginseng craze emerged in New York as Mohawks and colonists roamed the woods together harvesting the roots for export to London and from there to China. One observer in 1752 encountered over 100 Oneidas and Cayugas digging in the woods for roots. It appears that Haudenosaunee harvesters of ginseng could command the price, for when Sir William Johnson sent a string of wampum to them to inform them of his willingness to purchase their ginseng, the Tuscaroras replied with a long list of trade goods they wished for him to bring.[38]

Mohawks and Oneidas were important participants in the cash economy of the Mohawk Valley as well. They obtained their material goods from merchants and traders in exactly the same way as European farmers. Sir William Johnson's tenants, for instance, paid for goods from an Albany general store with potash, peas, wood, butter, cows, and cash. Iroquois people paid for their goods in nearly identical fashion with potash, corn, cranberries, venison, wampum, and cash. They continued to bring in beaver, marten, otter, and deer skins and pelts. They also paid cash. They worked as wage laborers on farms along the Mohawk River. Settlers bought baskets and brooms from them, as well as shoes, "Indian gartering," cups, and herbal remedies. They lived as well as their neighbors, productive members of a thriving regional Anglo-Iroquoian local economy. They creatively responded to encroaching forces of commerce in ways that lessened their detrimental effects on Iroquois culture. They continued to hunt and farm, they transformed the goods they acquired, and they continued to employ goods they produced or acquired as currency. They were getting by in a world of change.[39]

And they remained important to the function of the British Empire in America as well. In the middle of the eighteenth century, imperial reformers called for the appointment of superintendents of Indian affairs to more effectively manage the empire's relations with native peoples, recognizing the importance of the fur trade to the empire. Cadwallader Colden, active in imperial politics and an expert on the Six Nations, wrote in 1749 that the fur trade was not only "a very considerable branch of the British Commerce in North America but likewise the Security of the Colonies in North America depends upon it." Colden worried about the lack of effective oversight of Indian trade. The French, he believed, had a great advantage over the English. "Their affairs among the Indians," he wrote, "are all directed by one Council, and no expence is thought too great, which is necessary for their purposes." He called upon the Crown to centralize Indian affairs under a single official. Like Colden, Thomas Pownall believed that the best way to maintain the Covenant Chain was to remove the administration of Indian affairs from the hands of locals and to place Indian affairs in the northern colonies under the direction of a "disinterested superintendent," funded by the king.[40]

The eventual superintendent, Sir William Johnson, wrote to the governor of Pennsylvania and explained to him the importance of a well-regulated trade to the function of the empire. The best way to protect the Pennsylvania frontier, Johnson said, was to "open an advantageous trade for the Indians and to have it put under such authoritative regulations as may convince the Indians how much it is for their interest to maintain peace & friendship for the English." Trade, he continued, "is undoubtedly the strongest cement to bind the Indians to our Alliance" and would help "dislodge the French from their alarming encroachments, with less Expence of both blood & treasure, more speedily & more effectually, than we shall perhaps be ever able to do by meer force."[41]

By the middle of the eighteenth century, however, British imperial officials found themselves confronting powerful pan-Indian, nativist movements against English expansion into the west. These militants, among other things, sought to break their people's dependence upon European trade goods. The Six Nations, with a small number of exceptions, did not participate in these movements. They were too central to the functioning of British imperialism, too much a part of the world of goods and imperial patronage. They were willing to travel the same stream, in parallel paths, as long as they could do so on their own terms.[42]

Imperial policymakers in the metropolis sought a peaceful and orderly frontier. They recognized that hostile Indians might provoke expensive warfare that could drain already-depleted imperial treasuries. They understood that disaffected Indians might easily align themselves with their imperial rivals, for these Indians retained their autonomy and their freedom of movement. Imperial officials recognized that warfare rendered more difficult mission work. So they took steps to preserve peace and order on the frontier. They nurtured alliances with native peoples. These alliances were delineated in councils and, occasionally, in treaties, and given form and meaning for the Haudenosaunee through trade—the exchange of goods. Parallel lines. "Trade and peace," Peter Wraxall noted in his *Abridgement of the Indian Affairs*, imperial officials understood "to be one thing"; so, too, did the Haudenosaunee.[43]

CHAPTER 2

....

Broken

The English empire in North America began to fall apart in a spectacular fashion in the middle of the eighteenth century. At least in part, its collapse originated with problems involving Indian affairs and the empire's inability to prevent disorder on the frontier. As early as 1761, during the closing years of that Great War for Empire that pitted France against Great Britain for control of the continent, Seneca warriors who lived closest to the fighting in Pennsylvania and the Ohio Country sent wampum belts to the Delawares and Shawnees, inviting them to join in raids against Anglo-American settlements. These warriors saw in the imperial conflict an opportunity to roll back the tide of settlement. The Senecas sent messages to the Potawatomis, Hurons, Ottawas, and Ojibwes in the western Great Lakes, testifying to the range of their travels and their many connections to native communities over a vast area.

They took part in a "spirited resistance," in the words of its finest historian, a militant campaign by religiously inspired nativist leaders to wipe out the Europeans who had brought so much destruction to their communities, restore their rituals and traditions, and eliminate every taint of colonialism.[1] Others in the Six Nations remained neutral in the conflict, which came to a close in 1763 with the Peace of Paris. England acquired all the lands in North America from the Atlantic to the Mississippi, and with it oversight of the problems that remained in the west. Many Senecas joined with their Ohio Valley allies in Pontiac's Rebellion, a massive pan-Indian uprising involving native peoples across several Anglo-American colonies that began in 1763. That September, Farmer's Brother and the "Chenussio" Senecas he led ambushed a

24

British convoy traveling the portage around Niagara Falls. Almost 100 soldiers died at the so-called Devil's Hole Massacre. The Senecas made amends, granting to Sir William Johnson Grand Island and the smaller islands in the Niagara River in 1764, and the fighting came to a close formally in 1766, when Sir William met with representatives from the Six Nations and warriors from farther west at Oswego.[2]

The British wanted a peaceful and orderly frontier. Warfare came with a heavy price. To this end, Parliament issued its famous proclamation late in 1763, declaring that a line ran the length of the continent from north to south, and that colonists must remain to its east, Indians to its west. Neither side could cross the line without the approval of imperial officials. The king's superintendents of Indian Affairs, Sir William Johnson in the north and Edward Atkin in the south, met with the Iroquois and the Cherokees to formalize the proclamation line. Two treaties resulted, Fort Stanwix (1768) and Hard Labor (1768), with overlapping boundary lines. Iroquois emissaries surrendered land below the Ohio River that Indians living in the valley and in parts of Pennsylvania and Virginia wished to retain. Lands north of the Ohio River were closed to white settlement. The Six Nations at Fort Stanwix, in this sense, agreed to open land to Anglo-American settlement that was not theirs to give, in an effort to direct the flow of settlement away from Iroquoia. Cherokees, Shawnees, Delawares, and others, who lived in the region and believed that it still was theirs, fought to retain it. The disputed zone became a battleground, one that would be contested for the next quarter-century. Murders became common, racial hatred the norm.[3]

The British government began its ill-fated and unsuccessful effort to tax the American colonies in order to raise a revenue to pay some small part of the colonies' defense. These taxes provoked a colonial resistance movement that flared by 1775 into a war and revolution. Sir William Johnson, watching these events from his seat in the Mohawk Valley, worked to persuade the Six Nations to continue to hold the Covenant Chain, to maintain their alliance to the British Crown. The Senecas, who retained their ties and connections to native allies in the west, and who obviously felt little affection for the British, raised special concerns for Johnson. Should the Senecas choose to take up arms against the empire as some of their warriors had done in the 1760s, or should they choose to avenge the insults and murders their people had suffered from frontier settlers in northwestern Pennsylvania, the entire western frontier might once again be set ablaze. As it attempted to crush the colonial rebellion, Britain did not want to fight an Indian war in the west. Iroquois allegiance was critical.[4]

The American rebels, gathered for their part in their Continental Congress, told representatives of the Six Nations at a council held at German Flats in the Mohawk Valley in the summer of 1775 that the war with Great Britain was a "family quarrel" and that "you Indians are not concerned in it." Although some in Congress saw the Iroquois as potentially valuable allies, the commissioners told the Iroquois to stay out of the fight. The choice was a difficult one for the Iroquois, with enormous stakes. Many of the growing numbers of white settlers who migrated into the Oneida territory in the years preceding the American Revolution, for instance, came as refugees fleeing the carnage of Pontiac's Rebellion. Many of these settlers hated Indians. Warren Johnson pointed out that some wore "an Indian's skin for a tobacco pouch," a grisly symbol of frontier violence. The Oneidas aligned themselves with the Americans as a result, not out of any devotion to the patriot cause, but because they feared the consequences of alienating their Indian-hating and territorially aggressive white neighbors.[5]

With the exception of the Tuscaroras and Oneidas, however, the rest of the Iroquois held fast the Covenant Chain, agreeing to assist the British in the war against the rebels. They calculated that they had less to fear from a British victory than an American triumph. The British, however ineffectively, took steps to curb encroachments on their lands. The British possessed the resources, and the trade goods, necessary to sustain an alliance. The British, so much more than the rebels, at least attempted the heavy lifting necessary to preserve the Covenant Chain.[6]

For the Iroquois, the fighting began in earnest in 1777. Senecas traveled east to Fort Stanwix, in present-day Rome, New York, at the invitation of British officers to "come and see them whip the rebels." At Oriskany Creek, however, they found themselves involved in an intense firefight with a rebel force escorted by Oneida guides. The Senecas lost many. Mary Jemison, a white woman adopted by the Senecas as a child, recalled the wailing and suffering that accompanied the loss of so many warriors and leaders. "Our town," she recalled, "exhibited a scene of real

sorrow and distress, when our warriors returned, recounted their misfortunes, and stated the real loss they had sustained in the engagement." Thirty-six warriors died, an enormous toll. The grief, Jemison
continued, "was excessive, and was expressed by the most doleful yells,
shrieks, and howlings, and by inimitable gesticulations."[7]

In her memoir, Jemison described the Senecas' world of intercon-
nected towns and villages. Senecas moved frequently back and forth
from one village to another, visiting relatives, conducting trade, and
attending religious observances. The village at Buffalo Creek stood
along the creek with that name, not far from today's downtown Buffalo.
Thirty-five miles south and west along the shore of Lake Erie stood
Cattaraugus, which itself stood nearly 100 miles west from Little
Beard's Town, located in today's Livingston County. Squawkie Hill,
"a great resort for the Indians to enjoy their sportive games, gymnas-
tic feats, and civic festivals," stood about two miles south of Little
Beard's Town. Farther south and east, near today's Dansville, the village of "Can-ne-skrau-gah" stood. A number of smaller towns still
stood along the Genesee River in the northern parts of today's
Livingston County, and to the north and west, along Tonawanda Creek,
stood the Tonawanda Indian village.[8]

After Oriskany, Iroquois warriors sought vengeance. Sometimes
led by Joseph Brant, the Mohawk leader thoroughly a part of Britain's
transatlantic empire, and sometimes accompanied by Loyalist Rangers,
they attacked frontier settlements throughout New York. At Cherry
Valley in November 1778 Iroquois warriors from several nations
joined in an attack that killed thirty-two civilians and sixteen American
soldiers. Seneca raiders destroyed settlements along the Susquehanna
River in Pennsylvania. Oneidas assisted the Continental soldiers. But
Iroquois peoples, whether they fought alongside the British or the
Americans, avoided fighting each other. Oriskany was the first occasion
during the war where Iroquois fought Iroquois; it was also the last.
Iroquois warriors shared intelligence, negotiated exchanges of prisoners, and in other ways worked to mitigate the effects of the war
upon the Longhouse.[9]

The attacks launched by British-allied Indians did significant
damage along an expansive American frontier. Iroquois attacks de-
populated large portions of Pennsylvania and New York, as settlers
sought safer quarters farther east. The attacks struck the rebels'

breadbasket, forcing the abandonment of farms rebel leaders hoped might feed the Continental Army. The attacks, from the perspective of the Continental Congress and General George Washington, demanded a response. The Onondagas first felt the wrath of American arms when a New York militia force attacked Onondaga Castle in the spring of 1779. Washington ordered a much larger operation against the western Iroquois. Major-General John Sullivan led four brigades of Continental soldiers into the Finger Lakes region of western New York in the summer of 1779. The Senecas offered minimal resistance in the face of this superior force. Sullivan's invading army, which Jemison said burned and destroyed our "huts and cornfields, hogs and horses, and cutting down the fruit trees belonging to the Indians throughout the country," did enormous damage. This was total war, with the American invaders looking to deprive the king's Indian allies of their food, shelter, and clothing. Sullivan's men destroyed two dozen Seneca and Cayuga towns.[10]

Five thousand Senecas and Cayugas fled toward British Fort Niagara after Sullivan's campaign. There they joined large numbers of native peoples already drawing rations at the post. Mohawks, Oneidas, Onondagas, Cayugas, Tuscaroras, and Senecas were there, but so too were Nanticokes, Conoys, Delawares, Shawnees, and many others. They settled in camps on the flatlands around the fort. With their crops destroyed so late in the planting season, they had little food, and the winter of 1779–1780 was especially cold. Many refugees died of starvation and exposure. They depended upon the British for provisions.[11]

Still, the king's Iroquois allies fought. Joseph Brant led forces in the Mohawk Valley. His warriors remained in the field when word of the Peace of Paris arrived, the agreement that ended the war between Britain and the newly independent United States. The treaty made no mention of Britain's Indian allies, who now found themselves living within the territorial limits of the United States.

Imperial officials in Canada surely understood the feelings of abandonment voiced by their allies. If few of these officers believed the British Prime Minister Lord Shelburne's assertion that "the Indian nations were not abandoned to their enemies" but "remitted to the care of neighbours, whose interest it was as much as ours to cultivate friendship with them, and who were certainly the best qualified for softening and humanizing their hearts," they tried to convince the Indians who came to them "thunderstruck" that their lands belonged to them still, and all that Britain had surrendered in Paris was the right of pre-emption, or the right to first purchase, to the Americans. In helping the empire, one Iroquois emissary told the Tory Colonel John Butler, "it seems we have wrought our own ruin." The British had abandoned them "like Bastards," said another, handing them over to an enemy who had committed so "many Acts of Treachery & Cruelty . . . on our Women and Children."[12]

New York's first state constitution, approved during the heart of the Revolution in 1777, asserted the state's exclusive right to acquire Indian lands within its bounds. Four years later, James Duane, a leading New York politician, called upon the legislature to enact "a liberal system for appropriating and settling our western country," much of it possessed still by the Iroquois. In 1782, the state government set aside a huge chunk of Iroquois lands to distribute as bounties to the state's soldiers. Iroquois lands were thus viewed as essential to a state government looking to satisfy its debts to veterans. Those lands not distributed might be sold to settlers and speculators, offering a means to finance state government more palatable to a hard-pressed population than taxation.[13]

The state's leaders, especially Governor George Clinton, argued that the United States possessed no authority to deal with Indians within New York's claimed boundaries. This he based upon his reading of the first U.S. constitution, the Articles of Confederation. Article IX, which listed the powers of the Congress, stated that the United States had "the sole and exclusive right and power . . . of regulating the trade and managing the affairs with the Indians, not members of any of the states, provided that the legislative right of any state within its own limits be not infringed or violated." The Iroquois were members of the state, Clinton argued, and any attempt by the American government to conduct diplomacy with the Six Nations, he believed, violated his state's rights.[14]

Clinton made claims for a state over which he exercised very little real control. The war left much damage in its wake. "The most beautiful country in the world," one observer noted in May 1784, "now presents only the poor cabins of an impoverished population who are nearly without food and upon the verge of starvation." The signs and symbols of battles only recently past stood everywhere. The British retained their posts at Fort Niagara and Oswego. Farther east, the two counties that later became the state of Vermont stood in open rebellion and state leaders feared, as James Duane put it in 1782, that "a *second Vermont* may spring up in our western limits." The Iroquois did not respect the state's claims to their lands. Despite the devastation they had suffered, they did what they could to resurrect their communities. Haudenosaunee people continued to travel, visiting their longhouse kin and restoring ties severed by war.[15]

Most of the Iroquois had taken up arms against the United States and they had been defeated. Now, state leaders believed, they must pay. In March 1783, the state legislature appointed commissioners to negotiate "an exchange of the district claimed by the Oneidas and Tuscaroras for a district of vacant and unappropriated lands within this State." They had lived closest to the line of white settlements. The legislature instructed the commissioners to explain that this exchange was in their best interest.[16]

Many members of Congress agreed with the state's assertion that the Indians, by siding with Great Britain, must surrender their lands. "A bare recollection of the facts," the Congress declared in 1783, "is sufficient to manifest the obligation they are under to make atonement for the enormities which they have perpetrated." New Yorker Philip Schuyler, a man closely involved in the formation of the nation's Indian policies during the Confederation, informed the Six Nations that "as we are the Conquerors, we claim the lands and property of all the white people as well as the Indians who have left and fought back against us."[17]

That New York possessed an exclusive right to conduct diplomacy with the Six Nations, however, was not a position that all in Congress shared. The commissioners it appointed—Oliver Wolcott of Connecticut, Richard Butler of Pennsylvania, and Arthur Lee of Virginia—headed for Fort Stanwix in the fall of 1784 to meet with representatives from the Six Nations. There they found the New York state commissioners already engaged with the Indians.[18]

Clinton instructed his commissioners to begin drafting a treaty. He also wrote to the congressional commissioners, demanding that they enter into no negotiations "with Indians residing within the jurisdiction of this State, with whom only I mean to treat." Lee and

Butler responded several days later. They asked Clinton to consider conducting the business of his state "at the same time with, and in subordination to the General Treaty" negotiated by the United States. This, the commissioners hopefully pointed out, was the course Pennsylvania had agreed to follow, a course the commissioners saw as consonant with the Articles of Confederation.[19]

Clinton was not dissuaded. He had been advised by James Duane to abandon the traditional protocols that had governed councils with the Iroquois and their neighbors. Duane, in his effort to justify New York's claims to exclusive jurisdiction over the conduct of Indian policy, told Clinton that the Indians must not be "considered as Indian nations," and no one "should suffer the word 'Nation' or 'Six Nations,' or 'Confederation,' or 'Council Fire at Onondaga' or any other form which would revive or seem to confirm their former ideas of Independence to escape." Rather, "These tribes should be treated as *antient Dependents on this State*," even though Duane doubted that the Indians of the Six Nations would "Submit to being treated as *Dependents*."[20]

Clinton opened his council in early September, only partially attentive to Duane's advice. He told the gathered Iroquois delegates that it was his hope, after a long war, "to reestablish the antient harmony and friendship which had so long subsisted between this state and the Six Nations residing within its limits." He wanted to resolve "those differences and animosities which have arisen between us by reason of your Conduct during the late war" and "to establish Boundary lines between you and us on such just and equitable terms as will be satisfactory & prevent all future Animosities." He had hoped to promote trade and commerce "and renew that former friendship and Compact antiently made between the Six Nations and our Dutch ancestors, and afterwards frequently renewed by the late colony now state of New York."[21]

The Iroquois listened to Clinton's speech but declined his invitation to negotiate. Joseph Brant and the Seneca leader Cornplanter told the governor that they would get back to him after they met with the congressional commissioners. Wolcott, Lee, and Butler paid little attention to the protocols of Iroquois diplomacy. They treated the Six Nations' representatives like conquered people. They wanted those Iroquois who had sided with Great Britain to submit, and to surrender to the United

States hostages to be held until all their own captives had been released. They demanded of the Iroquois a cession of all their lands *west* of a line drawn generally four miles *east* of the Niagara River. Only for the Oneidas and the Tuscaroras, "who preserved their faith to them, and adhered to their cause," did the commissioners recognize "the full and free enjoyment" of the lands they held.[22]

Presumably the commissioners, through their interpreter, explained what "full and free enjoyment" meant. They conveyed these words, in English, to their interpreter, most likely Samuel Kirkland, who in turn thought it over and attempted to convey this concept into something the Indians might have understood. When he did so, what might the Oneidas and Tuscaroras have heard? What Oneida concepts most closely equated with the English-language meaning of "full and free enjoyment" of their lands? It's a difficult question to answer. The finished treaty used sparse language, noting in its second article that "the Oneida and Tuscarora Nations shall be secured in the possession of the lands on which they are settled" and in the third article that the rest of the Six Nations "shall be secured in the peaceful possession of the lands they inhabit east and north" of the cession line, with the exception of a six-mile buffer zone around the fort at Oswego, which they ceded to the United States. After the United States and the Six Nations finished their business on October 22, the Iroquois ceded to Pennsylvania all their lands in the state save for a small tract along the Allegheny known as the "Cornplanter Reserve," a tract set aside for the Seneca leader and his descendants that some suspected came as payment for his cooperation.[23]

These cessions were significant. At Fort Stanwix, the United States dictated a treaty that defined the western border of Iroquoia, and not its eastern, where settlers already had gathered in significant numbers. The strip of federal land along the Niagara isolated the Six Nations from the British in Canada and separated them by an international border from their allies and kinfolk in the west. The buffer around Oswego limited contacts between the Iroquois and the British, who still occupied the fort. The Fort Stanwix border, in other words, threatened to curtail the freedom of movement that Iroquois peoples had struggled to preserve over the course of many decades. Their lands, no longer located on the frontier, or as part of a permeable borderland, lay now entirely within the asserted boundaries of the United States, a new nation committed to the dispossession of the Six Nations and the transformation of Indian land into white agricultural settlements. They no longer could claim the river, nor a right to fish and hunt along the Niagara. The United States hoped that by limiting Iroquois access to the British in Canada, the Fort Stanwix treaty reduced the threat to frontier settlements and exposed the British posts by eliminating their Indian buffer. The United States made no offer to pay for this cession and agreed only "to give peace to the Senecas, Mohawks, Onondagas, Cayugas, and receive them into their protection."[24]

Relatively few Iroquois attended the treaty. Illness ravaged the settlements around Fort Niagara and kept many from attending. Those who signed felt that they had been coerced. The congressional commissioners obtained exactly what they wanted. Other U.S. commissioners negotiated similarly harsh treaties with the Cherokees at Hopewell in 1785 and with the Ohio Valley tribes at Fort MacIntosh in 1785 and at Fort Finney one year later. These treaties did little for those Indians who signed them, and the congressional pledge to protect their remaining lands, it turned out, ended up meaning little.[25]

Half a year after Fort Stanwix, New York's agents tried to obtain a cession of Oneida lands. The attempt grew out of a land dispute involving a Revolutionary War veteran named John Harper, who had persuaded some Oneidas to sell him twenty-four square miles of territory along the Pennsylvania border. Grasshopper, a sachem of the Oneidas, told Governor Clinton of the unauthorized sale to Harper and asked that the "writing might be destroyed." Clinton told the Oneidas that he wished to "perpetuate that harmony and friendship between you and us, by preventing Frauds and Impositions, which might be attempted to be committed on you by our white people." He seemed sympathetic, but the Oneidas, he said, must decide their course with "dispatch." He tried to rush them to make a hasty decision.[26]

The Oneidas did not want to be rushed. That is not how Iroquois diplomacy worked. The great Oneida leader Good Peter responded to the governor's address. The United States, he knew, had guaranteed the Oneidas the possession of their lands. Now he asked the governor to take action to prevent New Yorkers from violating that pledge. Settlers at German Flats, for instance, had taken Oneida lands without payment. Good Peter now "was willing to lease one tier of farms in the manner they are done by the White People, along the

Boundary Line throughout the extent of our Country, and that People of influence might be settled on those Farms to prevent encroachments, and that a person might be appointed to collect our rents annually." Good Peter wanted friendship, and he was willing to lease a small tract if doing so formed a buffer that could protect the Oneida heartland from further encroachments on their lands.[27]

But Governor Clinton would not accept these terms. Clinton would not tolerate having an Indian community as landlords for white people. The Oneidas had believed that they were meeting with the state to brighten a chain of friendship that existed between them and that had survived a war, but not to sell their lands. Clinton told the Oneidas that he felt betrayed. The Oneidas, out of a desire to placate the angry governor, then expressed a willingness to sell lands along a "line from the Mouth of the Unadilla River with a direct course to the Chenango River and so down the same." Good Peter cautioned the governor. His offer had been premised more upon a desire to preserve "friendship, than out of a pecuniary reward, and that they could not part with more." He did not want the governor to misunderstand the Oneidas' motives. Clinton continued to press for a larger cession. The Oneidas, through the terms of the resulting Fort Herkimer treaty, reluctantly sold to the state 200,000 acres for $11,500.[28]

Thus began years of intense, state-sponsored aggression against Iroquois land rights. The number of settlers moving onto lands bordering Iroquoia grew rapidly in the 1780s. They hunted woods and fished streams upon which Indians had relied for their subsistence. They chased Indians from the fields they had farmed for many years. The growing numbers of settlers in much of New York no longer feared Indians, and some used the opportunity provided by their strength relative to the Iroquois to settle scores, real and imagined, left over from the Revolution.[29]

Not all the assaults on Iroquois land were launched by the state. Massachusetts, whose colonial charter had specified no western limits, claimed much of the land in New York. In December 1786, representatives from the two states met in Hartford to hammer out their differences. The "Articles" to which they agreed gave to New York "all the claim, right, and title which the Commonwealth of Massachusetts hath to the Government, Sovereignty, and Jurisdiction of the Lands and Territories so claimed by the State of New York."

Massachusetts received, for its part, "the right of pre-emption of the soil from the native Indians," which it promptly sold to a group of speculators headed by Oliver Phelps and Nathaniel Gorham. The right of pre-emption, or the right to sell, was based on the notion that actual title to the land was vested in the European discoverers and their successor states. All that native peoples possessed in this formulation was a right of occupancy. They might remain upon their lands, but they could only sell them to the holder of the right of pre-emption. Massachusetts looked forward to profiting from the title it claimed to Iroquois lands.[30]

The speculators met with the Senecas and others of the Six Nations at Buffalo Creek, the political center of the relocated Iroquois League, where 2,000 Indians lived in approximately 250 houses, in the summer of 1788. Phelps and Gorham persuaded the sachems to sell them a huge tract of land lying mostly to the east of the Genesee River and west of Seneca Lake in return for "two thousand one hundred pounds lawful money of the State of New York." Furthermore, Phelps signed a bond in which he promised to pay an annuity amounting to "two hundred pounds lawful money of the state of New York, the one half whereof to be cattle at a reasonable appraisment, the other half in silver and gold coined," with the payment to be made on the Fourth of July "annually forever thereafter to ensure to the use benefit and behalf of the said five Nations." Joseph Brant, who hoped to persuade Iroquois people to move to a rekindled council fire at Grand River, assisted the speculators, service for which they compensated him with $750 and a fine pacing horse.[31]

Many Senecas objected to this sale. Cornplanter, who signed the deed to Phelps and Gorham, received death threats. Others spoke of fighting to preserve their lands, or of ending their lives rather than living with the pain of a lost homeland. Cornplanter, in his own defense, charged that Phelps deceived him, that he had promised the Senecas twice the amount stated in the written deed, and that he had signed the treaty only on the advice of the missionary Samuel Kirkland, who worked for Phelps.[32]

In addition to the speculators backed by Massachusetts, Clinton and his allies worried about the activities of the New York Genesee Company of Adventurers, a wealthy and influential group of land barons led by John Livingston, a member of the New York state assembly. On November 13, 1787, the Livingston Company negotiated a lease with "the Chiefs and sachems of the Six Nations of Indians" for a term of 999 years for "all that certain Tract or Parcel of Land, commonly called and known by the Name of the Lands of the Six Nations, situate, lying, and being in the State of New York, and now in the actual possession of the said Chiefs and Sachems." Livingston and his investors agreed to pay "the yearly Rent or Sum of Two Thousand Spanish Milled Dollars, in and upon the fourth Day of July." Two months later, the Company negotiated an additional lease with the Oneidas, for the same term of 999 years, to all their lands for a sum gradually rising up to $1,500 per year.[33]

The Livingston Company men came cloaked with the mantle of state authority—Livingston's associates Peter Schuyler, Abraham Cuyler, and Martin Visscher, as well as Samuel Kirkland, all had represented the state in past negotiations. They intended to evade through a long-term lease the state constitutional prohibition against sales of land without its permission. The Livingston Company used deception to skirt the requirements of law. These transactions involved millions of acres of land open now to white settlers and speculators who felt little regard for their native neighbors. It is worth asking why the Six Nations delegates put pen to paper, agreeing to sell their lands to Phelps and Gorham. Why did they lease their lands to Livingston and his associates? Did they understand what they were doing?[34]

Iroquois peoples complained about the relentless pressure placed upon them to cede their lands. They found confusing the multitude of forces that approached them. Iroquois leaders could see the growing numbers of white settlers who encroached upon their homelands, a force no authority seemed able to control. These settlers were coming, they might have reasoned, whether the Iroquois sold the lands or not. Best to receive something for lands that white settlers already had begun to clear, and that they risked losing outright to squatters. But the Iroquois were experimenting as well, learning their way in the new world created by the American Revolution. Their attempt to sell their lands in return for annual payments—however paltry those sums appear to us now—might be best viewed as an attempt, on highly unfavorable terms, to transform their lands into cash payments. Efforts to lease lands, like those the Oneidas proposed in 1785 and like the agreement with the Livingston Company, might have allowed Iroquois people to derive an income from lands they feared they might lose outright to expanding white settlements. Haudenosaunee leaders struggled to hang on to their lands, their autonomy, and their way of life in the face of numerous challenges, and in so doing, they suffered many setbacks.[35]

The deeds negotiated by the state with the Onondagas and Oneidas at Fort Schuyler, the former Fort Stanwix, in the summer of 1788 illustrate the nature of the problems Haudenosaunee people faced in the years after the Revolution. Governor Clinton and his allies in the state legislature saw the Livingston Lease as a threat, and they acted with energy to consolidate state control over the conduct of Indian policy in New York and the disposition of those lands they might obtain from the Iroquois. The legislature declared that the leases were void and that no purchases of land from Indians, "within the limits of this State, shall be binding on the said Indians, or deemed valid, unless made under the authority, and with the consent, of the Legislature of this State."[36]

Clinton did not tell the Indians about the revocation of the Livingston Lease. Instead, he invited them to the fort not to purchase their lands but to protect them and "by a new agreement place matters on such a footing as to prevent these things for the future." The Livingston Company had taken their lands against the state's wishes; Clinton promised to protect them from this illegal act and to set things right. If they did not meet with him, and chose not to gather at the Council Fire, he would do nothing to help them collect their rents.[37]

The Iroquois may have been confused about Governor Clinton's intentions. Certainly officers employed by the Livingston Company attempted to disrupt the proceedings. They told a Seneca named Onyegat that "the Governor's Business at this proposed Treaty is to purchase your Lands, but you have leased them to us. He means to pay you all at once for them, and then in a few years to drive you off and tell you that you have no Property here." A Frenchman named Dominique Debarges, a fur trader from Montreal and a Livingston Company agent, along with an Indian known as "the Infant," told sachems on their way to Fort Schuyler that "it will be your Destruction if you go down to the Treaty." Clinton intended to acquire their lands by fair means or foul, and "when you return you'll have no place to set your Foot on."[38] That the missionary Samuel Kirkland served as an interpreter at Fort Schuyler might have aided the governor's campaign of deceit. The minister and missionary, after all, had served at the federal Fort Stanwix treaty in 1784, and his presence at Fort Schuyler may have granted a veneer of legitimacy to Clinton's efforts and supported the governor's claim to represent the only jurisdiction with a legitimate right to negotiate with the Six Nations.[39]

Clinton and the commissioners met first with the Onondagas. At the council, after a lengthy and misleading negotiation, the Onondaga orator Black Cap told Clinton that "we have chosen to convey to you our Country in a way in which we may receive a continual Benefit; that when the Cold comes we may be kept warm, and when hungry we may have something to subsist upon." This is what Kirkland wrote down in English as he listened to and interpreted Black Cap's speech. What Black Cap thought he was agreeing to, however, and what the New Yorkers wrote into the treaty were significantly different. The state of New York acquired, on paper, title to a vast swath of territory stretching from Lake Ontario to Pennsylvania. The Onondagas, on the other hand, believed that the treaty established something akin to a shared-use or commons arrangement in exchange for an annual payment. In the large quantity of lands that the Onondagas ostensibly had ceded to the state of New York, for instance, the Indians were guaranteed "the free right of Hunting in every part of the said ceded lands, and of fishing in all the waters within the same." The fourth article of the treaty, similarly, guaranteed equal access for both New Yorkers and Onondagas to a strip of land one mile around Onondaga Lake. Nothing in the language of the third or fourth articles of the treaty, in short, would have led the Onondagas to any conclusion other than that their willingness to share a large portion of their lands with the citizens of the state of New York had been recognized by the governor.[40]

Governor Clinton's speech after the parties had signed the treaty could only have confirmed the Onondagas' interpretation of its terms. The governor once again reminded the sachems that this treaty was held for "our mutual interest" and that "in making this Covenant we have regarded what appeared to us to be the true interest of both the Parties." Black Cap agreed. "Friendship and a tender regard for our interest has marked every step of your conduct towards us on this occasion," he said. The 1788 treaty, Black Cap believed, guaranteed the Onondagas a tract for their exclusive use; the rest of their enormous territory they would share with the New Yorkers, firm in the belief that "every privilege arising from our Whole territory we enjoy and continue to enjoy." They and their posterity, the 1788 agreement reads, "forever shall enjoy the free right of hunting in every part of the said ceded lands, and of fishing in all the waters within the same."[41]

It is, once again, worth remembering that Black Cap spoke his own language. He spoke, Kirkland listened, and then the missionary searched through his stock of images and ideas to express what Black Cap said in written English. The treaty was read back to Black Cap and the Onondagas by Kirkland, who interpreted the commissioners' English into something the Onondagas could understand. The Onondagas "ceded" land to the New Yorkers but, in doing so, insisted that they continued to enjoy "every privilege" deriving from those lands, including the right to hunt and fish. The Onondagas, and Indians in North America generally, did not have a concept of real property similar to that of the Americans. The Iroquois divided their physical world into woods and clearings, one a zone of hunting and warfare, the other a place of peace. Iroquois women planted crops and tended farms in the villages. Men ventured into the woods to hunt and fish and make war. It is at least possible, if we take seriously Iroquois conceptions of the land and how it was used, that Black Cap did nothing more than grant the commissioners access to their lands.

In the years following the treaty of 1788, the Onondagas and their neighbors continued to travel across lands they ostensibly had ceded to the state. At Kanadasaga, near today's Geneva, New York, Kirkland ran into Senecas, Cayugas, and Onondagas. The Onondagas, after the Fort Schuyler treaty, acted on the understanding that they had entered into a joint-use arrangement with the citizens of the state of New York. They shared their lands. They shared the tract around Onondaga Lake, trading with the growing numbers of white settlers there. They continued to travel through and hunt and fish on the lands they supposedly had ceded as well. When the explorer Elkanah Watson traveled through the Onondagas' country in 1791, he encountered Indians everywhere. Along the Onondaga River they taught him "the mode of catching eels . . . in weirs." They taught him how to catch the many salmon that ascended the river on their spawning runs. At Three River Point, where the Onondaga River flowed from the east into its junction with the Seneca River, Watson again encountered Onondagas. He met "several troublesome Indians of the Onondage tribe" looking for rum, but he also met "Old Kiadote the Chief of the Onondago Indians," who "with several warriors and the Queen who brought us several excellent salmon and eels for which we gave them in exchange rum and biscuits."[42]

After leaving Three River Point, Watson began to ascend the Seneca River. After "about one mile," he came to "a considerable rapid." He and his associates encountered there "a party of Indians . . . encamp'd for the purpose of the eel fishery." The next day, along the western shore of Onondaga Lake, Watson and his fellow travelers "passed several birch canoes with Onondago Indians returning from fishing, accompanied by all their families—Children, dogs, cats, &c." Watson took time to visit with the Onondagas. He and the Indians spent "time together talking by signs and trafficking biscuit and rum for smoked eels and salmon." Watson was surprised, he wrote, "that Indians who reside near the influence of white people and even when mixed with them, should preserve their native Customs so tenaciously."[43]

It is a revealing quote. Watson found Indians drunk and Indians trading, but he also found Onondagas exploiting regional resources in ways that they always had done, lots of them, enjoying the "peaceful possession" of what they had left. They feared the aggressiveness of the New Yorkers in trying to lure them to negotiate the sale of their lands. They recognized that they faced a relentless enemy, determined to gobble up their remaining lands. But those they still held, by their standards, they continued to use in ways that they always had done.[44]

After Clinton and the commissioners finished with the Onondagas, it was the Oneidas' turn. That Clinton said he would protect the Oneidas from the Livingston adventurers pleased Good Peter. At the close of the council, where the Oneidas entered into an agreement similar to that signed by the Onondagas, Good Peter proudly announced to Governor Clinton that "my nation are now restored to a possession of their property which they were in danger of having lost." The agreement, Good Peter continued, secured for the Oneidas "so much of our property which would otherwise have been lost." Like Black Cap, Good Peter offered to share the bulk of the Oneidas' lands with the New Yorkers, reserving a right to hunt and fish in the opened lands, and a tract of land for their own use that the settlers could not enter. Only when surveyors arrived in the fall of 1790 did Good Peter realize that what he viewed as a lease of sorts was, under law, a sale.[45]

Treaties, deeds, and councils: During the Confederation era at both the state and national level these became the instruments of Indian dispossession. At times, Indians wanted to meet with American officials. At times these councils addressed issues of consequence to native communities. But the written documents that emerged from the negotiations served the interests always of those who possessed the power to write. The actions of New York, and of more aggressive states like North Carolina and Georgia, both of which extracted cessions of Indian lands through fraudulent or coerced written treaties, posed a significant danger to the fragile young republic.

Governor Clinton had good cause for rushing the Oneidas and Onondagas at Fort Schuyler in the summer of 1788. New Yorkers overwhelmingly had opposed the new federal Constitution drawn up at the convention held in Philadelphia in the summer of 1787, and the governor led the "Antifederalist" forces within his state. Advocates of a stronger national government felt the need to replace the Articles of Confederation for a number of reasons, but the "father of the Constitution," James Madison, listed high on his list of "Vices of the Political System of the United States" the aggressive Indian policies pursued by the states. Article I, Section 8 of the new Constitution replaced the vague and ambiguous language of Article IX of the Articles of Confederation, with an assertive statement of federal authority over the conduct of Indian affairs: Once the Constitution became the "Supreme Law of the Land," Congress would possess the exclusive authority "to regulate Commerce with foreign Nations, and among the several states, and with the Indian tribes."[46]

CHAPTER 3

....

Critically Circumstanced

The United States came into existence, Henry Knox wrote, "embarrassed with a frontier of immense extent." It presented to the new nation enormous problems of governance. Georgians, for instance, had pushed the powerful Creek towns, already armed and supplied by the Spanish on the Gulf Coast, to the point of armed resistance. Settlers in North Carolina and in the short-lived "State of Franklin" had done the same with the Cherokees. In each of these areas, settlers deployed violence against native leaders who sought an accommodation with white settlers, destroyed Indian towns, and assaulted their ways of living. Militant Chickamauga Cherokees kept in close contact with a powerful Indian confederation growing in the Ohio Country—Shawnees and Delawares played leading roles, but also important were Ottawas, Potawatomis, Miamis, Wyandots, and many others. Together native peoples in the north and south believed that no peace could be achieved with murderous white frontiersmen, and they vowed to resist further white expansion onto their lands.[1]

In December 1786, Congress received the speech delivered to them by "The United Indian Nations at their Confederate Council" held near the mouth of the Detroit River. The Ohio Valley tribes were there in force, but so were Cherokees and representatives from the Five Nations. They told the Americans that they wanted peace, but only on their own terms. They repudiated the postwar treaties and asked that new treaties be negotiated. If the Americans wanted peace they should take "such steps as become upright and honest men." The Northwestern confederates pledged to look past the murder of their leaders by frontier thugs, but only if the Americans promised not to cross the Ohio

River and hold to the line negotiated at Fort Stanwix in 1768. Further, they asked the United States to negotiate with the Northwestern confederates as a whole, rather than with individual nations, and to acknowledge that any agreement involving "any cession of our lands should be made in the most public manner, and by the united voice of the confederacy." They expected the Americans to attempt to divide in advance of conquest. They would as a consequence hold "all partial treaties as void and of no effect."[2]

Joseph Brant and other Iroquois from Grand River attended the conference and joined in the call for a restoration of the 1768 Fort Stanwix treaty line separating Indian from non-Indian lands. The treaties that congressional commissioners had negotiated in the mid-1780s had, at least in part, been directed toward separating the Iroquois from their western allies. The 1786 conference showed the enduring strength of these ties. The Northwestern confederates proposed an alternative to the border that the Americans attempted to define after the Revolution, one that separated the British in Canada to the north from the sovereign American states to their south. Instead, they called for a line that separated an Indian domain above the Ohio from white settlements to their east.[3]

Many of the Iroquois in New York state shared the anger of the Northwestern confederates. They complained of the relentless efforts by the state and speculators to acquire their lands. They complained of violence, and of hunger.[4] The British saw in this disaffection an opportunity. The American republic had a population that dwarfed that of British Canada, and the disparity they knew would continue to increase. The British worried about American expansion and saw cooperation with the Northwestern confederates and the Six Nations as a way to curb it. Cooperation, furthermore, might allow the British to retain control of the region's trade in furs. The British government had already decided to hold on to their posts on American soil—Niagara, Oswego, Detroit, and others—an act that the American states' persecution of Loyalists justified. If American state governments would ignore the peace treaty that ended the Revolutionary War by dispossessing loyal subjects of the Crown, the British would ignore the treaty's demands that they abandon the forts.[5]

British officers did not want war with the United States, but they were willing to quietly arm and equip native warriors determined to

Joseph Fayadaneega, called the Brant, the Great Captain of the Six Nations, Engraving by J. R. Smith, based on painting by George Romney, Library of Congress Prints and Photographs Division, Washington, DC. Smith erred; Brant's name was Thayendanegea. Romney painted Brant's portrait when the Mohawk leader visited Great Britain during the early years of the American Revolutionary War.
Courtesy of the Library of Congress Prints and Photographs Division, LC-USZC4-4913

prevent American settlement beyond the Ohio. By the middle of the 1780s, British officials began to express the hope that a neutral Indian barrier state might arise, with its southern border running along the Ohio. Through 1786 and 1787, the British Indian Department held a number of councils with the Iroquois in Canada and at Buffalo Creek, expressing this aspiration.[6]

The United States confronted a frontier that was, in the words of Henry Knox, "critically circumstanced," and the United States met with some 200 Indians from several nations at Fort Harmar in January 1789 in an attempt to begin addressing the challenges it faced. Secretary of War Knox hoped to learn more about "the causes of uneasiness among the said tribes," and after that, to settle "all affairs concerning lands and boundaries, between them and the United

States." A small number of Iroquois—Senecas from the Allegheny and from the Genesee, mostly—attended the treaty. Cornplanter told the governor of the Northwest Territory, Arthur St. Clair, that his people could not live without their land. They hoped that the United States would repudiate the cessions it had extracted several years before at a time when his people were in no position to resist.[7]

St. Clair could not do this. He would not relinquish the lands that the United States had acquired by treaty. He did offer to pay them for what the United States had acquired: $3,000 for the land the Iroquois had lost at Fort Stanwix in 1784 and $6,000 for those lands relinquished by the Ohio Valley tribes at Fort McIntosh and Fort Finney. Cornplanter signed. Few of the men who joined him seem to have spoken with much authority. In return for his signature, Cornplanter received a payment in goods that he could carry home to the Allegany and distribute to his followers. Frontiersmen robbed him of most of these goods on the trip home. He also negotiated an agreement with Pennsylvania, ceding to the Keystone State the so-called Erie Triangle. In return, and "to fix his attachment to this state," he received 1,400 acres of land, which he thereafter sold, and a small quantity of goods. Living remote from the British post at Niagara, and between land-hungry settlers and angry western Indians, Cornplanter felt that he needed the friendship of the United States.[8]

Fort Harmar did not set things right. Too few leaders, from too few communities, with too little influence signed the document, and many important leaders stayed away. The president knew that his work was not finished. He and Knox wanted frontier order, and they recognized that the pretense of conquest, coupled with the government's inability to control its settlers and the sovereign states, must bring to the young republic a continuous cycle of expensive warfare. So they abandoned the conquest policy and adopted a program reminiscent of that employed by the British empire: negotiation, the giving of gifts, a regulated trade, and guarantees that Indian lands would be protected from the territorial aggression of the frontier population. To achieve this, in the summer of 1790, Washington signed into law the first federal Indian Trade and Intercourse Act.[9]

The law established licensing procedures for Americans who wished to engage in trade with native peoples and penalties for unlicensed traders. With regard to the purchase of Indian land, the law

Cornplanter. Seneca Chief, Ki-On-Twog-Ky, also known as Cornplanter
(1732/40–1836), by F. Bartoli, 1796.
Courtesy of the New York Historical Society

read that no sale "shall be valid to any person or persons, or to any
state, whether having the right of pre-emption to such lands or not,
unless the same shall be made and duly executed at some public
treaty, held under the authority of the United States." The law also
held that American citizens committing crimes would be prosecuted
as if they had committed the same crime against a white person.[10]

Congress enacted the Trade and Intercourse Act to provide the
president with the power to oversee the orderly expansion of American
settlement, something that Washington and Knox believed could best
be achieved if peace was maintained with the Indian tribes. Washington
hoped to exert federal control over Indian affairs and to limit the ability
of frontier whites to poison the nation's relations with its Indian neighbors. By establishing licensing procedures for traders entering Indian
country, Washington secured in theory at least one means to prevent
unsavory characters from cheating Indians and so provoking an expensive Indian war. By requiring that whites guilty of crimes against the

Indians be treated as if they had committed the crime against another white person, the Indian Trade and Intercourse Act at least on paper committed the United States to a principle of justice defined by Americans for Indians. Washington wanted for the United States the Indians' land, but he wanted to acquire it peacefully and inexpensively.[11]

Indeed, Washington wrote to Secretary of the Treasury Alexander Hamilton to complain that peace with Indians was impossible "while land-jobbing and the disorderly conduct of our borderers is suffered with impunity, and whilst the States individually are omitting no occasion to interfere in matters which belong to the general Government."[12] Washington was frustrated. He knew he lacked the real power to keep order. Aware that power claimed but not exercised effectively was power lost, he fumed in his correspondence with cabinet officers but still expressed his increasingly forlorn hope that he might restrain the worst of the abuses, while "advancing the happiness of the Indians" and attaching "them firmly to the United States."[13]

These attachments could be formed only if the Indians looked past their grievances, and that was something many of them were not yet prepared to do. Good Peter, the Oneida leader, pointed out that under the republic, "it seems to us we are not really free men." The Oneidas' struggles continued through the era of the American Revolution, an unabated contest for independence. Good Peter complained of the fraudulent land transactions carried out by the state of New York. Senecas complained of the Phelps and Gorham purchase and, most of all, the loss of the Erie Triangle, which included the Lake Erie post of Presqu' Isle, both in agreements that Cornplanter had signed. As Pennsylvania began to make plans to survey the lands, even Cornplanter regretted his actions.[14]

The loss of the Erie Triangle, that tract that ensured Pennsylvania's access to the southern shore of Lake Erie, threatened to tear asunder connections between the Six Nations and the Northwestern confederates. It represented not just a loss of land, but a loss of autonomy, an ability to move through a greater Iroquoia. Leaders like Cornplanter, who found themselves living in close quarter with violent and aggressive settlers on the Pennsylvania frontier, and who believed as a result that they must reach an accommodation with the United States, received the scorn of both the Northwestern confederates and the hatred of frontier settlers. But other Senecas, "young men" who could not easily be controlled, found themselves attracted to the message of militant western Indians who identified the source of their communities' problems in the aggressions of white settlers. Cornplanter warned the Pennsylvania government. He sent a petition to the assembly, noting that despite his friendship to the state, "we are often disturbed by bad people." The situation was urgent. "We must hunt very hard for the skins to keep our wives and children alive," he noted, and when they found them, they carried them downriver to Pittsburgh, where "our camps are plundered, our horses and canoes stolen, and also some of our people killed by bad people." Trade and commerce were breaking down. When they complained, nobody came forward "to hear, to Judge, or interpret for us, that the wrongs done us may be redressed." Cornplanter wanted peace, he said, and he offered a lot to get it. He asked the Pennsylvania assembly to "appoint some persons, in Pittsburgh, to judge, and interpret, that if our bad people do mischief we may deliver them up to your law, and that if your people do us harm, they may also be found and delivered up to your law." He offered, at heart, to make Pennsylvania law the arbiter in all disputes between Senecas and Pennsylvanians, an enormous concession that not all Indians would willingly have made. Cornplanter pointed out that he needed an answer. "Our families, and skins, our lives and property are in danger" both from the Northwestern Indians and the white people.[15]

Less than three months after Cornplanter's petition, in June 1790, four settlers killed two Senecas they found hunting along Pine Creek in northern Pennsylvania. The Pennsylvanians, Samuel Doyle and the three Walker brothers, met the Senecas in a tavern, evidence in itself of the great range of interactions that might occur in the borderlands. The Walkers believed that the older of the two Senecas, a man in his fifties, had killed their father during the Revolutionary War. They wanted vengeance. That night, they surprised the sleeping Seneca hunters, and killed the younger man with a tomahawk blow to the skull and the older man with a gunshot to the head.[16]

The Senecas learned of the murders despite the efforts of the killers to hide the bodies. The Senecas asked Pennsylvania authorities to set things right, not to punish the murderers so much as to come and condole them for their losses, and in so doing to respect traditional Iroquois cultural protocols that prevented unassuaged grief from spiraling into warfare. They asked the Pennsylvanians to perform the rituals of condolence that rested at the heart of Iroquois League traditional culture. The goal was to find peace of mind, to calm those who grieved. They asked the Pennsylvanians to act according to cultural norms and values that stretched back into the mythic past. They asked the authorities to send presents to Tioga, "where you will meet the whole of the Tribe of the deceased, and all the Chiefs, and a number of warriors of our nation, where we will expect you will wash away the blood of your Brothers and Bury the Hatchet, and put it out of memory as it is yet sticking in our Head." They told the Pennsylvanians to act quickly. They warned that some of "our young warriors are very uneasy."[17]

Pennsylvania attempted to arrest and try the murderers. The state's agent, Robert King, who not only "carried the public dispatches to the Seneca Nation respecting the murders" but also worked "to bring the offenders to justice," was forced thereafter "to abandon his place of residence through the fear of being assassinated by the supposed murderers, who have repeatedly menaced his life." The Walkers' friends and neighbors did not see the murder of an Indian as a crime.[18] The Pennsylvania assembly, recognizing the gravity of the situation, appropriated funds to pay for presents to "cover the graves," but Governor Thomas Mifflin asked the federal government to assume the more expensive responsibility of meeting the Senecas in council and delivering the presents. President Washington seized the opportunity. He and Knox had wanted to assert federal supremacy in Indian affairs, and the Pine Creek murders gave them their chance. Failure, he feared, might lead young Seneca warriors to join with the growing number of Northwestern confederates attacking American settlements.[19]

Washington confronted a complex problem. He hoped to maintain a friendship with the Senecas and the Six Nations in the face of frontier outrages, while preventing them from joining the growing war in the west. The Northwestern confederates raided American settlements in the Ohio country. Washington would not grant them the boundary line they wanted along the Ohio, and he feared that the hostile natives might find additional support from the British. While he pursued peace with the Six Nations, then, in June 1790 his secretary of war issued orders to General Josiah Harmar, commanding him to march out against the western Indians, burn their towns, and "to extirpate, utterly" the enemy.[20]

The president, shortly thereafter, appointed Timothy Pickering as his agent to meet with the Senecas. Pickering had been born in Salem, Massachusetts, in 1745. He graduated from Harvard in 1763, just as the colonists' protest movement began. He served during the war initially in the Massachusetts militia before joining the Continental Army in 1776. He rose through the ranks, eventually becoming the army's Quarter-Master General. Here he learned first-hand about the challenges sovereign states might cause under a weak central government. Pickering became an early and ardent Federalist and felt strongly that the states must be subordinated to national control.

Pickering moved to Pennsylvania after the war. He took up residence in Wilkes-Barre. In 1788, he found himself taken captive by

Timothy Pickering, 1806, engraving by Charles Balthazar Julien Fevret de Saint-Memin.
Courtesy of the Library of Congress Prints and Photographs Division, LC-USZ62-54942

"Wild Yankees," the descendants of New England settlers who claimed lands in the northwestern corner of the state and resisted its authority. His abductors had been characterized as "a dangerous combination of villains, composed of runaway debtors, criminals, [and] adherents of Shays," the western Massachusetts agrarian rebel who took up arms against his own state government in 1786 to protest rising economic injustice. The Wild Yankees' protest movement, at times quite violent, was far more complex than this simple characterization suggests, but it had the effect of educating Pickering about the sorts of men who inhabited the Pennsylvania frontier.[21]

By 1790, Pickering was looking for work. He served in the state constitutional convention that met in Philadelphia, and he approached both Washington and his treasury secretary, Alexander Hamilton, seeking some appointment. The president had something in mind. On September 7 Pickering wrote to his brother John, informing him that Washington had "requested me to undertake a mission to the Seneca Nation of Indians, to give them satisfaction for the murder of two of their people on the West Branch of the Susquehanna in Pennsylvania." Pickering threw himself into the endeavor, even if it was less than what he wanted. He looked forward to meeting the grieving Senecas at Tioga at the end of September. He could not know it at the time, but Pickering would spend the next five years at the center of America's relations with the Six Nations.[22]

Washington instructed Pickering to make known, through the presentation of gifts, "that the murders committed at Pine Creek on some of their tribe are causes of great displeasure to the United States." Looking to assert federal supremacy over the conduct of diplomacy and to bring order to the frontier, the president also instructed Pickering to explain to the Senecas the federal Trade and Intercourse Act and "that all business between them and any part of the United States is hereafter to be transacted by the general government" and not by states acting by themselves.[23]

Pickering sent out his invitation. He asked "the relatives of the deceased" to travel to Tioga and receive the American government's assurances of friendship. Clearly he received some advice on how to frame his invitation, for Pickering drew upon the language of the Covenant Chain. At Tioga, he wrote, "the chain of friendship between us shall be brightened; and may the Great Spirit lead your nation and the United States to keep it always bright while the sun shines." He hoped that the number of attendees would be few. He understood the importance of economy. Still, he began to stockpile supplies to feed 200 Indians for twelve days.[24]

Pickering approached the work with an open mind. He asked for advice. He was told to plan for more Indians and to find, as Oliver Phelps put it, "an interpreter that you can confide in." Washington instructed him to keep the gathering small, but Pickering quickly learned that he had little control over the number of Indians who were coming. He realized that he needed more supplies, and he began to grasp the enormity of the challenge before him.

Late in September, for instance, residents from Chemung, having heard of the council, expressed their alarm. Large numbers of Senecas would pass through their town on the way to the treaty grounds. Even small numbers of Indians, the petitioners charged, "distressed and injured the inhabitants by killing & pilfering their property." With an even greater number coming, the Chemung men feared that Indians will "for lack of provisions destroy much of our property which perhaps may so exhaust some of the inhabitants to so great a degree as to lead to bloodshed."[25]

Pickering assured them that he would do all in his power to prevent this problem from occurring. He ordered provisions placed along the way to ease the Senecas' advance. But many more were coming than he anticipated. "Great numbers will come to see you," the Seneca leader Little Billy told Pickering, perhaps 500 from Buffalo Creek and 300 from Geneseo. They would need provisions, and they wanted to talk about much more than the murders committed at Pine Creek.[26]

While Pickering made plans to meet the Senecas at Tioga, Harmar marched out from Fort Washington, the future site of Cincinnati, against the Miami towns. Washington and Knox had hoped to avoid war. They worried that "blood and injustice" might "stain the character of the nation." The price for this, they feared, might exceed "all pecuniary calculation." But settlers persisted in pushing across the Ohio, the line the Northwestern tribes had determined would serve as a boundary. As reports of raid and counter-raid poured in from the west, the secretary of war felt pressure to act.[27]

Harmar's force consisted of 320 regulars and nearly 1,200 militia. They headed north, burning five Miami towns and some 20,000 bushels of corn. But the Indians would not engage the American forces on fields of Harmar's choosing. They bided their time, retreating, waiting for an opportunity. Finally, on October 21, and again the next day, the Northwestern confederates struck, ambushing detachments from Harmar's army. He lost more than 100 men and 500 horses. Shawnees following Blue Jacket and Miamis following Little Turtle, along with Potawatomis, Delawares, and others, forced Harmar to retreat. Washington understood the gravity of the situation. The expedition had produced only "expence without honor or profit" and was a "disappointment" that came to "a disgraceful termination." Settlers in the western parts of Kentucky, Virginia, and Pennsylvania expressed their growing distrust of a central government that seemed incapable of protecting them. Indians, buoyed with confidence, launched a new round of assaults the length of the frontier. The situation was indeed critical.[28]

Timothy Pickering left Wilkes-Barre on October 17. He arrived at Tioga three days later and immediately set to work ensuring that supplies were in order. The Seneca chief Little Billy arrived from Buffalo Creek on the 30th, along with four runners. Pickering welcomed them to the treaty ground, and Little Billy sent two of the runners to hasten the rest of the Senecas' arrival. The council was supposed to begin on the 25th, and the Senecas were late. Pickering learned that diplomacy with native nations demanded patience.

Little Billy stayed in camp and offered Pickering an opportunity to learn how the Senecas conducted their business. "On all occasions," Pickering wrote, Little Billy gave "decisive proofs of his good sense and great prudence." He told the truth, conducted himself "as a man of honor," and possessed "a delicate sense of propriety and decency, in his whole behavior." Pickering appreciated immensely the help Little Billy gave him and, he recalled later, "I have derived much pleasure from his acquaintance, and I shall always value him as my very particular friend."[29]

Pickering waited. He gathered intelligence. He obtained additional supplies. With the help of his interpreters, Joseph Smith, Jasper Parrish, and Israel Chapin, he learned what he could from Little Billy. He learned that the British attempted to prevent the Indians from attending the treaty. So, too, Pickering learned, did Horatio Jones, an interpreter favored by the Geneseo Senecas, who was a highly talented "but an unprincipled fellow."

Pickering remained optimistic. On November 11 he wrote to his friend Samuel Hodgdon. He had been waiting for over two weeks and complained of interference by the British. Still, he thought "the issue of the business will be satisfactory to both sides." Pickering wrote this letter one day before a Pennsylvania jury acquitted the only Pine Creek killer who stood trial for the crime. Pickering was mortified to learn "that the bulk of the frontier inhabitants consider the killing of Indians in time of peace, to be no crime." He thought the settlers "far more savage & revengeful than the Indians."[30]

The Senecas arrived at Tioga on November 14. The chiefs visited with Pickering that evening, but he recognized that one in his position "must serve at least a short apprenticeship in learning their manners and customs." He had much still to learn, and he knew it. He met at Tioga the men with whom he would work to preserve order on the frontier and the autonomy and independence of the Iroquois. In addition to Little Billy, he met Farmer's Brother, "dignified and fluent," and Red Jacket, the great orator. They wanted peace, and they would help Pickering understand how to secure it.[31]

The next morning, Pickering formally welcomed the Senecas, although he lamented the cause of the meeting. He showed to them the commission he had received from the president and explained that "I was appointed to wash off the blood of our murdered brothers, and wipe away the tears from the eyes of their friends." He hoped that the council might result in an agreement "to brighten the chain of friendship between you and the United States." Pickering was a quick study. Clearly advised by Chapin and Parrish, he made use of the council rhetoric Haudenosaunee peacemakers expected to hear. He also was honest about his inexperience. "Brothers," he told the Senecas, "as this is the first time that I have held a treaty with you, it cannot be expected that I am well acquainted with your customs." He would do his best, and he was willing to learn, and he pledged that "what I speak to you shall be the truth, which I am sure you will think more important than a strict observance of ceremonious forms." Pickering acknowledged the Senecas' grief. "You said the hatchet was yet sticking in your head: I now pull it out." He handed to Farmer's Brother strings of wampum, to make his words real.[32]

Farmer's Brother, rising to speak, apologized for their tardiness. Red Jacket then rose and spoke. An enormously talented orator, with a poor reputation as a warrior, it would be the first of a number of exchanges between him and Pickering over the next several years. Red Jacket spoke of grief, of covering graves. "A man of great ambition" in Pickering's view, and an outstanding debater and public speaker,[33] Red Jacket appreciated Pickering's honesty. He understood that Pickering lacked experience but promised that "we will describe the ancient practices of our fathers." At the outset, he offered to Pickering some gentle correction. Not so fast, Red Jacket said. "You say you have pulled the hatchet out of their heads," he said, "but you have only cast it behind you." So long as it remains unburied, he continued, "we cannot rest easy on our seats."[34]

Red Jacket said that the murders on Pine Creek had caused great grief. "The two men you have killed," he said, "were very great men." Eleven others had been murdered since the end of the war, he

RED JACKET.
SENECA WAR CHIEF.

Published by Campbell and Jones.

Red Jacket, who sat for King late in his life, wears the medal given to him by Washington. Red Jacket, Engraving based on original by Charles Bird King.
Courtesy of the Library of Congress Prints and Photographs Division, LC-DIG-ppmsca-05086

continued, and all their relatives still grieved. The matter must be set right, "for our young warriors are very uneasy." Red Jacket knew of Harmar's defeat, and he issued a menacing warning. He hoped, he told Pickering, "that our troubles will now have an end, but our eyes are not yet washed that we may see, nor our throats cleared so that we may speak."[35]

Pickering learned from Red Jacket. He pulled the hatchet from the Senecas' heads, he said, and would "now bury it, and pray God that it may remain buried, that its edge may nevermore be seen." He said that the United States had "no wish but to live with you as brothers in perpetual peace." *Guswenta*: The principle emerged again. As Jasper Parrish or Joseph Smith took Pickering's words and transformed them into Seneca, this may very well have been what they heard. A round of rum was served at the end of Pickering's speech and, following Red Jacket's advice, Pickering addressed the women. He took them "by the hand as sisters" and shook each of their hands.[36]

Concerns remained. On the 18th, Pickering once again addressed the Senecas. He cautioned them against avenging the murder of their people. It was best, he said, to leave the matter "to be done by judges, who act coolly and without passion; and by a careful examination, distinguish the innocent from the guilty." This was the way of the white people.

Red Jacket replied. He wanted to bury the difficulties, to move past them. But there were other issues, larger than the murder of Senecas by white frontiersmen. Red Jacket called for an acknowledgment of his people's autonomy and of their right to move about freely between Pennsylvania and New York. "Now Brother," he told Pickering, "you must caution your people of Pennsylvania that your brothers may pass and repass unmolested." The Senecas would permit the same for white settlers, traders, and travelers. "We sit side by side," he said, "& it ought to be done."[37]

One solution to a host of problems, Pickering believed, was for the Senecas to deal only with the United States. Once again he explained to the Senecas the terms of the Indian Trade and Intercourse Act. Red Jacket appreciated this. He was glad the trade was now regulated, for the traders "have cheated us out of all our money" and cheated in the fur trade. Calling for equality, Red Jacket said that "it will be right if both sides will behave alike and do not cheat one another." Fair play. The cheating was not solely in the fur trade but in the buying and selling of land. Red Jacket finished. Farmer's Brother rose and complained, once again, of the Fort Stanwix treaty in 1784 and the Phelps and Gorham purchase. The Trade and Intercourse Act, Pickering hoped, might prevent fraudulent sales for the future, but the Senecas still felt the sting from transactions past. Fort Harmar had not helped, and significant grievances remained.[38]

Pickering could do little about this at Tioga. On the 22nd, he prepared to close the council. He addressed the Senecas one last time about the murders at Pine Creek. Speaking to the "Mothers, Brothers & Sisters" of the victims, he asked them to allow him to assuage their grief. "You enjoy the satisfaction of remembering the good qualities of your deceased sons & brothers, of reflecting that they were worthy men, and of hearing their names mentioned with honour." He continued:

> Let those considerations afford you some comfort. Death, you know, is the common lot of all mankind; and none can escape its stroke. Some, indeed, live many years, till, like well-ripened corn, they wither and bend down their heads. But multitudes fall in infancy and childhood, like the tender shooting corn nipped by untimely frosts. Others again grow to manhood, are then cut off, while full of sap, and flourishing in all the vigor of life. The latter, it seems, was the state of our two deceased brothers.

They were gone now, Pickering said, and nothing could bring them back. It is our duty, he said, "to bear our misfortunes." But he wanted to set things right, and addressing specifically the mothers, Pickering offered them two wampum belts "to manifest the sorrow of the United States for the loss of your sons."[39]

The Senecas accepted the gift, and Pickering, at the close of the council, wrote proudly "that the matter has been settled in the most friendly manner, that the said Indians are satisfied, that the chain of friendship between them and the United States has been brightened, and that they are now returning home in peace, with their minds easy."[40]

While Timothy Pickering met with the Senecas from Buffalo Creek and the Genesee Valley in Tioga, Cornplanter of the Allegany Senecas, along with Half Town and Big Tree, commenced a journey of their own to Philadelphia to meet with officials from Pennsylvania and the United States. Pressed upon by the Northwestern tribes and closer to Pittsburgh by water than to the British along the Niagara, Cornplanter needed to secure the ability of his people to travel safely through western Pennsylvania. Also known as Abeel or O'Bail or Obeal, after his white father, John O'Bail, Cornplanter was described by Samuel Kirkland as a man of "uncommon genius," a leader known for his sobriety and intellect and, to Henry Knox, as "the fittest person to make use of to manage the six nations, Brandt excepted." He was also proud to a fault.[41]

They arrived in Philadelphia on October 22 and addressed the Pennsylvania assembly the next day. Cornplanter expressed his people's friendship for Pennsylvania but pointed out that all was not well. Cornplanter recalled for the assembly the murder of an Allegany Seneca several years before. Addressing the "Fathers of the Quaker State," Cornplanter said that "you have now got the most of our lands, and have taken the game upon the same." All that his people retained, he said, was "the privilege of hunting and fishing thereon." He knew little could be done to reverse this new reality, but he did request that the Pennsylvanians establish a post at Pittsburgh "for the accommodation of my people and the other nations when they go to hunt, and where they may purchase goods at a reasonable price." The ability to move, and to trade, still mattered. Autonomy and freedom mattered as well. He and his people wished "to live peaceably and quietly with you and yours," but their losses required gifts, a payment. Cornplanter asked for $830 to make things right and "bury in the earth all ill will and enmity to each other."[42]

Pennsylvania stood in a constitutional crisis. Conservatives had organized to supplant the radical revolutionary state constitution of 1776 with a new compact, and until that work was completed, and the new government sworn in, little action could be taken. Still, Governor Mifflin responded to the Senecas' complaints. Bad things happened, he said. "Evil disposed men exist in every society." The government of Pennsylvania would do what it could. In the meantime, Mifflin gave gifts and good wishes, hoping that the Senecas would leave the capital and "arrive at your own homes in good health, and find your families in the possession of the same blessings."[43]

The Senecas were not going anywhere. They had business to attend to with the federal government. Knox sent letters to Governor

Clinton in New York. He knew that the Phelps and Gorham purchase continued to anger the Senecas but did not thoroughly understand the issues. He called upon Kirkland to repair to the capital to
serve as an interpreter. Cornplanter told the missionary that he intended, like Red Jacket and Farmer's Brother at Tioga, "to represent
& state the abuses which the Seneka nation had suffered from the
white people."[44]

Cornplanter, Half Town, and Big Tree delivered their address to
the "Great Concillors of the Thirteen Fires" on December 1. They stated
their respect for Washington as a warrior, as the "Town Destroyer" who
conceived of the Sullivan campaign in 1779. When your name is heard,
Cornplanter announced, "our women look behind them and turn pale,
and our children cling close to the necks of their mothers."[45]

The Senecas made peace with the United States in 1784 by giving
up an enormous cession of land. The Pennsylvanians came and took
a chunk as well. They could not resist these demands for land. The
Americans told them, Cornplanter recalled, "that we are in your
hand, and that, by closing it, you could crush us to nothing." Humiliated,
some Senecas thereafter contemplated suicide.[46]

"Father," he continued, "when that great country was given up,
there were but few chiefs present, and they were compelled to give it
up." At Fort Stanwix the United States "compelled us to do that
which has made us ashamed." The Indians to the west, who occupied
the lands the Iroquois ceded in 1784, treated them with scorn.
"When, last spring, they called upon us to go to war, to secure them
a bed to lie upon, the Senecas entreated them to be quiet." But an
American army was marching. The peace, to Cornplanter, seemed
quite fragile.[47]

Cornplanter was willing to work with the United States. He was
willing to accommodate himself to what he saw as the new realities of
a post-Revolutionary world. "The game which the Great Spirit sent
into our country for us to eat, is going from among us," he said. "We
thought he intended we should till the ground with the plough, as the
white people do, and we talked to one another about it." They would
make changes to how they lived, selectively altering elements of their
culture, but it only could work if they still controlled their lands. "We
must know from you," they asked the president, "whether you mean
to leave us and our children any land to till."[48]

Washington took his time composing a reply. He responded on December 29. He wished that "the miseries of the late war should be forgotten, and buried forever." He knew about the murders, and the government offered rewards that he hoped would lead to the apprehension, trial, and conviction of the guilty parties. He understood that they grieved still the loss of lands at Fort Stanwix. He understood their anger over the state treaties in New York. There was little he could do about these things, he said. Cornplanter, Half Town, and Great Tree, he pointed out, had confirmed the cessions of 1784 at Fort Harmar in 1789, and the state treaties took place before the present constitution went into effect.[49]

He could not undo the past, but he had taken steps for a better future. Now, he said, only the federal government could purchase Indian lands. No state purchase without federal support would be recognized. "Here then," he said, "is the security for the remainder of your lands. No state, nor person, can purchase your lands, unless at some public treaty, held under the authority of the United States." Washington wanted to be clear, and he restated the point a number of different ways. In the future, he said, "you can not be defrauded of your lands; that you possess the right to sell, and the right of refusing to sell, your lands; that, therefore, the sale of your lands, in future, will depend entirely upon yourselves."[50]

And now that the Indians understood the land was theirs until they chose to sell it, they could begin to till the ground like white people. He would help them. Washington would send farmers to teach them to farm, teachers to instruct their children how to read and write. The president would help the Iroquois make this important change, to allow them to enjoy the many benefits of civility. He would appoint for them an agent "to reside in some place convenient to the Senecas and Six Nations," to represent the United States. He would help keep peace, and help them to live more like their white neighbors.[51]

The Senecas replied. Washington's speech, Cornplanter said, "is to us like the first light of the morning to a sick man, whose pulse beats too strongly in his temples and prevents him from sleep. He sees it, rejoices, but he is not cured." Washington had not adequately addressed their concerns about Fort Stanwix. The United States demanded from the Six Nations too much land. It did so in anger, and so behaved in a manner that was "unreasonable and unjust."[52]

They asked that the president restore to them a portion of the land taken. They objected to the four-mile strip along the Niagara River, included in the original treaty to separate the Iroquois in New York from the British and their own Canadian kin. The Americans, Cornplanter said, were free to pass through the region. That was no problem at all. "But let us," he pleaded, "also pass along the same way, and continue to take the fish of those waters in common with you." They might share it, and in so doing preserve access to a critical resource—the fishing on the Niagara River—and the ability to move and to travel that came with it.[53]

By restoring to the Six Nations this small piece of land, Cornplanter said, "you will satisfy the whole of our nation." Those chiefs who had ceded those lands in 1784 and confirmed that cession in 1789 "will be in safety." A small part of the damage will have been undone. "Every man of our nation will then turn his eyes away from all the other lands which we then gave up to you, and forget that our fathers ever said that they belonged to them." And with their lands held securely, they could commit themselves to farming on an American model. "We ask you to teach us to plough and to grind corn, to assist us in building saw mills, and to supply us with broad axes, saws, augurs, and other tools, so as that we may make our houses more comfortable and more durable; that you will send smiths among us, and, above all, that you will teach our children to read and write, and our women to spin and weave."[54]

Washington was elated by the Allegany Senecas' seeming willingness to transform critical parts of their culture, to extract a living from the soil like their white neighbors. He was pleased that they pledged to help work out a peace with the Indians in the northwest. But he would not help them with the treaties. The cession had been negotiated before his presidency, and "the boundaries therein have been twice confirmed by yourselves."[55]

Cornplanter, Half Town, and Big Tree saw some of their concerns addressed, but other issues lingered. Shortly before leaving town on February 7, they thanked the president for their presents, pledged once again to help prevent a war that very likely could bring them suffering, expressed their hope that the president would follow through on his promise "to instruct us in raising corn, as the white people do," and thanked him for preventing "bad men coming to trade among us."[56]

Cornplanter and his associates left without obtaining all that they wanted. Quickly, the president and his secretary of war must have realized that they also had not achieved all they wanted. Less than a month after he departed from Philadelphia, Cornplanter sent a message that found its way to Henry Knox. Militiamen from Westmoreland County in Virginia crossed into Pennsylvania. They murdered four Senecas near Big Bear Creek. The militiamen took nine horses and all the trade goods the Seneca party carried. The victims were three men and one woman, Cornplanter wrote, all good people. "Your people are killing them as fast as they can," he wrote. He promised he would not join in with the "warrior nations," he wrote, but "if we cannot do it, do not blame us: you struck the innocent men first."[57]

Knox understood the stakes. "Decisive measures" must be taken, he told Governor St. Clair, or "this matter will be attended with the most pernicious consequences." He wrote to Cornplanter that the president "will do all in his power to bring the murderers to justice." In the meantime, they should hold on to the Covenant Chain and not let the actions of bad men cause it to fall apart. A few days later, Knox learned that a small number of Senecas had joined in an attack with Delawares and Wyandots that killed nine men, women, and children twenty miles from Fort Pitt. By the second week of March, locals reported that they saw Cornplanter in the area. They suspected his involvement in the attack. They tried to kill him and failed, but they did plunder more of this goods. Knox sent reinforcements to protect Allegany Senecas from their white neighbors, but with the western Indians requesting arms and ammunition from the British and the violence increasing, the prospects for peace seemed increasingly forlorn.

CHAPTER 4

....

St. Clair's Defeat and Its Consequences

Timothy Pickering wrote to his friend Samuel Hodgdon late in February 1791. He admitted that despite the work he had done the previous fall, he still knew very little about native peoples. Nonetheless, based upon his "small experience," Pickering thought it entirely possible "to make peace with the western nations, without the loss of much more blood." The Indians who defeated Harmar's force, he believed, were a lot like the Iroquois he met at Tioga. "They feel sore of the many injuries they have received from the white people, and that in their mode they have been taking revenge." The problems began and ended with the white frontier population, Pickering believed. The Indians would stop fighting "when the frontier white people cease to provoke them."[1]

Henry Knox, writing six weeks later to New York Governor George Clinton, was much less hopeful. "The involved state of things, arising from circumstances not under the control of the general government," he wrote, "have proceeded from one state to another, until it seems but too probable that force only can decide the contest" in the west.[2] He retained some small hope that diplomacy might keep the Iroquois out of the conflict. Pickering would meet once again with the Six Nations. Emissaries sent by the United States, meanwhile, would travel west to attempt to arrange a peace. And while these diplomatic efforts played themselves out, and in the event that they failed, territorial governor Arthur St. Clair prepared to march at the head of an army and destroy the confederacy.

In March 1791 Knox sent Colonel Thomas Proctor on a mission to the Miami and Wabash Indians with instructions to take with him Cornplanter and as many Senecas as he could collect. Proctor attended a conference at Buffalo Creek on April 22. Red Jacket attended the council, as did the important leaders Young King and Farmer's Brother. Horatio Jones served as Proctor's interpreter.[3]

Proctor made his pitch to the Senecas at Buffalo Creek. Accompany Cornplanter and me on a diplomatic mission into the west, he said. You have influence with the hostile Indians, and you can assist us in ending this war. He waited for an answer. Two days later, Red Jacket, accompanied by Farmer's Brother and the Cayuga Fish Carrier, responded. They wanted to consult with the British at Fort Niagara first. Proctor was angry. He would carry home to the Town Destroyer "a negative report." The Senecas found themselves in a tough spot. British officials told them that assisting the Americans would anger the western Indians. Robert Morris, the wealthy land speculator, was on hand at the council as well. He had acquired from Phelps and Gorham the pre-emption rights to Iroquois lands in the western part of the state. Morris's efforts to buy land at the council, something Proctor should have prevented, raised the ire of native people who saw abundant evidence that the white people loved Indian land more than Indians themselves.[4]

Proctor's threat seems to have worried especially the Clan Mothers. The leaders of the individual lineages that made up Iroquois clans and communities, it was they who appointed the league sachems. They wielded considerable influence, and Red Jacket was their spokesman. "The elders of our women," he said, "have said that our sachems and warriors must help you over your difficulties, for the good of them and their children." He would accompany Proctor, but enthusiasm for the effort otherwise was limited. The Young King told Proctor that "we desire to be still and to be at peace." Proctor tried to charter a boat to carry him westward on Lake Erie, but the British refused to allow him to visit the Northwestern confederates. It was, for Proctor, the end of the line. He could go no further.[5]

The United States expected that obstacles might arise, and Knox did not rely solely upon Proctor. While Cornplanter and he attempted to persuade Iroquois settled along the Niagara to participate in a diplomatic journey into the west, the Mohawk leader Joseph Brant departed on his own for the Ohio Country. Brant knew well that the Americans hoped to enlist the Six Nations, whether in Canada, or at Buffalo Creek, or along the Allegheny, in its war plans.

Brant thought war might be averted if the British intervened as mediators, but the conduct of Proctor, and Knox, and St. Clair in the west, made clear to him that the Americans viewed any British offer to mediate as unwelcome.

It is not difficult to imagine how the Ohio Indians perceived this state of affairs. The United States expressed a desire for peace. Its agents and emissaries sent numerous messages to that effect. But their armies already had once invaded the Ohio Country, its diplomats turned down the assistance of the British that the Indians believed might bring peace, and it was preparing once again to send an army against them. And the United States showed no interest in accepting the Ohio River as a boundary line. Brant listened to the Shawnees and the Delawares and the Miamis. They no longer had any interest in peace, not on the terms offered by the United States. Militias from Kentucky had attacked a number of Kickapoo and Wea towns in southern Ohio and taken women and children hostage. St. Clair's preparations were well known to the Indians. Brant might have hoped that Proctor made it west, but he would have had to conclude as well that the Northwestern confederates had a point: It was not a party of American peacemakers, but St. Clair's army, that seemed to be closest to them.[6]

While Proctor floundered in western New York, Knox looked to assemble yet another council with the Six Nations under the direction of Timothy Pickering. Governor Clinton thought it a bad idea. He wrote to Knox and pointed out that the Six Nations were divided, and "that this disunion produces impotency and secures inaction, and that, if we should revive their importance by renewing their union, we may give power and vigor, which we cannot with certainty direct, and over which we shall, with much trouble and expence, have an uncertain control." The governor likely thought of his state interests, putting those ahead of the Union. A unified Indian confederacy might place obstacles in the path blocking New York's plans to gobble up the Iroquois estate.[7]

The meeting with the Six Nations, Knox replied, would deal mostly with Seneca concerns, but he thought "it would have been impolitic to omit inviting the other tribes." Knox hoped that Pickering would prevent them joining with the western Indians and, as well, "induce them, as a security to the continuance of their friendship, to join some of their young warriors to the troops of the United States."

Knox needed Clinton's assistance as well. He wanted the New York governor to do what he could to persuade Brant to visit the president. Knox doubted Brant's willingness to attach himself to the United States, and he thought Brant's views, dating back to 1786, "may be dangerous." But the effort was worthwhile. Get him to Philadelphia, Knox urged. The government would cover all expenses.[8]

Pickering sent Israel Chapin to carry word of the council he hoped to convene at Painted Post, on the Chemung River, on June 15. Why another meeting? Pickering posed the question and answered it for the "Brothers, Sachems, and Warriors of the Six Nations." "We had managed a peace at Tioga," he said, but he now feared that "enemies of the United States may again endeavor to persuade you to engage in the war" in the west. With "misrepresentations and lies" they might "prevail on some, contrary to their own interest and the interest of the Six Nations" to take part. The war in the west, he wanted the Six Nations to know, was for the United States "not a war of choice, not of oppression, not of injustice, but of necessity, to defend our frontiers and to save the settlers from destruction." He asked them to join him at the Painted Post "to make the chain of friendship with you still brighter, and to keep it always bright."[9]

Pickering received his instructions from Knox. He would explain to them that the United States wished for the Six Nations, on all occasions, to "be treated with entire justice and humanity." Pickering must "impress on the minds of the Indians," Knox wrote, "that their interest and happiness depend upon the protection and friendship of the United States." About the continuing problems caused by the violence of frontier settlers, Knox asked Pickering to reassure them, once again, that the United States would do all it could "to make atonement to the Indians aggrieved."[10]

Pickering had few problems with this part of his instructions. Nor did he have any problem letting the Iroquois know that the president wished for them to learn husbandry and the arts of civilization, and for their children to learn to read and write. What bothered him was the president's expectation that at least some Iroquois warriors would join in the military campaign against the western confederates. The Six Nations should not "only abstain from joining the enemy" but must as well "manifest their friendship by sending their young warriors to join our army, for which they shall be well paid." Pickering should labor this point, Knox said. The young men likely would fight, and in his view they would probably "join the western Indians unless they join us." The best way to avoid "so dangerous a situation," he said, was to persuade them to join our forces.[11]

Pickering believed that this was asking too much. Bring order to the frontier. Show the Indians the benevolence of the United States, its philanthropic desire to educate and assimilate native peoples. But do not go after them like this. When Pickering wrote to the chiefs and warriors and sachems of the Six Nations in May, he said nothing about a military contribution to the American war effort. He wrote of the provisions of the federal Trade and Intercourse Act, of polishing the chain of friendship. He said that "the Great Spirit has given to us as well as you land enough on which to lie down. Why then should we quarrel?" Whether he knew it or not, he spoke in terms of *guswenta*. He told Knox that he had heard from his sources that the Senecas might join in the war against the western nations, but only if the United States pledged to protect their towns from attack.[12]

Pickering began to make his way toward the Painted Post. As always, the traveling was tough. Joseph Sansom, a Quaker who traveled the same road as Pickering two weeks later, described the hardships. "Good water is rare," he said, and "often a half mile distant." Meat was hard to find. Bread was scarce, and when "flour is to be had it is generally molded up brown (not to say black)." The food was terrible, but also "uninterrupted sleep, the last and worst want of all, is often wanting here, amidst foul linen, fleas and gnats."[13]

Pickering arrived at Painted Post on June 15. The Iroquois had not yet arrived. He decided to move the meeting to Newtown, an easier place for supply. On the 19th, a runner brought Pickering news that twenty Indians from the Oneida country, a party that included Stockbridge and Tuscaroras as well, would arrive at the council fire. Young Peter, the son of Good Peter, spoke first, invoking the language of the condolence council. He condoled Pickering for Harmar's dead soldiers. "Brother," he said, "we see the tear rolling down your face, for the loss of your officers and warriors, whose blood was spilt last year." He wiped the tears from his face, and "we put our hands to your throat, & take them away, that your throat may be clear, so that you may speak freely and moderately."[14]

Pickering thanked the Oneidas and their neighbors for the kind words. He wanted peace, he said, and the war in the west caused him grief for both the American and Indian lives lost. He believed that war might still be averted but that if it resumes, "the Western Indians must be destroyed." He could use their help to avert that possibility, he said.[15]

Pickering met in his quarters after this exchange with the Stockbridge leaders. The descendants of New England Algonquians chased out of Connecticut and western Massachusetts late in the colonial period, the Oneidas welcomed their resettlement on the eastern margins of their homeland, a buffer against the surging white population. Hendrick Aupaumut, "a slender, pale-faced young man, in a scarlet cloak and leggings," just beginning a long career in intercultural diplomacy, delivered a long address to Pickering in English. His people had "done more service for the United States than any other Indian nation." He felt sorry about the war in the west. He believed Pickering when he said the war was not one the Americans chose. But he raised a point that Pickering understood well. The problem, Aupaumut said, was that despite your intentions, "your people on the frontiers," with their "inhuman practices . . . have set bad examples." Here was the obstacle Pickering must overcome: The western Indians, Aupaumut said, "think all the people of the United States are as bad as those on the frontiers." Among the Six Nations, he continued, "there is a common opinion of white people—that they are not true friends to the Indians, but the friends to Indian lands." Aupaumut offered to go west and attempt to work out a peace, but he saw little chance for success while St. Clair's army marshaled its strength in advance of its march against them.[16]

More Iroquois began to arrive. Four Senecas, on the 21st, indicated that the rest soon would follow. Pickering noted the arrivals. On the 22nd, "Steel Trap, and ten more Cayugas arrived"; a day after that a small party of Oneidas, Onondagas, and Tuscaroras, and Beech Tree with thirty Oneidas; Good Peter, on the 24th, with seventy-four Oneidas and Onondagas; and on the 29th, "the Seneca and other Indians dwelling in their country arrived, in number about 700." The women, he said, began to gather the bark from trees and to construct housing while the men, maybe 300 strong, drew up in a line outside Pickering's tent and fired a salute. Nearly 1,000 Indians, Iroquois, and their close neighbors, had encamped at Newtown.[17]

Pickering came with an agenda. So, too, did the Six Nations, and at Newtown, Pickering found himself parrying the arguments of the Seneca orator Red Jacket. A Quaker observer named John Parrish was impressed by Red Jacket and believed that his "appearance and manner, his eloquence & person . . . would cut no inconsiderable figure on the floor of a British Parliament or an American Congress." Thomas Morris, sent by his father Robert to observe the proceedings and learn if the New York frontier was a suitable place for his abode, came to Newtown as well. Red Jacket, Morris thought, "was a cunning talented man without a particle of principle" but also "very fluent," and "the most graceful speaker that I have ever heard address an audience of any description." Red Jacket poked at Pickering. He was witty and graceful. Sometimes, according to Morris, Pickering would "become indignant at Red Jacket's sarcasms and discover much irritation." This would "delight Red Jacket," who was more than a match for the American commissioner.[18]

Pickering delivered to the gathered Iroquois a speech that some of them had heard before. The representatives from the Six Nations must have been appreciative that Pickering understood the source of frontier disorder. They listened, once again, as he described to them the legislation Congress had enacted to preserve peace on the frontier. But Red Jacket seemed interested in turning the discussion toward other ends, and in other directions.

Red Jacket was "very sensible" of his great abilities as an orator. "Before he rose," Morris recalled, "he took great pains so to place the blanket round his shoulders and to arrange the silver bracelets on his arms so as to give the most graceful appearance." He addressed the Indians, and then he addressed the commissioner. He told Pickering on July 10 that the Six Nations retained their autonomy. He happily would participate in discussions about polishing the chain of friendship with the United States. "We do the same with the British to this day," he continued. "But we do not give ourselves entirely up to them; nor lean altogether upon you." The Six Nations were independent, following their own course. "We mean to stand upright, as we live between both."[19]

Red Jacket knew that Cornplanter had invited the United States to bring its "civilization program" to Allegany. Red Jacket wanted to make sure that Pickering understood where "all the Six Nations here" stood on this issue. His people would make changes, abandoning some old cultural practices and adopting some new ones, but only "by degrees." He was willing to accept "your advice and your rules, which we think are good, and put them by the side of ours, for we would have our rules live with yours," side by side, parallel lines.[20]

To Pickering's charge that the Senecas, in particular, leaned more toward the British than the Americans, Red Jacket said that his people looked to their own interests first. "You do not know our old customs," he told Pickering, "but what shall we say? Shall the way of doing business be all on one side? In one way? And we not follow any of our ancient customs?"[21]

Pickering responded in anger. "Brothers," he warned, if you "lay aside your prejudices," you will understand "that it is your true interests so to conduct that the United States may place a confidence in you." He asked the Six Nations to consider their interests and their safety. Those who resist the United States will be destroyed. This for Pickering was established fact. It might take time, but those who fought would ultimately lose. "Let me give you some idea of the strength of the United States," he said. Three million citizens in the American republic; calculate that one in ten is a soldier, "and the whole number of warriors will be three hundred thousand." And that population was increasing rapidly. The American population would double every quarter-century. "In twenty-five years, we shall have six hundred thousand warriors." We will bury you if you choose the wrong side, Pickering warned. The United States was strong and growing stronger, but also wise and just. Make the right choice, he said. Do not trust the British.[22]

He quickly had to backpedal. Red Jacket explained that his words had done damage. Pickering learned that he must treat the Six Nations, and the individual nations, as independent and autonomous communities. He could not bully. He could not threaten, not when he needed from them a commitment to peace and alliance. He said little more about Knox's request that the Six Nations join St. Clair's forces. He wrote to the Allegany Senecas, stating that "if any of your young warriors choose to rise up, we shall not refuse their company." But he did not push it with the rest of the Six Nations any farther than that. He invited them to send a delegation of chiefs to the capital to meet with Washington, and he announced that he would obtain for them an agent to reside near their towns. Pickering had committed some serious missteps at Newtown, but the Six Nations respected him, so long as he understood the importance of their culture and their autonomy. He was willing to learn, and they must have seen in him a man with whom they could work.[23]

American settlers, meanwhile, felt the blows delivered by the Northwestern confederates, part of the Indians' "Spirited Resistance" to white encroachment on their lands and all the disruptions that approaching settlements brought. If they restored their rituals and rid themselves of the influence of the Anglo-Americans in their communities, they might set the world aright. By early in 1791, well before Pickering met with the Six Nations, Secretary Knox received reports that eight counties each in Virginia and Kentucky, all of western Pennsylvania, and parts of the Carolinas and Georgia faced attacks by native warriors.[24]

From Knox and Washington's perspective, something had to be done, but Arthur St. Clair, a weak and ineffective leader, obese and hobbled by gout, was not the man for the job. He could not maintain discipline. Militiamen deserted and then threatened his army's supply lines. St. Clair detached half his army to protect the pack trains.[25]

Warriors led by the Miami Little Turtle and the Shawnee Blue Jacket watched St. Clair's slow advance. The British Indian agent Simon Girty recalled that "the Indians were never in greater heart to meet their enemy." St. Clair marched twenty-nine miles north from Fort Jefferson. There, along the banks of the Wabash River on the morning of November 4, the warriors attacked. They struck shortly before dawn. They rushed St. Clair's camp. The soldiers broke and ran. They threw away their weapons and begin fleeing toward Fort Jefferson before St. Clair could order the retreat. Few of them arrived uninjured. Of St. Clair's force of 1,400 men, 914 were killed or wounded. The army lost 1,200 muskets, hundreds of horses, six artillery pieces, and an enormous sum of other resources. Twenty percent of the entire United States army was wiped out in one morning, the worst defeat ever experienced by the American military at the hands of Indians.[26]

In the immediate aftermath of the battle, the warriors constructed a "large, painted encampment" where they celebrated. They painted the saplings with "hieroglyphicks." They attributed their victory to their spiritual power, the potency of their rituals. And while the warriors felt the strength of the spiritual forces that allowed them to triumph over their enemies, American settlers and statesmen shuddered. Virginians were "miserable," Kentuckians demoralized, by this "alarming affair." Thomas Mifflin, Pennsylvania's governor, passed along to the president a petition from the residents of Pittsburgh, who asked for a garrison and for arms and ammunition. The Indians would attack them, too, they believed, and "should this place be lost, the whole country is open to them." Along the New York frontier, Ontario County Sheriff Judah Colt worried that the settlers, "scattered promiscuous over a large tract," a population "undisciplined, without guns or ammunition or anyone to take command of them in case of invasion," might easily come under attack. Othniel Taylor told Oliver Phelps that the "defeat of our army at the southward . . . gives our people no small degree of uneasiness respecting the Indians."[27]

Confident and unified warriors; frightened and defeated settlers. Add to that mix opportunistic imperial officials, like the new Lieutenant Governor of Canada John Graves Simcoe, who thought that St. Clair's defeat "may be productive of beneficial consequences to the government of Upper Canada." They saw in the Indians' victory an opportunity to construct a neutral Indian barrier state with its southern border running along the Ohio River. The republic, Simcoe believed, was weak, and its finances stood on shaky ground. Only with enormous difficulty could they continue to fight the Indians. Indeed, Simcoe's friend, and the deputy-quartermaster for Upper Canada, Captain Charles Stevenson, reported on "the terror which the victory of the Indians has spread over the country," and he believed that "the continuance of the Indian war," from the British perspective, "is to be desired." They believed that eventually the United States would have to negotiate with the western Indians, whom the British might continue to supply. Because any peace delegation would have to pass in the vicinity of the posts the British retained on American soil, they hoped to be able to influence the outcome in ways that might curb the already-apparent expansionism of the young United States.[28]

Knox wanted to make sure that the Senecas, or others of the Six Nations, did not join in a movement that legitimately threatened the American republic. Knox heartily endorsed Pickering's plan to invite

Six Nations leaders to the nation's capital. Knox wrote to Cornplanter, letting him know that "the number of men we have lost, we can easily replace; and, therefore, although the continuance of the war will be troublesome, yet, in the long run, we must conquer." Perhaps he was right. But it was difficult to forecast at the time, and diplomacy seemed like a strategy wiser than bluster and threat. Knox sent Samuel Kirkland that winter overland to Geneseo to meet the chiefs and escort them by way of Tioga to Philadelphia. He should make sure "that they are not insulted on the road, but kindly received." Much, indeed, hung in the balance. The United States needed the Six Nations as allies.[29]

A rapid flurry of diplomatic activity thus followed the defeat of St. Clair's army. Pickering invited Iroquois leaders to Philadelphia. He hoped to secure their neutrality and to persuade them to adopt his program for their assimilation and improvement. Kirkland, Knox wrote, must act to persuade the Six Nations leaders to accept Pickering's invitation, and keep his ear to the ground for information on "the effect which the late defeat of our army has had upon the minds of the six nations, particularly the Senecas." Hustle to Geneseo, Knox told Kirkland, see what you can find out, and bring a delegation with you back to Philadelphia.[30]

Kirkland set out early in January, accompanied by Hendrick Aupaumut, the Oneidas Good Peter and Skenandoa, and a handful of others. It was tough traveling—it always is in January in western New York. Invitations went out, meanwhile, to the Allegany Senecas and to Joseph Brant who, the secretary of war hoped, may have a heart "filled with a true desire to serve the essential interests of your countrymen."[31]

What Kirkland saw troubled him. Unless a peace was arranged with the western Indians, Kirkland expected a fissure in the Six Nations. Young warriors, subject to no one's authority, had marched off piecemeal to join the westerners. Those in the west, and those camped around Fort Niagara, received plentiful supplies of clothing, arms, and ammunition from the British. Should the Iroquois from Buffalo Creek, Grand River, and Geneseo come together to join the western rising, Kirkland feared that New York's frontiers "and that of Pennsylvania, would be in my apprehension, the most defenseless part of the United States."[32]

Kirkland could not persuade Brant to accompany him, but nearly fifty other chiefs made the journey to Philadelphia. Yet if the United

States wanted neutrality and a commitment to civilization, the Iroquois delegates came for different reasons. Some wanted to air their growing list of grievances—encroachment and theft mostly—while others sought trade goods, regularly supplied, and a pledge to protect them from the hostile Indians. They wanted protection and alliance, and a commitment to respect their autonomy and nationhood. Some of them feared for their safety on the journey down. Some of them feared as well the western nations. For these Iroquois diplomats much stood in the balance; meeting with the United States could bring down upon them the anger of the Northwestern confederates.[33]

The Iroquois delegation included a heavy contingent from Buffalo Creek. Red Jacket, once again, played a leading role in the negotiations. They arrived in Philadelphia on March 13. Escorts met them on the road into the city, greeting them at the edge of the woods. A detachment of infantrymen guided them through the streets of Philadelphia to their hotel, where Governor Mifflin ordered a cannon salute. Once the Iroquois League had been viewed as a vital part of the Anglo-American empire, whatever the actual scope of its power. In the immediate aftermath of the Revolution, they had been treated by the congressional commissioners as defeated enemies. What a change since the Fort Stanwix treaty of 1784. American officials lost no opportunity to fete the Iroquois delegates, including holding an elaborate state funeral replete with a grand procession after the unexpected death of an Oneida sachem.[34]

All of this caught Pickering a bit off guard. He did not know the Seneca delegation was on its way until he had heard from a Moravian that they were at Nazareth, roughly sixty miles away. Later that day, passing Knox on Chestnut Street, the secretary of war told Kirkland that "the Indians were at Bethlehem, and said 'I believe I must get you to negotiate with them.'" Everyone but he seemed to know what was going on. Pickering had extended the invitation to the Six Nations and expected to continue his involvement in the country's Indian diplomacy. Not only did Knox appear to ignore him, but he seemed determined to derail the meeting's purpose by leaning on the delegation once again for military assistance against the Northwestern tribes.[35]

When Pickering caught word of what the president intended to say, he could quiet his tongue, and his pen, no longer. The president would say nothing about the plans to bring "civilization," American-style, to the Six Nations. Instead, like Knox, he intended to address them only on matters diplomatic and military. Joseph Brant, according to Kirkland, already had warned the Buffalo Creek leaders that the Americans had lied about the purpose of the meeting, that talk of plows and agriculture and spinning wheels was nothing but a ruse to draw them in.[36]

Pickering understood how the Iroquois might react to such an address, and he felt himself, he wrote the president, "peculiarly interested that the negotiations . . . conform with the direct object of the invitation" he had extended to them. To speak with them of military alliance and war made it appear that the United States acted on the basis of fear. The invitation was "confined to this simple object": the introduction of "the knowledge of husbandry and a few other important arts connected with it." Stick to the plan, he wrote, and we stand a better chance of convincing the Six Nations that we really are interested in their friendship. For Pickering, the matter was simple: "Indians have been deceived so often by white people," he continued, "that *white man* is among many of them, but another name for *Liar*." He told the president that the government's actions risked damaging his credibility. "I am not indifferent to a good name," Pickering concluded, "even among Indians."[37]

By early 1792, Pickering no longer needed a job. Recognizing his service and his capability at Tioga and Newtown, Washington appointed Pickering the U.S. Postmaster General in August 1791. He still was learning the ropes of a demanding job. Pickering intervened for two reasons: He did not want the work he had done undermined, and he legitimately felt that it was as important for the United States to keep its word and to behave honorably as it was for an upright individual. His letter to Washington had an effect. Knox met with Pickering the next morning. He apologized to Pickering for neglecting his advice and invited him to attend the conference.[38]

The next day Washington delivered a speech to the gathered Iroquois leaders that conformed closely to Pickering's original invitation. The Indians had been invited by Pickering, the president said, "in order to remove all causes of discontent, to devise and adopt plans to promote your welfare, and firmly to cement the peace between the United States and you, so as that, in the future, we shall consider ourselves as brothers indeed." He told them that the United States wanted no land "but those obtained by treaties, which we consider fairly made" in 1784 and 1789. And he called upon Congress to appropriate the funds for an annual gift of $1,500 to purchase for the Six Nations clothing, tools, and livestock.[39]

Between council sessions, much went on. It was during this visit that Good Peter related to Pickering his history of the Oneidas' misfortunes at the hands of the state of New York and its land-hungry settlers. Members of the delegation sat for portraits. Red Jacket received the large silver medal that he wore on public occasions for the rest of his life, one that encapsulated Pickering's goals for the meeting. It depicted the president, extending the hand of friendship to an Indian smoking a pipe of peace. In the background, another Indian worked at plowing his fields behind a team of oxen.[40]

On the last day of March, Red Jacket replied to the president's speech. A large audience, including members of Congress, had gathered to witness the proceedings. Red Jacket recapitulated the main points of Washington's address. Red Jacket expressed his happiness that a "peace might be established between your brothers of the five nations,

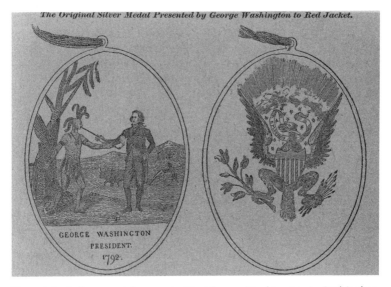

The original silver medal presented by George Washington to Red Jacket, Etching.
Courtesy of the Library of Congress, LC-USZ62-125642

so firmly that nothing might move it." He was happy, as well, that "we might share with you in all the blessings of civilized life."[41]

He then picked up a belt of wampum and asked "the great Council of the Thirteen United States" to hear what he had to say. President Washington "observed to us that we of the five nations were our own proprietors, were freemen and might speak with freedom." The president had acknowledged that we are "the sole proprietors of the soil on which we live." He continued. The Iroquois consider "ourselves by your own acknowledgment as freemen" and this "has given joy to our hearts." It was a powerful statement that the Iroquois would join with the United States as friends, but only if their autonomy and independence were respected.[42]

Pickering addressed the Iroquois delegates two weeks later. He felt optimistic about the civilization program. And after discussing it again at length, and blaming the war on the western Indians, he finally came around to the point that so concerned Washington and Knox: Might the Six Nations send delegates to the west? Might they help broker a peace with the western Indians?[43]

Farmer's Brother, the Seneca, did not think so. The source of the differences in the west, he said, had been the conduct of the American commissioners after the Revolution. Red Jacket replied by telling Pickering that "the burthen of bringing you and the Western Indians together . . . tis too heavy for us to bear without your assistance."[44] But Pickering kept after them, and a small number of sachems from Buffalo Creek agreed to meet with the western nations in the fall. Knox, meanwhile, appointed Israel Chapin to serve as U.S. agent to the Six Nations, a good choice, Pickering thought. The agent, Pickering believed, should be "one who was no speculator in Indian lands, and who has too much honesty ever to be made the instrument of deception."[45]

Chapin would keep the peace between settlers and Indians, distribute gifts and presents, and demonstrate hospitality to Iroquois guests at his Canandaigua home. He would enforce the federal Indian Trade and Intercourse Act on the New York frontier. He would also oversee the spending of funds for the Indians' "improvement," and Knox drew up detailed instructions to guide Chapin's conduct. For schoolmasters, blacksmiths, and carpenters, Chapin must hire men who "sustain fair reputations; men of perfect temperance, or unblemished integrity, and unaffected reverence for religion."

The wives of these men should "teach the Indian girls to spin, sew, knit, and do all sorts of business proper for farmers wives to be acquainted with." Children should learn to read and write, and to do the work of farm children. The teacher should not hit the children, as that was foreign to them, and he should not ask of them any work that white people did not do. On Sundays the schoolmaster should "instruct them in the duties they owe to each other as members of society, and to all people of whatever color as children of the great spirit, whose parental kindness extends to all."[46]

Pickering, Knox, and Washington agreed on the proper ends of American policy with regards to native peoples. They disagreed only slightly on means. They wanted a peaceful and orderly frontier. They hoped American settlement would advance and that native land would peacefully become part of the United States, a process the central government would oversee. They hoped to bring the Indians within the pale of civility. In this sense, they believed that Indians had the capacity to become something else, and they did not envision a future where Iroquois people remained Iroquois. Set aside the polite language, and it is obvious that native peoples faced policies that were replete with aggression and that demanded of them a great deal.

Timothy Pickering hoped that Joseph Brant might join the Six Nations emissaries who visited Philadelphia, but he chose to stay home. Brant understood Anglo-American farming. He understood husbandry, the practices of civility. Literate and educated and familiar with the ways of Anglo-Americans, Brant long had made the arts of civilization his own. Truly a creature of the Anglo-American empire, his life reflected the transatlantic connections that linked Iroquoia—religiously, economically, and diplomatically—to the imperial state. A council called ostensibly to discuss the government's civilization program offered Brant little of interest.[47]

Still, with the support of the American government, Kirkland kept after him. They had known each other for years. Kirkland understood something of the difficulties Brant faced. He learned that illness had confined him to Grand River while warriors from his community traveled west. He had not succeeded in restraining them. The Northwestern Indians sent along a message to him with some of these returning warriors, a message that showed their lack of respect. They sent to him the scalp of Richard Butler, the American officer and commissioner who died with St. Clair's forces. Brant had deserted them, they said. "You Mohawk Chief," they complained, "time was when you roused us to war, and told us that, if all the Indians would join the king, they should be happy people, and become independent." But since then "you have changed your voice, and went to sleep, and left us in the lurch." Brant's power had declined in the west, and he no longer spoke for the Six Nations.[48]

Nevertheless, as a Mohawk leader, and as "one who has a general interest in the soil and the welfare of the western Indians," the president and the secretary of war thought him an important voice and one they must win over. Escorted to Philadelphia by Israel Chapin, Jr., the agent's son, Brant arrived in the capital on June 20.[49]

Brant met briefly with Washington but spent most of this time with Knox. The secretary of war said that the western Indians acted on the mistaken notion that the United States wanted to take their lands. This was not the case. Knox, flattering Brant for his "general character for intelligence and attachment to the Indians' interest," asked that he travel west and let them know that the United States did not want their lands and wanted to make peace. If a payment to the western Indians in the form of an annuity would help, Knox authorized Brant to make the offer.[50]

Knox told Brant to let the western Indians know that the United States considered "that all their lands not fairly ceded are their own, and that they cannot be dispossessed thereof excepting by a fair and voluntary sale, made under the authority of the United States." Brant surely understood that this was the problem. The United States assumed the validity of the Confederation-era conquest treaties and their confirmation at Fort Harmar early in 1789. The western Indians did not, and for them the Ohio River line remained nonnegotiable. Brant understood that the United States asked the westerners to settle while a new army prepared to march out against them, to negotiate, in effect, with a gun pointed at them. Brant assured Knox that he would journey westward and that he would see what he could do.[51]

CHAPTER 5

·······················

Disaffected

Washington, Knox, and others in charge of Indian affairs prepared for another round of war in the west, but they also harbored still a belief in the importance of diplomacy. The United States needed the assistance of the Iroquois. It needed an assurance that the Six Nations would not join with the Northwestern confederates. It relied heavily upon intelligence provided by Iroquois travelers and diplomats. Washington and Knox did not expect the western nations to back down—not after they had defeated two American armies. They worried still that the British might use the disorder to push for a mediated end to the conflict that curbed American dreams of expansion and resulted in the establishment of a neutral Indian barrier state north of the Ohio. They believed that working with the Iroquois might offer opportunities for solving the grave crisis the new nation faced in the west.

Some American officials did not trust the leaders of the Six Nations. When Cornplanter, New Arrow, Big Tree, and Guyasuta visited General Anthony Wayne's camp downriver from Pittsburgh in March, they must have sensed the General's suspicion. Wayne told Knox just two weeks before the Seneca delegation arrived that he could not trust Cornplanter, who, he had heard, recently offered a toast to the western Indians in which he pointed to the Ohio and expressed his hope that it will "remain the *boundary of lasting peace*, between the Americans & the Indians on its opposite shores." In Wayne's view, Cornplanter played both sides of the street, telling the western nations and the United States what he sensed each wanted to hear.[1]

Map of part of the state of New York with parts of the adjacent states, 1793–1794, New York State Archives, A0448-79, Recorded Indian treaties and deeds, 1703–1871 (bulk 1748–1871). Vol. 1, p. 45. *Courtesy of the New York State Department of Archives and History*

But what choice did the United States have? Haudenosaunee warriors and hunters long had traversed the contested region. They served as the eyes and ears of the United States in the Ohio Country. They hoped to preserve their people's right to travel, to hunt, and to trade, and they did not want to be hemmed in by the restrictive boundaries dictated to them by the United States at Fort Stanwix in 1784, and reaffirmed at Fort Harmar in 1789.

Iroquois diplomats, and diplomats from other pressed-upon New York Indian communities, traveled west in the spring, summer, and fall of 1792, looking to the interests of their own people as they served as intermediaries between the western nations and the United States. Hendrick Aupaumut led the first group of New York Indians. He would attend a "great council of the Indians" in the summer "at the Miami river of Lake Erie, in order to convince them of the moderation, justice, and desire of the United States for peace." The United States, Knox told Aupaumut, desired peace not out of fear but "for the sake of humanity." The Northwestern confederates should send their emissaries to Fort Jefferson to meet with the American general Rufus Putnam, whom the government had authorized to negotiate a truce.[2]

Aupaumut traveled with Israel Chapin. They found the Iroquois at Buffalo Creek "extremely disaffected." Chapin, nonetheless, thought these differences might be resolved. The Iroquois, he told Knox, "manifested gratitude to Congress for their intention of erecting schools among them, and providing them with blacksmiths." A school built west of the Genesee, and adequately supplied with funding from the national government, Chapin thought "might prove of infinite service, both in conciliating the affections of the Indians, and in laying a foundation for their civilization."[3]

Aupaumut delivered to the Northwestern confederates the message of the United States. They thanked Aupaumut for the speech. They told him that they "never had such a pure good message from the White People." All but the Shawnees, Aupaumut thought, would consider peace with the United States. American preparations for war, however, derailed the proceedings. "Before they came to a conclusion," Aupaumut wrote, "an alarming voice reach to their ears—that the Big Knife," the Americans, "were coming to fight against the nations."[4]

The Senecas returned home from Philadelphia after agreeing to Pickering's request that they travel west "to assure those Indians of the sincere disposition of the United States to make peace with them." They understood that the problems in the region lay far beyond the solutions proposed by Knox and Washington. Explaining to the hostile western nations the bounds claimed by the United States as a result of the treaties at Fort Stanwix and Fort Harmar would not conciliate Indians who rejected those cessions in their entirety. Farmer's Brother and other chiefs at Buffalo Creek informed Israel Chapin shortly before the Senecas headed west that "the disturbance" there "between our Brethren and your people is entirely owing to your detaining the lands."[5]

A large party made the journey. General Wayne thought that as many as 500 accompanied Cornplanter, Red Jacket, and the other chiefs, Seneca leaders from the Allegany and from Buffalo Creek. They needed the numbers for safety. Wayne thought it possible that Cornplanter would not survive the meeting, for the western Indians had threatened his life.[6] He seemed to some too close to the Americans. At the same time, however, Cornplanter had extended his influence to Buffalo Creek. Many of the chiefs did not support his pro-American policy, but because so many of the clan mothers at Buffalo Creek favored peace, and friendship with the United States, they agreed to accompany him. They met the western Indians at the Glaize, where the Maumee and Auglaize rivers come together near present-day Defiance, Ohio. The Glaize was a gathering place for militants from many tribes, committed to holding the line at the Ohio.[7]

The council began on September 30. The Shawnee leader Painted Pole, who had led warriors into battle against the Americans, passed the pipe and announced to the Iroquois that he would serve as the principal speaker for the western nations. He told the Seneca leaders, in a speech inflected with sarcasm and disappointment, that he had not seen or heard from the Six Nations in quite a while.

Red Jacket delivered the Senecas' reply. The "white people," Red Jacket said, always are "the instigators of our quarrels." We must "unite and consider what will be best for us, our women, and Children, to lengthen our days, and be in Peace." This did nothing to satisfy the Shawnees and their allies, nothing to convince them that the Iroquois were more interested in standing up for the rights of native

peoples than in delivering messages for the United States. When Red
Jacket pointed out that the Americans wanted peace, and when he
advised the gathered western Indians to not "be too proud spirited"
to reject it, "lest the Great Spirit should be angry with you," he appeared as an enemy to their cause and an errand boy for the armies
that invaded their homelands.[8]

Red Jacket's speech offended the Shawnees. The next day the
leaders met in private, hoping to patch up their differences. But when
the council reopened, Painted Pole made clear his disdain for the
course the Iroquois had followed. They had sold out to the Americans.
While the armies of the United States marched against the western
allies, the Iroquois listened to their sweet speeches. If you want to
serve as messengers, Painted Pole said, here is a message you can deliver to the President. He reminded Red Jacket of the 1768 Fort
Stanwix treaty line, the Ohio River boundary "that was made between us and the English & Americans when they were one people."
Red Jacket had told the western Indians that the United States might
offer additional compensation for the lands its settlers had taken.
Tell the President, Painted Pole said, that "we do not want compensation, we want restitution of our Country which they hold under false
pretences." The Shawnees' demand, "a determination of all the nations present," was simple, really. "If the Americans want to make
peace with us," Painted Pole continued, "let them destroy these forts"
on the north side of the Ohio. They must cease their encroachment,
their invasion of the Ohio Country. We will meet them in Sandusky
in the spring, as Red Jacket had suggested, but the old 1768 Fort
Stanwix line was a demand that would not change. They were willing
to fight over the line.[9]

The speech must have rattled the Senecas. After listening to
Painted Pole, Red Jacket pledged to the Shawnees that "we now join
you and will put our heads together, and endeavor to get all our lands
back, where the Americans have encroached upon us." They would
look forward to meeting with the western nations in the spring. The
council ended, and the Six Nations delegation hastily returned home.
They left in fear.[10]

Hendrick Aupaumut had struck out. Red Jacket's delegation
feared they would not be able to leave without a fight. Brant arrived a
week and a half after the Senecas left and enjoyed no more success

than they had. He shared a commitment to the western nations' vision of pan-Indian unity, of native people coming together to keep the assault upon their lands and way they lived at bay, but in his vision the Mohawks would predominate. His visit to the Glaize must have made clear to Brant that the time for that had passed.

The Northwestern confederates expressed their confidence. Creeks and Cherokees in the south and Shawnees and others at the Glaize launched assaults on white settlements. Warriors the length of the frontier worked together frequently and effectively. And they did so without the assistance of the Iroquois. Their help was not needed, and for the westerners, the "Iroquois mystique" clearly had worn off. Even many Americans pointed out that the Indians in New York had become "poor enervated creatures." Confined to their state reserves, some observers thought them "contemptible compared with their former greatness." The Iroquois, if they were to protect their communities' interests, would have to do so in an arena where their real power had declined significantly. The western Indians did not fear them. The United States feared only that their disaffection with fraudulent land sales, settler encroachment, and white violence might reach a point where they joined with the more menacing western nations.[11]

The first issue George Washington addressed in his annual message to Congress in November 1792 was the war in the northwest. He regretted that he could not announce that "the Indian hostilities which have for some time past distressed our Northwestern frontier have terminated." He wanted peace, he said, and told his audience that "an earnest desire to procure tranquility . . . to stop the further effusion of blood," and "to arrest the progress of expense" led him to undertake "strenuous efforts through various channels" to bring the conflict to a close. Although Washington still hoped for peace, he said, success was "not promised by anything that has yet happened."[12]

The president planned to try again. Early in 1793 he asked Timothy Pickering to enlist himself once more in the effort to avoid even more costly warfare in the northwest. Pickering accepted Washington's invitation, as did Benjamin Lincoln and the Virginian Beverley Randolph. Two Quaker observers from the Philadelphia Meeting of the Society of Friends, William Savery and John Parrish, also joined the emissaries as witnesses, as did the Moravian missionary John Heckewelder, a fluent and talented cultural broker.[13]

Lincoln, Randolph, and Pickering headed west with detailed instructions, the thoroughness of which testifies to the planning that went into this latest peace mission. Henry Knox drew up the instructions. The American people, he asserted, opposed war in the west and favored "a peace upon terms of justice and humanity." Bring the conflict to a close, Knox told his commissioners, and bring peace to the frontier. But Knox told the commissioners that the United States regarded the 1789 Fort Harmar treaty as a "fair purchase and sale," an agreement "having been formed on solid ground." Those who signed the treaty did so "with their free consent and full understanding."[14]

No change here: The Washington administration seemed unwilling to budge on what the western Indians considered absolutely fundamental—the injustice of the postwar treaties and the rushed and unrepresentative quality of the Fort Harmar accord. The commissioners would attempt to persuade the tribes to accept "the boundary established by the said Treaty of Fort Harmar" that they already had clearly rejected. The commissioners received authorization to pay to the aggrieved nations $50,000 in goods and a total of $10,000 in annuities.[15]

When the commissioners met with the Indians, Knox expected them to attempt to disrupt their unity. Divide, and then conquer. "Form separate contracts, or treaties," if possible, "relative to boundaries," and avoid doing anything in council "to confirm the idea of an union, or general confederacy of all the tribes, or of any patronage of the whole over the lands of any particular tribes, or subdivisions of tribes."[16]

While the Americans planned for a council to be held at Sandusky, British Indian department officials made their own arrangements to play a role in the proceedings. Well aware that the Indians had defeated two American armies, they hoped to be there to mediate any end to the conflict in the west. Six Nations emissaries returning from the council at the Glaize in 1792, at the suggestion of British Indian agent Alexander McKee, invited the British to help with mediation. This the United States refused, but Secretary of State Thomas Jefferson did permit British agents to attend the council and assist the Indians. McKee and John Butler planned to attend the treaty council, and Governor John Graves Simcoe refused to allow American agents to purchase supplies in Canada, and he intended to restrict their movement once they arrived. Simcoe hoped to wield his power at Sandusky to show the Indians that the British, despite the ignominious end to the Revolutionary War, still mattered very much and that the power of the English Crown was real.[17]

While Simcoe laid his plans, the commissioners began their journey. They met with Red Jacket, Farmer's Brother, and others along the Genesee in mid-May and encouraged them to attend the council in Ohio. Upon arriving at Niagara, they sent Jasper Parrish to the Allegany Senecas in hope of finding interpreters who could speak with the Shawnees and Delawares. Parrish, while along the Allegheny, should try to obtain as much white wampum as possible (they had enough black, they thought), at least 80,000 beads. It was hard to find. Pickering hoped to obtain a supply in New York City or Albany, but he was disappointed. He wrote to an American officer at Pittsburgh, with instructions to acquire as much wampum there as he could, "if it can be minted at Pittsburg." Pickering wondered in a letter to Knox whether the British might be persuaded to loan the United States wampum for the council. Parrish, meanwhile, believed that he had seen two million beads of white wampum stored in Philadelphia.[18]

They also gathered intelligence, and kept in touch with the native diplomats with whom they most recently had worked. Brant arrived at the Miami Rapids in late May and received rough treatment from the western nations. The Shawnees refused to speak to him. Brant came to them with a compromise proposal, a boundary line based not on the Ohio but on the Muskingum River. Under Brant's proposal, the United States would give up a significant chunk of the lands it claimed as a result of the Fort Harmar treaty, while the Indians would concede to the United States the posts and settlements already established beyond the Ohio.[19]

The Shawnees and Delawares would have none of this, but Brant did gain some support among the Potawatomis, Ottawas, and Ojibwes. They lived closer to the Great Lakes, were closely tied to the British trading posts there, and lived more distant from the Ohio than did the Shawnees. A long war with the United States would not help them, and setting the Muskingum rather than the Ohio as a boundary line cost them relatively less.[20]

Brant hoped to assert Iroquois influence in the west, to restore the power of the Iroquois League based at Grand River. Meanwhile, the commissioners did what they could along the Niagara River. Simcoe and his men watched the American commissioners closely. Pickering instructed Hendrick Aupaumut to travel west with the suggestion that the Northwestern tribes accept a revised line along the Great Miami River, considerably farther west than the compromise proposed by Brant. Land to the west of the Great Miami would belong to Indians. Aupaumut should ask them to consider "the advantages you derive from the lands which the United States wish to retain." They hunted these lands. Pickering understood that much. "But, suppose the Commissioners should offer to pay a large annual rent for these lands, in money, in goods or provisions; would not such terms be better than war?" Aupaumut should relay this to the Indians, and ask them to keep their minds open.[21] But the British Indian department would not let the commissioners meet with Indian visitors at Fort Niagara without their men present. James Monroe, who learned about the negotiations from afar, complained about the British conduct in a letter to Jefferson. The United States had forced the British "to abandon those very Indians in her treaty with us," yet now "we accept, if not solicit, her aid to make our own peace with those whom they had sacrific'd." The commissioners, and American officials in Philadelphia, worried that the British were trying to delay the proceedings to a point where it would be too late in the year to follow the failure of negotiations with a military campaign. And few in the government had much faith that the council would succeed.[22]

Pickering wanted to clear out. He wanted to head to Detroit, with a British escort, and then on to Sandusky. Bad weather kept them from leaving in June, and while they waited for better conditions, Brant and about fifty western Indians arrived. Brant presented to Pickering his compromise and asked Pickering whether the commissioners had the authority to draw a permanent boundary line. This pleased Pickering. On June 10, as the commissioners prepared once again to set sail on Lake Erie, he noted that they did so "with better prospects of success than before."[23]

This optimism, it turns out, was not warranted. Brant, Pickering learned, did not speak for all the Northwestern Indians. In fact, four different positions seem to have been at play when Pickering and his fellow commissioners arrived at the home of the British Indian agent Andrew Elliott at the mouth of the Detroit River. The Shawnees and Delawares and their allies stuck to the Ohio as a boundary line. The Iroquois delegates to the conference, almost 120 in number, along with the Potawatomis and the western Great Lakes tribes with close ties to the British at Detroit, would settle for the Muskingum line Brant proposed. The British would accept either line, so long as an Indian buffer territory might emerge between the United States and British Canada. The United States, of course, wanted as much of Ohio as it could get, and recognition of the validity of the lines agreed to at Fort Stanwix and Fort Harmar.[24]

Elliott kept the commissioners close by, and they could communicate with the Northwestern confederates only through mediators. Pickering, on the last day of July, sent to them a proposal to "finally relinquish to the United States, some of the lands on your side of the River Ohio." He would pay them for what they gave up "such a large sum, in money or goods, as was never given on this island." To replace the "skin and furs" that they acquired in what Pickering and the commissioners dismissed as little more than hunting territory, the United States would deliver to them every year "a large quantity of such goods as are best suited to the wants of yourselves, your women, and children."[25]

They replied on August 13. They rejected everything the commissioners offered. They rejected the Confederation-era conquest treaties, and they rejected Fort Harmar. They rejected American claims to hold a right of preemption over the Ohio Country that the commissioners said derived from the British Crown. "We never made any agreement with the king, nor with any other Nation," they said, that would give "to either the exclusive right of purchasing our lands." The United States could keep its money, they said, something that "to us, is of no value, & to most of us unknown." Nothing the United States could offer "can induce us to sell the lands on which we get sustenance for our women and children." Instead of paying us, they suggested, why not buy out the settlers who squatted on their lands? However great that expense, it must be less than the amount you offered to us and "the great sums you must expend in raising and paying armies."[26]

"Our only demand," they told the commissioners, "is the peaceable possession of a small part of our once great Country." They asked the commissioners to try to understand their historical experience. "Look back and view the lands from whence we have been driven to this spot, we can retreat no further, because the country behind hardly affords food for its present inhabitants." They had resolved never "to leave our homes in this small space, to which we are now confined."[27]

The commissioners returned home. There was nothing left to do, no compromise acceptable to all parties. Pickering blamed the British for the Indians' insistence on the Ohio boundary. In this he was mistaken, however, for the Indians themselves had determined upon this course long before the British got involved, a course they knew would cause the war to resume, but one that, given the assaults they had suffered, they could not avoid.[28]

General Anthony Wayne arrived at Pittsburgh in the summer of 1792 with forty recruits and a handful of dragoons. He got to work. He instructed local militia officers to move carefully, to defend American settlements but to avoid any action that Indians might construe as provocative. He wrote to Knox, requesting more troops, preparing for war while the commissioners tried to negotiate peace. By early August, he had 1,100 men in camp. On August 25, 1793, the commissioners informed Wayne that negotiations had failed. There would be no peace settlement with the Northwestern tribes, and the war would resume.[29]

Despite the efforts made by Brant to broker a compromise with the Northwestern nations, and their confidence that the Iroquois from Grand River would not join in any conflict, American officials could not be certain where Iroquois peoples living within New York stood. Considerable disaffection remained. There was no doubt about that. In October 1793, in the presence of Israel Chapin and the British Indian Superintendent John Butler, the Seneca Farmer's Brother delivered an address in which he spoke for the Shawnees, Delawares, and others. The Shawnees thanked the Six Nations for their efforts to avert war. The Shawnees and Iroquois had pledged to protect each other in time of war many decades before. They renewed that agreement at Buffalo Creek. Well aware that the Iroquois, too, faced pressure upon their lands, the Shawnees invited them to join them, to accept their offer of shelter. "We now see that you are in distress, that you are surrounded by water, and have not dry land to stand upon," and "that a large white beast stands with open mouth on the other side ready to destroy you." The Iroquois need not remain in so exposed a position. "We have dry land for you to stand on and we now take you by the hand, and invite you to come and bring your beds and sit down with us."[30]

Joseph Brant, who spoke two days later, reiterated his proposal for a compromise line. It began "where the Ohio falls into the Mississippi, to follow the course of the Ohio to the Muskingum, to ascend that river up its most easternmost Fork to a Lake at its Head, the carrying place between the River & the Cayahoga, & then from then to follow a direct course . . . till it strikes the old Pennsylvania line proceeding easterly on that till it is intersected by a line running Southerly, to Chenesee River, till it falls into Lake Ontario." Unless this line was agreed to, Brant saw little reason to meet again with the Americans. But the Six Nations did not commit to assist the Northwestern confederates.[31]

Chapin forwarded to Henry Knox a record of the proceedings, and Knox forwarded them to the president. On Christmas Eve 1793, Knox wrote a reply to the sachems, chiefs, and warriors of the Six Nations. He thanked them for their efforts. He pointed out that "peace is best for the whites as well as the red people," and he asserted that the United States had done all it could to avoid war. The president would consider the proposed boundary line, Knox continued, even though "the lines you mention are considered as liable to considerable objections." He would not give a precise answer, and the president wanted to hold a general council for the Six Nations and "the chiefs of all such Western Tribes" the Six Nations might wish to invite. The meeting should take place at Venango, south of Presqu' Isle, in the middle of May.[32]

This offer disturbed the Six Nations. Cornplanter and the Senecas at Allegheny would not attend a council at Buffalo Creek in February to discuss the proposed meeting because "the sickness that we got at the Sandusky is very bad among us." Big Tree of the Genesee Senecas had died, and the Allegany Senecas suspected poison administered by the Northwestern tribes. Red Jacket and Iroquois from the Niagara did attend and so did Joseph Brant, who expressed the Six Nations' frustration. The American position caused them "great uneasiness." Respond to our boundary line proposal, he said, but why kindle "a council fire at a distant place?"[33]

Their uneasiness only increased. Anthony Wayne sent a message to the Six Nations. The Delawares, he said, were cowards. They poisoned Big Tree, leaving him "melancholy & deranged until the last moment of his death," when he stabbed "himself with his own knife." New Arrow, Wayne had since learned, died as well, and Cornplanter was ill. "This mode of making war is cowardly & base," he wrote, and Big Tree "was determined to have revenge had he lived." It was a bald attempt to sow divisions between the Allegheny Senecas, the Iroquois in New York in general, and the Northwestern tribes against whom Wayne prepared to march. He attempted to shame the Iroquois into joining him.[34]

By the time they received Wayne's letter, it is likely that many Iroquois had learned of the speech delivered in February by Lord Dorchester, the governor-general of Canada. In it, Dorchester suggested that war between the United States and Great Britain was inevitable. At war with France, Britain refused to honor America's rights as a proclaimed neutral nation. Israel Chapin described the address as "inflammatory," and it was. At yet another council held at Buffalo Creek in April and attended by Chapin and John Butler, the British tried to line up the assistance of the Iroquois. That is what Chapin suspected. Butler lavished gifts upon the Six Nations. Frontier settlers in New York, Chapin wrote, could see that all was not well, and according to Chapin they felt "very much alarmed at the present appearance of war." They were poorly equipped, and "the scattered inhabitants of this remote wilderness," Chapin admitted, "would fall an easy prey to their savage neighbors, should they think proper to attack them."[35]

The state of New York respected neither the authority of the United States over Indian affairs nor the Iroquois League itself, and it moved aggressively to acquire Iroquois lands in the center of the state. The New Yorkers exploited divisions between Iroquois people who still lived in the refugee centers at Buffalo Creek and those who remained in or had since reoccupied their homelands. Commissioners appointed by the state legislature, John Cantine and Simeon DeWitt, failed in their efforts to acquire land from the Oneidas in 1793, but they had better luck with the Cayugas and Onondagas. The state's commissioners visited the Onondagas in November 1793. They hoped "to enquire of you which lands you are inclined to lease, and which to keep for yourselves to live upon." Kakitikon, an Onondaga sachem who had signed the 1788 accord at Fort Schuyler, gently corrected the New Yorkers' misapprehension. Although they may have heard rumors that the Onondagas were willing to part with some of their lands, "it is not our voice you have heard but that of some . . . who live to the westward." A refugee sachem at Buffalo Creek, Kakitikon pointed out, "wishes to dispose of the whole of our lands but we are deaf to him." The Onondagas would gladly meet with the governor's messengers, Kakitikon said, but not to sell land.[36]

Cantine and DeWitt promised the Onondagas that they did not want to buy their land. Rather, they told the sachems, they wished "to make your reservation productive to you." Rent paid on lands the state leased from the Onondagas would bring the tribe more cash than its members could acquire through farming. The Onondagas considered the agents' proposals, but even Cantine and DeWitt recognized that "their only inducement to part with their property was their apprehension that those of their Nation who resided at Buffalo Creek would sell the whole of their reservation and leave no part of it for them to remain upon." If the Onondagas did not want to part with their land, other Iroquois at Buffalo Creek would sell their lands from underneath them. The Onondaga sachems, as a result, agreed to a limited lease of their lands. When the treaty was written and recorded, however, the extent to which Cantine, DeWitt, and the state had defrauded the Onondagas became clear. The first article of the November 1793 agreement showed that the Onondagas did "release and quit-claim to the People of New York forever all rights reserved to the said Onondagas in and to so much of the lands appropriated to their use by the said state commonly called the Onondaga Reservation." The rest of the agreement specified the precise bounds of the cession.[37]

Four months later, in February 1794, New York officials met again with the Onondaga sachems, this time at Albany. It was winter, and the federal agent charged with overseeing Indian policy lived 200 miles to the west at Canandaigua. At this meeting, Kakitikon told Clinton that while the Onondagas' neighbors had frequently complained to the young national government of the injustices they had suffered at the hands of the state, his people had "always stayed at home peaceably and never troubled you." Delivering to the governor a message "from the women that we have left at home," Kakitikon expressed their wish "that the path may be forever kept open between us and that there may be no obstructions." He presented to Clinton strings of wampum from the women and announced that "the land belongs to them [the women] and they are fully satisfied with the Agreement" that the Onondagas and the citizens of the state of New York had entered into in the summer of 1788—if only the state would honor its obligations.[38]

The Onondagas complained, in fact, that the citizens of the state of New York had violated the spirit of the shared-use agreement negotiated at Fort Schuyler. They had taken too much from the Onondagas. Gastontegachte, who had not signed the treaty, complained that too many settlers had occupied the eastern shore of Onondaga Lake to erect salt works, effectively deforesting the area in search of the fuel they needed to boil brine from the nearby salt springs. The Onondagas, he said, would allow the settlers to remain on the eastern shore, but only "if you will allow us to have the west side for our use." Other lands used by the New Yorkers, Gastontegachte continued, the Onondagas had never intended to share with state citizens. The Onondagas had thought that under the terms of the 1788 treaty that "we were to have a mile on each side of the River at the Eel weir or fishing place, since which we have heard this is not the case which is contrary to our expectation." It was a serious matter, and the Onondagas expected to have exclusive use of this vital resource. Fishing, Gastontegachte told Clinton, "is almost the only support we have to keep us and our Women and Children alive in the Spring when our corn and provisions is gone [and when] we then go there and draw our living from the fishing place." Some things, Gastontegachte explained, simply could not be shared.[39]

When Chapin arrived at Buffalo Creek to meet with the Six Nations, he "found the minds of the Indians much agitated" by two issues. The first, Cornplanter said in a speech he delivered on June 18, was the distressing fact that "a number of our warriors are missing and we know not what has become of them, but suppose they have been killed by the Americans." He suspected that the "American army" may have played some role in the death of Big Tree. The violence continued, an old issue indeed, and Cornplanter wanted it to stop.[40]

The Six Nations wanted justice. The Americans wished to live as free people, but so, too, did the Iroquois. They needed land. We "want room for our children," for "it will be hard for them to have no country to live in after we are gone." This brought Cornplanter to his second issue, the Erie Triangle. It was he who had signed the quit claim to Pennsylvania. Now, in the face of increasing criticism from his own people, Cornplanter became an assertive critic. When the Pennsylvanians began to occupy the lands, survey them, and garrison them, some Senecas contemplated attacks. Cornplanter said that he had never officially consented to the sales, and he repudiated the treaties of Fort Stanwix and Fort Harmar. He wanted the United States to remove the Pennsylvanians from these lands. If they left, "we shall consider them as our friends," he told Chapin, but "if not, we shall consider them as no friends."[41]

This opposition earned for Cornplanter some respect from the Iroquois. Chapin departed from Buffalo Creek and traveled with sixteen warriors to Fort LeBoeuf in the Triangle. They met with Andrew Ellicott and Ebenezer Denny, two Pennsylvania officials, who declared that the state "fairly and openly made the purchase of all the lands to which they lay claim." They could not move off the lands without orders from the governor, and they expressed to the Iroquois delegates their sorrow "that our continuing on the lands which you have sold to your Brethren of Pennsylvania should be the cause of any uneasiness."[42]

Henry Knox made it clear, meanwhile, to Pennsylvania Governor Thomas Mifflin that conditions in the Erie Triangle, in light of the problems in the west and the deteriorating relationship between the United States and Great Britain, "concern not only our peace, but other great interests of our country." Cornplanter told Chapin that the Pennsylvanians were liars. You know what we want, he said. You have heard our proposal for a boundary line, he told Chapin, and you know how we feel about the Erie Triangle. President Washington needs to act to set this right. "If you do not comply," he warned, the Six Nations would consider their options. "You know that we are a free people, and that the Six Nations are able to defend themselves." Chapin must understand what he said: "We are determined to maintain our freedom," he said, and, he warned Chapin, "do not imagine that our minds are corrupted by other people," for "the only thing that can corrupt them will be a refusal of our demands."[43]

Cornplanter was serious. He told a surveyor named John Adlum that the British offered to assist them if they decided upon war. Adlum and Cornplanter met at Allegheny. As they smoked a pipe, the young men heckled, saluting him, he wrote, "with an universal roar, *vulgarly called farting.*" Some women joined in, claiming that Adlum's talk of surveying was "scandalous." Cornplanter told them to be quiet, as did a clan mother, and the meeting continued without further distraction. Cornplanter aired for Adlum all his grievances: the violence, the fraudulent treaties. Although they allowed Adlum to carry on and to complete his survey, Cornplanter and the other chiefs made clear to him that they did not see why Wayne would fare any better than Harmar and St. Clair.[44]

Knox wrote to Mifflin once again. The intelligence streaming in from Pennsylvania and New York made clear the disaffection of important parts of the Six Nations. If the Pennsylvanians curtailed their activity in the region, however, this small gesture might placate the Iroquois. Mifflin agreed. Knox would call a council of the Six Nations to discuss their grievances. It would take place at Canandaigua in the fall. The Pennsylvanians would produce evidence documenting their claims to the Erie Triangle. They would await the results of the council before moving forward to survey and sell lands in the disputed territory, although Mifflin made clear that "no assent is given to any proposition, that shall bring into doubt or controversy the rights of the state."[45]

CHAPTER 6

....

Fallen Timbers

F ear hung over the borderlands in the spring of 1794. Rumors of
what the Senecas might do coursed through white settlements
in Pennsylvania and New York. The Iroquois, too, discussed the
future. White people continued to encroach on native land. This was
true for the many frontiers of the republic. Their numbers increased
each year. Should we strike before more arrive? Native peoples could
point to the two American armies the Northwestern confederates
already had repulsed. Should they wait—for something—to see what
the western Indians did, or what might result from additional diplomacy? Or might they consider fighting an act of futility? Might it be
better to accommodate themselves to the American presence, to
learn to live as much as possible with the newcomers, and to take the
white government up—selectively and conditionally—on its offers
for sponsored culture change? Perhaps then they might be able to
remain on their homelands.[1]

Rumors and reports, fears of violence: In May a settler killed a
"Friendly Indian" in the vicinity of Fort Franklin. The fort's com-
mander, a General Wilkinson, noted that the Indians distrusted
American justice, even with the suspect in custody. "The Indians say
the white people always tell them they will punish crimes of this kind,
but never yet have done it, and they are determined not to let this instance pass without having justice." Wilkinson and his officers paid
to the father of the victim $100 to cover the grave, and set things
right. Wilkinson thought that the Pennsylvania state government
could not do too much "to keep the Six Nations friendly." Wilkinson
was optimistic that he had solved this problem, but fears remained.[2]

Six weeks later, five Senecas along with five men from the Fort Franklin garrison found two missing white men "shot, scalped, and tomahawked." Six Nations warriors had nothing to do with the killing, but that did not keep white settlers from clinging to their suspicions. They heard frightening stories. The British had bought canoes for Cornplanter's men to enable them to strike white settlements along the Alleghany with speed and strength.[3] As one Pennsylvanian noted, "the fluctuation and inconsistency of our news is such that it is difficult to form a proper opinion" of the threats they faced. Rumors and stories and fear hung thick. One Pennsylvania officer at Pittsburgh reported to Governor Mifflin that in June a Seneca had tried to kill a white man at Cornplanter's town. Cornplanter prevented any violence against the visitor by telling the aggressor that "the time was not yet come for them to strike." The Senecas, to this observer, "appeared very surly and ill-natured" and certain to join with the Northwestern tribes. Traders in the western part of the state who knew the Indians well broke up their stores and headed for safer quarters. An officer at Fort Franklin possessed "not a shadow of doubt, but that a plan was formed to destroy all the posts and settlements in this quarter" should Great Britain and the United States go to war.[4]

Western New Yorkers shared their neighbors' fears. They worried about the Iroquois and about the British. Settlers in the vicinity of Canandaigua petitioned Governor Clinton early in May. They wanted him to understand "the exposed situation of this country as the frontier of this State." They needed immediate help to withstand an invasion by British soldiers or Indian warriors. "Our inhabitants are totally destitute of arms and ammunition," they wrote, "so much as to render the militia of this country useless in case they are called into action." Secretary of War Knox ordered Governor Clinton to take whatever actions "as may tend to shelter and secure the inhabitants on a sudden emergency whom it would be advisable to furnish with arms and ammunition."[5]

The notion that Great Britain and the United States might go to war was not at all far-fetched in early 1794. The problem between the two countries was not solely Indian policy or the question of northwestern posts. Beginning in 1793, Britain found itself embroiled in warfare with Revolutionary France. It was an alliance with France dating back to 1778 that in part had enabled the United States to triumph over Britain in the Revolutionary War. With France descending into the violence of its "Reign of Terror," some American "Federalists" urged a retreat from the commitments the French alliance entailed. Some advocated closer ties with Great Britain, the greatest commercial power in the world. For the "Republicans," the followers of Thomas Jefferson and James Madison, the French Revolution had produced excesses to be sure, but France was now a sister republic, engaged in the same struggle against tyranny and monarchy that the Americans had waged. The alliance, as a result, must still be honored.

But the British refused to recognize America's rights as a neutral nation. Its navy stopped American ships on the high seas and pressed American sailors into service in the Royal Navy. To remedy these problems, the president appointed John Jay, the Chief Justice of the Supreme Court, as his emissary to Great Britain. The resulting foreign policy questions—to adhere to the French alliance or to move toward an accommodation with Great Britain—produced deep fissures in the political system. Jay had little real bargaining power. He possessed little clout and could offer few reasons for the British to listen to him. Federalists and Republicans mobilized their supporters around this and a host of other issues, all of which connected fundamentally to the question of whether the American nation could succeed in a world seemingly hostile to republican forms of government. Politics reached a fever pitch, with Republicans denouncing Federalists as "Monocrats" and monarchists, while Federalists described Republicans as anarchists and radicals sympathetic to a movement that seemed hell-bent on destroying all the institutions that kept civil society in order. The fear that the American nation might break apart under the strain, that it might not survive this test of republican institutions, loomed large in the political conflict of the 1790s.[6]

Anthony Wayne, of course, could not await the results of Jay's diplomatic mission. Wayne moved cautiously. He trained his men. He readied his raw recruits for battle. He treated deserters harshly, branding them on the forehead with the label "Coward." He worked to keep order, to crack down on indiscipline. Of course he knew well the mistakes Harmar and St. Clair had made, and he devoted most of his energy to trying not to repeat them.[7]

While Chapin and others conducted their slow diplomacy with the Six Nations, as they undertook their efforts to keep the Six Nations and the western tribes apart, Wayne moved forward, cautiously applying pressure to the westerners. Brant, and spokesmen for the Senecas, Delawares, and Miamis, denounced these efforts as provocative, and as actions that showed the insincerity of the Americans' talk of peace. In January, a detachment from Wayne's main force constructed Fort Recovery at the site of St. Clair's defeat. From this base, small contingents marched out against towns along the Auglaize River. Wayne's men took some casualties, but his invasion force kept the Indians on their toes.[8]

Wayne conducted diplomacy as well, but the leaders Painted Pole, Blue Jacket, and Little Turtle rejected his offers to talk. They did not trust him, Wayne said, owing to the influence of the British. Dorchester's speech convinced many that the British, soon to be at war with the United States, would assist the Indians in recovering those lands they had lost since 1783. In May, Wayne learned that the British had occupied an old American post along the Maumee and garrisoned it with 400 men and enough artillery to offer a formidable defense. If true, it was a provocative act that showed that the British did not respect American sovereignty, that they believed that their plan to erect an Indian barrier state with the Ohio as its southern boundary just might succeed, and that the United States faced a formidable set of dangers. On June 28, 1794, Wayne's forces moved out, heading toward the Northwestern confederates' towns and that British post.[9]

While Wayne's forces marched, Pickering set to work readying supplies for the treaty council set to convene in the fall. Israel Chapin kept busy, too, gathering gifts and supplies, extending invitations to the meeting, and sending assurances that the United States wished to work out a lasting peace with the Six Nations. The council at Canandaigua, Chapin wrote to the chiefs of the Six Nations on August 15, he hoped "would produce an amiable agreement between both parties" and one that will "satisfy your minds and . . . give you a right understanding *in all things* whereby you make your minds uneasy."[10]

Chapin wrote these words three days after he had learned "by an Indian from the westward that General Wayne has had a battle with the Indians in which the Indians lost seventy men." He told Knox, upon receiving this news, that he believed that the Six Nations would not now join with the western Indians, and that at the Canandaigua council all the differences existing between the Iroquois and the United States "will be removed and more security will be rendered on the frontiers." Wayne, it seemed, might solve one problem, and Pickering and he could take care of another—placing relations between the Six Nations and the United States on a firm footing and bringing security to the New York and Pennsylvania borderlands—in the coming weeks.[11]

It was an opening battle. Wayne's men engaged in a number of brushfire skirmishes as they advanced on the northwestern towns. Supported by a good supply of artillery, and cavalrymen from Kentucky, his 3,000-man "Legion" fought like a force determined. The northern nativists expected that Wayne's forces would attack their settlement, defended on one flank by a large number of trees that had been blown down in a windstorm, on August 18. The warriors fasted and performed rituals to harness the sacred power necessary to succeed in battle, the same sacred forces that had assisted them against two previous American armies. Wayne was running late, however, moving cautiously and guarding his flank to prevent ambush. On August 20 he attacked, finally, catching the Indians in a weakened state. Wayne took the field, and although it was not an easy victory, and his men suffered casualties roughly equal to those they inflicted on the Indians, the Northwestern allies fled toward the British post on the Maumee a short distance away. The British officers ordered the gates kept closed. Once again, the British betrayed the expectations of their Indian allies. They demonstrated clearly that they would not come to the Indians' assistance if it meant an open conflict with the United States.[12]

Wayne's troops razed the countryside, burning fields and Indian towns throughout the Glaize. The Northwestern confederates were on the run. They were short of food, defeated in battle, and abandoned by the British. According to an officer at Fort Miami, the Northwestern confederates were "much dejected."[13] Within months, Wayne would dictate to them a conqueror's peace at Greenville, putting an end to armed resistance in the region that would last until the War of 1812. It was one of a number of significant defeats native peoples suffered in 1794. Farther south, the militant Chickamauga

Cherokees were defeated when Kentucky and Virginia militiamen destroyed their towns at Nickajack and Running Water. Connections between militants in the south—Creeks and Cherokees—were severed by the growth of Kentucky, which entered the Union in 1792, and Tennessee four years later. British support for these Indians, and Spanish assistance tendered to the Creeks from the Gulf Coast, dried up as war in Europe intensified. By the end of the summer of 1794, the threat of a western Indian force armed and supported by the British descending on American settlements had been eliminated. But there remained the issues that bothered the Six Nations.[14]

The treaty council at Canandaigua had originally been scheduled to begin on September 10, the day Pickering finally found an opportunity to escape his obligations as Postmaster General and depart from Philadelphia. Pickering believed that if he arrived in Canandaigua by September 18 he would be all right: Neither of the two councils he previously had presided over began on the date he expected, and he now understood how deliberately members of the Six Nations approached their diplomatic work. So he continued to make his preparations. Most of the gifts for the Indians, he was assured, would arrive at Canandaigua in time. He asked Chapin to arrange for him lodging in Canandaigua where he might entertain, and he carried with him supplies of "liquors, coffee, tea and chocolate" for his special guests. Even with the delays his own obligations imposed upon him, Pickering arrived before any of the Iroquois. He learned that the British were trying to delay the Indians, or to have the council held at Buffalo Creek where, in the words of the land baron Thomas Morris, they could watch "the business negotiated under their own eyes, and assist their Tawny friends with their advice." Pickering would not alter the site for the treaty, and he was willing to wait at Canandaigua for their arrival.[15]

Four Quakers followed Pickering for the purpose of attending the treaty: William Savery, James Emlen, John Parrish, and David Bacon. They traveled from Philadelphia "with the approbation of the meeting for Sufferings in conjunction with the Committee of the Yearly Meeting on Indian Affairs." The journals that Emlen, Savery, and Bacon kept, along with Pickering's own detailed writings, provide the best historical sources for understanding the council. Since 1790, members of the Society of Friends, as the Quakers were formally known, had watched closely the conduct of the nation's Indian policy, and they involved themselves as observers and witnesses with the blessings of Washington and Pickering. Unlike Samuel Kirkland, who had thoroughly thrown his lot in with the land speculators who coveted the Indians' estate, the Iroquois trusted the Quakers and, as Savery pointed out, "when treaties were about to be negotiated, the Indians generally solicited the attendance of some Friends to advise and assist them."[16]

The four Quakers left Philadelphia on September 15. They described the difficulties of traveling through a land that to them still appeared wild. Just a couple of days into their journey, they encountered rains that left them soaked, a rough environment where "neither the land nor the appearance of the country round this place appear very attractive," and "the worst Road that ever mine eyes beheld," often "so covered with Stones as to make traveling slow & tedious." They described shortages of food, because "the Inhabitants in some places are deterred from keeping Swine, as the Bears devour them when they come their way," and wolves preyed upon their cattle. Indeed, Savery noted that "the country so abounds with wild game, bear, deer, elk, foxes, and wolves, that it is difficult to keep hogs or sheep."[17] It was a rough life for the settlers in the borderlands of Pennsylvania and New York. "Ague" and "bilious fevers" struck down hearty settlers who migrated westward from New England. Everywhere Emlen went, he observed "their pale dejected appearance." Emlen thought the Genesee country a difficult place to live, and passing through it took its toll on him.[18]

It was not until the 25th that they arrived at Canandaigua. Emlen described a young settlement, planted just a half-decade earlier. It was, in his view, "beautifully situated in the borders of Canandague Lake" and "now contains about 40 Dwelling Houses, several of which are built in a style of elegance which we could hardly have expected in this remote country." He marveled at the house Morris was building, which "would make a respectable appearance on the Banks of the Schuylkill."[19]

They had arrived, and they took up residence in the lodging Israel Chapin had arranged for them. If they left Philadelphia pessimistic about the chances for peace, they received significant news when they arrived. By September 20, the day after Pickering arrived in

Canandaigua, word arrived "of a very important victory . . . over the hostile Indians near the British fort at the Rapids of the Miami." Word of the Battle of Fallen Timbers had made it to Canandaigua. Pickering learned that Wayne's army "had nearly surrounded and made a great slaughter" of the enemy. According to what Thomas Morris heard, "Wayne is said to have slaughtered a number of them [and] to have driven them 12 miles back as far as the fort & to have destroyed all their cornfields." The British did nothing to aid those Indians, Morris learned. The Six Nations now were isolated.[20]

Pickering might have pressed the advantage. He knew that no danger existed of an alliance between disaffected western Indians and the Six Nations, and he knew that when push came to shove, the British would not go out on a limb for native peoples living in the borderlands. Pickering told Savery that he believed that the cessions extracted from the Iroquois at Fort Stanwix in 1784 were reasonable. "That as the Indians did the United States a great deal of injury by taking part with the British in the late war, it was strictly just that they should make compensation by giving up the lands which they relinquished at that time." He also knew that the Iroquois were eager to negotiate and that "the Indians worked with uncommon zeal to get in their harvest of corn; the men and boys (which is not usual) assisting the women and girls, that it might be accomplished in time, & that they all might go to the treaty." But Pickering avoided the bluster of the congressional commissioners who met with the Six Nations in 1784. He thought of policy and longer-term goals. He wanted to achieve a peaceful and orderly frontier. The Iroquois still were numerous and they were still capable warriors. The British still had posts on American soil through which they could conceivably supply embittered Six Nations warriors. The threat remained. Settlers in increasing numbers still pressed upon their lands. And violence and the violation of native people's property rights remained a problem. Pickering waited patiently for the Iroquois. He would provide them with provisions once they arrived. And when the proceedings began, he remained attentive to the cultural values that rested at the heart of Iroquois diplomacy.[21]

The Oneidas arrived at Canandaigua first, 150 in all, accompanied by a "small number of Onondagas from their reservation." Pickering and Chapin were meeting with them when the Quakers arrived.

The Oneidas spoke of "what had befallen them" over the past several years. They expressed their hope that "we should discuss all the necessary objects of the treaty with candour and freedom, and for that purpose they now unstopped our ears that we might hear, and opened our throats that we might speak freely." Pickering appreciated the gesture. According to Savery, Pickering told the Oneidas that it was "his wish to conduct the business with the unreserved candour they desired." To facilitate this, Pickering "also opened their ears and unstopped their throats."[22]

It was an opening meeting, a chance to get acquainted, but more substantive business would await the arrival of representatives from more Iroquois communities. The four Quakers thus found themselves with an opportunity to explore. They visited a Friends' meeting house in Canandaigua, James Emlen wrote, with "the people and Indians behaving sober and orderly" while "the gospel was preached with power and demonstration." Emlen testified to the fact that not all encounters between natives and newcomers were violent and fraught with tension. But he also described those attending the meeting as "people" on the one hand and "Indians" on the other.[23]

The Friends traveled around. They saw sights. On September 30, they learned "of a few families of friends settled" a short distance from Canandaigua. Abraham Lapham, who lived with his wife and eight children roughly five miles from the town, told the Quakers of the difficulties of living in the New York borderlands. The first settlers, Lapham told them, had to travel more than 100 miles to reach a mill and had to confront the "great disadvantages" arising from "the scarcity of springs and rivulets, and the unhealthiness of the climate in its present uncultivated state." Some settlers lived "for many weeks under the shelter of bark and bushes before they could erect a hut." And though the white population increased every year, "the Indians are all round, and the settlement of whites very thin," so "there still is some danger to be apprehended."[24]

They returned to Canandaigua. The Senecas, Savery noted, "are very slow in coming to attend the treaty." He had traveled to the northwest in 1793, and the experience taught him the importance of "a patience which will always be needed by those who attend Indian treaties." Emlen also emphasized the importance of being patient, for the Indians, he believed, were people with "no extensive schemes in view, their wants confined within a narrow compass." He came across as peevish, dismissive. Time might be precious to white people, but to the Iroquois it was something held "in little estimation." But the Friends really had no choice but to wait. Savery was homesick already, but he had little control over the course of events.[25]

They were curious about the progress of religion, and when they learned of Friends or former members of the Society of Friends, the four Quakers tried to visit them. On October 8, they approached the settlement of Jemima Wilkinson, about twenty miles from Canandaigua. Born into a Quaker family in Rhode Island in 1752, she fell ill in her twenties and, in 1776, declared independence from her previous identity, taking for herself the title of "Publick Universal Friend." She and her followers believed that during this illness she had died, and was resurrected with the spirit of Christ in her body.[26]

Savery and Emlen, who recorded their thoughts in some detail, were not impressed. Her settlement consisted of "several hovels . . . which are the residences of women who have forsaken their husbands and children; and also of men who have left their families to become what they now literally are, hewers of wood and drawers of water to an artful and designing woman." Of Wilkinson herself, Emlen noted that "her deportment, dress, features &c are so very masculine that I think no one would suppose her to be a woman, who had not some previous knowledge of her." She began to discourse on matters religious. The Quakers tried to interrupt her. They took exception to her setting herself apart from the rest of mankind by taking the title of the Universal Friend. They made a number of attempts to "check her rhapsodies," but their efforts failed. The Quakers all thought her a schemer. They thought her unbalanced. And they believed, as Savery put it, that her followers were "declining fast; and both reason and religion inform us, that their fall is at no great distance, and perhaps the last days of this deluded woman may be spent in contempt, unless her heart becomes humbled and contrite, and the mercy of the Lord be eminently manifest to pity, and spare her." As settlers poured into the borderlands, schemers and dreamers and outcasts like Wilkinson found it even more difficult to get by. The Quakers undoubtedly told her about the council set to begin shortly at Canandaigua, and Wilkinson viewed the occasion as an opportunity to attempt to broadcast her message to a larger audience.[27]

On October 9, Parrish and Emlen rode out from Canandaigua to meet the Senecas who, Bacon reported, "are thought to be near." They headed toward the Genesee crossing, near today's Avon, New York, where an Irishman named Gilbert Berry operated a tavern and a ferry. They got little sleep for "about the Middle of the Night," Emlen wrote, "we were much alarm'd by some drunken Indians knocking at the Tavern door for Rum." Things got ugly. "An Irishman who was intoxicated the preceding evening was lying on the floor of the room where the Indians first enter'd." He attacked them, "whence a dreadful tumult ensued with the cry of Murder, Murder." Had not "some more sober persons" intervened, things might have ended quite badly.

Emlen and Parrish visited the Senecas' camp the next day and watched them performing a "brag dance," in which "any of the spectators have a right, after presenting a Bottle of Rum to make their Boast of what great feats they had done in the course of their Lives." Both Indians and whites participated, Emlen noted, including "a sensible doctor of the neighborhood." Instead of bragging about how many battles he had fought, or how many scalps or prisoners he had taken, the doctor said that he saved lives, and "that a child was capable of taking the life of a fellow creature, but that it required a man of judgment and skill to save it." The Senecas, enjoying the novelty of this boast, gave it "universal applause."[28]

The encounter at the Genesee crossing highlighted the challenges presented to men like Knox and Pickering and Washington who wanted to assert control over the borderlands. Berry showed to Emlen the "considerable tract" he had acquired from the Indians in a private purchase that violated the terms of the Trade and Intercourse Act. Berry knew that his title might be disputed, but he purchased the lands anyway. Berry's purchase appears not to have angered any Indians, but other encroachments did, and Berry's conduct shows the weakness of federal authority in the west. Encounters between Senecas and settlers at Berry's tavern included drinking and trading, but they could easily degenerate into violence. Alcohol was readily available, and a source of instability, despite the intention of the Trade and Intercourse Act to regulate its distribution. Law did not mean much in New York's borderlands.[29]

While Emlen and Parrish visited Berry's tavern and the camp of the Buffalo Creek Senecas at the Genesee crossing, Savery and Bacon accompanied Pickering to the Oneidas' camp. The Indians slowly were coming in for the council. On the 8th, Parrish estimated that nearly 450 had arrived, and by the time the treaty opened, Pickering believed, about 1,500 Iroquois would set up camp in the neighborhood. The Oneidas told Pickering that since the rest of the Six Nations had not yet arrived, they might take advantage of the opportunity to speak with him "of private affairs, which concerned only their nation."[30]

Pickering knew some of what was bothering them. He understood that "two parties had for some time existed in the Oneida nation, and altho' there had been an apparent reconciliation, yet that some heartburning remained, and that the breach was in danger of increasing." Pickering assembled the chiefs and warriors and hoped to remove the causes of difference and "restore their union." This was important work, he believed. "Such a union," he wrote, "at all times desirable, seemed to be particularly important at this time; the Oneidas forming a respectable portion of the Six Nations; and having been always attached to the United States." He delivered to them a short speech. He wished "to see them united among themselves," and "dwelling together on their own land, in our neighborhood, and having one common interest," that they "might live in harmony and love: observing, that this would be agreeable to the Great Spirit who delighted in the happiness of mankind, but that happiness was attainable only by union, peace and mutual kindness." He asked the Oneidas to explain the sources of their divisions, and he then handed to Young Peter, the head warrior, five strings of wampum.[31]

In the past, Good Peter would have spoken for the Oneidas. He had died the year before, however, and Captain John, a sachem, delivered to Pickering a speech addressing the "Causes of Dissention in the Oneida Nation." It was a simple message. "Our minds are divided on account of our lands," he said. It was not the Oneidas' fault. "'Tis you, Brothers of a white skin, who cause our uneasiness. You keep coming to our seats, one after another. You advise us to sell our lands, you say it will be to our advantage." Captain John recounted for Pickering the story of the Livingston Lease, and the fraud-filled treaty council held by Governor Clinton at Fort Schuyler in 1788. Captain John told Pickering how the Oneidas had always kept the peace with the United States, but now they struggled to keep the peace among themselves.[32]

That was, according to Peter, the head warrior, because the sachems had agreed to cessions of land without consulting with the warriors. According to Emlen's account, Peter complained that the sachems leased 61,440 acres of land to Peter Smith for twenty-one years at a rent of $200 per annum. Through transactions of this kind, the land was slipping away. Pickering did not respond to this immediately. It was late and it was a Saturday. Their meetings could resume on Monday. In the meantime, Emlen and Parrish having returned, the four Quakers visited the Oneidas' camp together on Sunday the 12th. It was a large meeting. The Oneidas sang the psalms they had learned from Samuel Kirkland, and Savery thought "that the melody and the softness of their voices in the Indian language, and the sweetness and harmony that attended, exceeded by far anything of the kind I had ever heard among the white people." Savery was moved, and he left the meeting inspired, feeling toward them "much love and sympathy, rejoicing in the midst of the wilderness, that the Lord is indeed everywhere." Emlen, peevish as always, conceded that the singers achieved some beautiful sounds, but he thought "that part of our meeting in which they were engaged in singing was to me the most exercising."[33]

Emlen had traveled through the wilderness to attend a treaty conference, and for him, religious services, while important, were not the reason they had come so far. He wanted to get started. On Monday the 13th he got his wish, as Pickering met again with the Oneidas to respond to the speeches of Captain John and Young Peter. Pickering had given their speeches a great deal of thought, he said. His principal object in this meeting "is to heal the wounds which have been given by the disposing of your lands." He reminded the Oneidas once again of the federal Trade and Intercourse Act, the most important provision of which regarded the sale and purchase of Indian land. Smith was not paying the Oneidas what the land was worth, Pickering said, and he offered them a concrete example to explain why. Three hundred farms might be carved out of the land that Smith had leased. "Those 300 farms would support 300 families upon them with good houses, and barns, horses, oxen, cows, sheep, hogs, wheat, corn, cloathing, and all the necessaries and comforts of life in great plenty." Those 300 families might consist of between 2,000 and 3,000 people, Pickering said. It was worth far more than $200 a year.[34]

Pickering did not blame the Oneidas, at least not entirely. They had men of understanding, "and minds equal to those of the whites." They lost their lands because they lacked the literacy and the knowledge of law that the land interests employed to transform Iroquoia into the Empire State. Learn to read and write. Learn the valuable things that white culture offered. "For bad people among the whites," Pickering told them, "knowing that you are incapable of computing the value of your lands, take advantage of your ignorance & deceive you: and knowing also your principal failing, they pretend to a great deal of generosity and provide a plenty of liquor; and when your hearts become cheerful, and your heads grow giddy, then they make their bargains with you, and get your chiefs to sign their papers."[35]

Nobody could purchase Oneida lands unless it was done "at a council Fire kindled by the United States and in the presence & with the approbation of the Commissioners appointed by the President." Do not believe agents from the state. Pickering told the Oneidas that they would lie. "Brothers," he said, "stop your ears when any men come to you with such talks, and do not believe them." It was a speech that the Oneidas liked, but they wanted to hear more. Captain John wanted Pickering to tell them whether it was the warriors or the sachems who had been in the wrong. Captain John told Pickering that "one of their customs was, for the sachems only to sit in council on civil affairs: but of late, their warriors appeared jealous of them, and had intruded into matters contrary to the ancient customs of the Indians." He spoke of divisions that long had occurred in Iroquois communities, but that had widened under the pressures of Anglo-American colonization and conflict. The sachems, the hereditary rulers of the league chosen by clan matrons, did not always agree with the war leaders, men who had risen in power owing to their abilities in battle and diplomacy. Like other outsiders who did not understand fully the function of the League, Pickering wrote little more about these divisions than what he was told. He recognized the divisions, understood the problem in its outlines, but could only offer that they come together, the sachems and warriors, to consider proposals to part with their lands closely, and not consent to a sale or a lease unless two thirds of the chiefs and warriors agreed that doing so was in the interest of the nation.[36]

The Senecas from Buffalo Creek arrived the next evening. They pitched their camp at the edge of the woods, about four miles from

Canandaigua, and sent word ahead so that the Oneidas, as younger brothers, might welcome them formally to the council. The Senecas, 472 strong, and led by Farmer's Brother, Little Billy, and Red Jacket, spent the morning of October 14 painting and ornamenting themselves for their public entry. They arrived in town about three in the afternoon. One hundred fifty Oneidas welcomed them, along with some Onondagas and Cayugas who also had just arrived. According to Savery, "the Oneidas, Cayugas, and Onondagoes were drawn up, dressed and painted, with their arms prepared for a salute, before General Chapin's door." The Seneca warriors "marched in, assuming good deal of importance, and drew up in a line facing the Oneidas &c., Colonel Pickering, General Chapin, and the many white people being present" at the public square on the grounds of today's Ontario County Courthouse. Both sides fired salutes, "making a long and loud echoe through the woods." The Senecas then sat down in a semicircle, and Farmer's Brother delivered a speech. He returned to Pickering the strings of wampum used to invite them to the treaty council. He apologized for their tardiness and gave his thanks that they had made it through the woods to this council fire. Pickering welcomed them. He answered them "in the usual complimentary manner," Savery noted, and then "ordered several kettles of rum to be brought." The Senecas from Buffalo Creek departed to set up their camp.[37]

Two days later the welcoming ceremony was repeated again, as Cornplanter and nearly 400 Senecas arrived from the Allegheny. The Senecas "drew up in three sides of a square, the Oneidas, Onondagoes, &c., facing them; each fired three rounds." They came into town "in full Indian dress, and painted in an extraordinary manner." They encircled Pickering and the Quakers and exchanged speeches with him. Once again Pickering brought out the rum, allowing the Indians to drink while they established their camps.[38]

There were now 1,600 Iroquois camped on the margins of Canandaigua. With a small contingent of Cayugas under the leadership of Fish Carrier due to arrive soon, Emlen at last had "grounds to hope [that] the Treaty will ere long commence." Nearly a third of the population of the Six Nations was in attendance, but not all nations were equally represented. The Mohawks did not attend, and only a small number of Onondagas made the journey. As the anthropologist William Fenton has pointed out, few of those present bore the titles of league sachems. The Thadodaho of the Onondagas, a "sensible old man" not fit to travel from Buffalo Creek to Canandaigua, could not attend. Most of the leaders were men who had come to their positions of influence owing to their ability to manage the important business of their nations, men like Red Jacket, Farmer's Brother, and Cornplanter. That they were not league sachems should not lead us to question their credentials or their capacity to speak for their nations. They were competent men, and they joined Pickering and the Quakers—interpreters like Horatio Jones, who traveled eastward with the Senecas from Geneseo led by Little Beard; Israel Chapin, ill and grieving, whose wife had died weeks before; and many scores of townspeople and observers who recognized that the events they were about to witness were of great significance for the security of the New York and Pennsylvania borderlands.[39]

CHAPTER 7

....

A Treaty at Canandaigua

William Savery spent part of October 17 "in company with an Indian queen." It was a quiet moment for him, and one that he seems to have appreciated. He said nothing about their conversation, or if they spoke at all. She had with her "a small child in one of their kind of cradles, hung with about one hundred small brass bells, intended to soothe the child to rest." Something about this small encounter interested him, struck him as worthy of note. Savery knew that in the coming weeks he would find little rest. "The attendance at Indian treaties is a painful task," he wrote, "wherein resignation is highly necessary." Small numbers of Anglo-Americans interacted with large numbers of native peoples, and not all of them were as easy as a mother with her sleeping baby. One had to be willing to adapt, to pay heed to the expectations of the large numbers of native peoples in attendance. "Sixteen hundred Indians are around us," Savery wrote, camped at several locations around Canandaigua. "Many of them," he continued, were "very noisy night and day, dancing, yelling, and constantly intruding upon us to beg for rum, but we uniformly resist their importunities for strong drink." Savery watched a sleeping baby and knew that he would need patience. He prayed that it might be granted.[1]

From the perspective of Timothy Pickering and his superiors, four major sets of issues needed resolution to consider the council a success. The first of course involved the land. Pickering understood well that the Iroquois felt aggrieved by their earlier cessions. He could do little about these transactions, but he could attempt to assert the authority of the federal government over the disposition of Indian lands and convince the Six Nations that sales undertaken without the approval of the United States were null and void and of no effect. He hoped to convince the Six Nations of the good faith of the United States. Second, although the western Indians had been defeated by Wayne at Fallen Timbers, Pickering could not have known yet how decisive this victory had been. Given the recent past, and the ability of native peoples to take blows and recover, Pickering could have anticipated that the Miamis, Shawnees, Delawares, and others would remain a force with whom the United States would have to contend. They were down now, so Canandaigua offered Pickering an opportunity to shut off the possibility once and for all that the Six Nations might combine with them. And, third, if the western tribes had been defeated on the battlefield at Fallen Timbers, there remained the question of the British posts. John Jay was negotiating these issues in London, but Pickering could know little of his progress. What he did recognize was that some American settlers had been enticed to move to Canada in response to the British government's generous land-granting policies, and that Oswego, Niagara, and Detroit remained in British hands. Nothing had occurred in the recent months that limited the ability of the Indian department to arm and equip Indians if its officers chose to do so. Pickering wanted to strengthen his ties to the Six Nations and, in so doing, isolate the British posts. And finally, there remained the hope expressed consistently by Pickering in nearly every piece of correspondence that passed between him and representatives of the Six Nations: that the Indians might accept the offer of the United States to teach them the arts of civilization. Pickering hoped to use the council to advance the government's efforts to "civilize" the American Indians. In this effort the Quakers hoped to play an instrumental role.[2]

The Six Nations, for their part, hoped to polish the rusted Covenant Chain that connected them to the United States. They hoped to eliminate the territorial barriers imposed upon them at Fort Stanwix a decade before. Pickering understood that they feared that "if they suffer the United States to inclose them, on all sides, they will become, like other tribes in the interior of the states, mere makers of baskets and brooms." They needed access to the Niagara River in order to preserve their capacity to move throughout a greater Iroquoia. They saw the Fort Stanwix border, reaffirmed by a rump at Fort Harmar, as a significant infringement on their liberty, a limitation on their autonomy, and a threat to their very way of life. They viewed the rapid settlement of the Erie Triangle in similar terms. The growing number of settlers in the Triangle trampled on the ability of Allegany Senecas to hunt and fish and move about their territory without the fear of violence. Some Senecas contemplated attacking the settlers, but for most of the Six Nations, the time when the interests of their community might be served by war had long since passed. Given the outcome at Fallen Timbers, and the unwillingness of the British to assist the Indians in any way, the treaty might provide the Six Nations with their last best opportunity to protect their lands, their ability to travel throughout Iroquoia, and their way of life.[3]

Red Jacket, Cornplanter, Farmer's Brother, Little Beard, and a number of others visited the Friends at their lodgings on the morning of October 18. Horatio Jones accompanied them as an interpreter. According to Savery, Cornplanter "congratulated us upon our safe arrival among them." They had passed through the woods without incident. He expressed his appreciation that the Quakers had accepted the invitation to come to Canandaigua. Cornplanter and the Seneca chiefs wanted to make sure they stood on solid ground in their relationship with the Friends. The Quakers, too, had matters they wished to discuss. A number of people from their community had taken up lands near Hopewell in Virginia. They wanted to pay for the lands, but they were not sure to which community the lands belonged. Cornplanter told the Friends that the Senecas had conferred about the matter in "many Conferences" and concluded that "the lands in Question were a part of the hunting ground of the Conestogoe Indians, whose limits extended to that Country." There were descendants of those Conestogas present at Canandaigua, and Cornplanter was optimistic that when time permitted the issue might be put to rest.[4]

Cornplanter could not pursue the matter now because Pickering had summoned the gathered Indians to meet in council. The Quakers attended. "We found a large body of them collected," Savery wrote, with "Colonel Pickering, General Chapin and three interpreters being in the center, and the surrounding assemblage presenting a very striking aspect." Captain John and another Oneida spoke first. They addressed the Senecas, Tuscaroras, and Delawares, "who lived westward." Captain John's speech was not publicly translated. It was business the Six Nations needed to address. Captain John spoke, and "handed to the Seneca chiefs one by one" a number of "strings of wampum and belts." One of the interpreters must have whispered what was said into the Quakers' ears for, Savery wrote, "we understood it was in the way of a condolence on account of the loss of many chiefs of the Six Nations by death, since they last met at a council-fire." According to Savery, Captain John and the Senecas to whom he spoke, younger brothers addressing the older, "expressed their desire to wipe the tears from their brethren's eyes, to brighten their countenances, and to unstop their throats, that they might speak clearly in the present council-fire." Fish Carrier, a Cayuga, the Onondaga Clear Sky, and Red Jacket responded to Captain John's address with what Savery thought "a brotherly salutation," handing the Oneidas "belts and strings of wampum, to unite each to the other, and thus to open the council as with the heart of one man." It took time for all of this, of course, but Pickering understood the importance of the condolence council, of approaching the work of peace with a good mind, and he told the Quakers that "it [was] needful to remove this stumbling block out of their way, preparatory to the Treaty."[5]

Pickering recognized the importance of Iroquois cultural norms. He recognized that the condoling of dead chiefs was an important League function. And he recognized that if he were to accomplish his own objectives in Canandaigua, he would need to honor and respect Iroquois practices. On the 20th he met again with the Iroquois, at a "very large Indian council," Savery wrote. Pickering "condoled with the Delawares for the loss of one of their people," and, Emlen added, he "inform'd them in their allegorical way that it had given him great sorrow that one of our hasty young men had killed one of their Nation that he now gather'd his Bones together, presenting a 15 string of black wampum." Through his speech and his gestures, with the help of his interpreters, Pickering "performed the ceremony of burying him after the Indian custom, and covering the grave with leaves, so that when they passed by they should not see it any more." Pickering "took the hatchet out of his head, and *in words* tore up a large pine tree and buried the hatchet in the hole then covered it thick with stones and planted the pine tree on the top of it again, so that it should never more be taken up." He then "wiped the blood from their beds, and the tears from their eyes, and opened the path of peace, which the Indians were requested to keep open at one end, and the United States at the other, as long as the sun shone." Farmer's Brother responded to Pickering, and he left Emlen impressed. The Seneca was "a man of Large stature, the Dignity & Majesty of his appearance, his sonorous voice & expanded arm, with the forcible manner of his utterance delivered in a language to us unintelligible reminded me of the antient Orators of Greece and Rome." The Six Nations, Farmer's Brother said, would take Pickering's words, consider them, and offer their reply tomorrow.[6]

The next morning Fish Carrier delivered the Six Nations' reply to Pickering. The death of their Delaware "nephew" saddened them, but Fish Carrier conceded that "accidents were liable in all Nations" and that they "were willing to bury his death in oblivion." They could move on. Handing to Pickering fifteen strings of wampum as he spoke, Fish Carrier announced that "it was the determination of the Six nations to keep hold of the chain of friendship with the fifteen fires." Pickering told the Iroquois that he had come to Canandaigua to speak for the United States, for the fifteen states gathered together. He formally introduced to them the Quakers whose presence, Pickering hoped, would lead the Six Nations to "rely on justice being done them" and to accept that "it was his sincere intention never to defraud them." With Parrish interpreting, the Friends then made an address that the gathered Iroquois "received with frequent expressions of *entaw* or approbation."[7]

Before Clear Sky could reply to the Quakers' address, Jemima Wilkinson and three of her followers, David Waggoner and Enoch and Rachel Malin, interrupted the proceedings. They fell on their knees, and with Wilkinson "dress'd in a compleat Clergyman's Surplice of black Silk," she began to offer "something in the form of a prayer," followed by a speech in which "she used many texts of scripture, without much similarity or connexion."[8] She saw the gathering, apparently, as an opportunity to convert the Iroquois to Christianity. If she could accomplish that feat, it seems, she might increase her fame. But her long harangue did not go over well. She preached until darkness fell, until it was too late to continue with the more important business of the council. Pickering, who had met with Wilkinson that morning and found her interesting and unusual, was greatly displeased by this interruption. Bacon wrote that her "performance was very disagreeable to me" and that he believed it "did not prove agreeable to Col. Pickering and not the Indians, I believe." Indeed, Bacon the next day relished the opportunity to denounce "her wild notions & conduct" and let her know that "I believed they were under delusions."[9]

Councils were like this: They could easily be sidetracked. Pickering tried to move things forward. Meanwhile, Captain John of the Oneidas visited the Quakers. He complained "about the many deceptions which had been practiced upon them by the white people." He conceded that some white men were good and honest but that "they were all deceivers when they wanted to buy Indian lands; and that the advantages of learning which they possessed, made them capable of doing much good and much evil." Dispossession and deception: These themes appeared as well later in the day when Pickering called the Quakers to attend the full council. Word had arrived, Pickering said, that one of the "antient men of the Oneida" had died. Pickering asked the Oneidas what they wanted to do. Captain John said that the death would not delay the council, even though carrying on "was contrary to their common custom." Pickering was pleased.[10]

But before he could move on, according to Emlen, "three elderly Squaws made their appearance, requesting that as some white women had been permitted to speak in council," they "also might be allowed the same Liberty." Red Jacket spoke for the clan matrons. If Jemima Wilkinson had asked the Indians to "repent & turn from their evil deeds," he thought the same should go for the Americans. White people, too, should repent. Red Jacket said that it was "the white people who had been the cause of all the Indians' distresses; that they had pressed and squeezed them together, until it gave them great pain at their hearts and that the whites ought to give them back the lands they had taken from them." Pickering knew what the Senecas wanted, Red Jacket said, and according to him the women "found themselves much distressed by being hemmed in." They wanted Pickering to return to them land that in their view had been unjustly acquired.[11]

Pickering spoke in reply. He recapitulated the speeches given by Cornplanter and Red Jacket the day before. The Seneca speakers had, according to Pickering, granted the first white settlers on this continent land, and they had continued to do so as their numbers increased, "til now they themselves were confined within a very narrow compass." They fought on the side of Britain during the Revolution but attempted to set things right at Fort Stanwix and Fort Harmar, councils they left feeling much "aggrieved." The U.S. commissioners at Fort Stanwix, they told Pickering, had "used such haughty & threatening Language, that they were intimidated to such a degree as to sign that which was contrary to their judgment." To brighten the chain of friendship, they told Pickering, they asked the United States to "confirm to them a strip of land about 30 or 20 miles wide from Lake Erie, & extending the length of the Seneca's country in the Westernmost Part of New York State to the Western Territory."[12]

Pickering conceded that the commissioners at Fort Stanwix had behaved harshly. He suggested that the Indians consider that they had done this at the end of a long war. According to Emlen, Pickering "appealed to the Warriors present whether in times of success in military enterprises they did not feel their Minds to exult & grow proud, which he believed was the situation of our Commissioners at that time." He asked Cornplanter and Red Jacket to clarify their claims for him. How far westward, he asked, did they believe the Six Nations' land extended? Cornplanter said that it included land within the state of Pennsylvania, "westward of the Allegauey River." It was these lands that the United States had purchased from the Delawares and Wyandots, Pickering pointed out, at the Treaty of Fort McIntosh in 1785.[13]

It was a difficult issue, Pickering observed. Identical pieces of land claimed by different Indian nations resulted in purchases that one party or the other would view as invalid. He hoped to carry on with the negotiations, but delays again intruded. It snowed all day on October 24, several inches according to Bacon. While the snow made it easy for Iroquois hunters to track deer, and while the resulting plenty of venison relieved townspeople of the occasional problem of stock stolen by the Iroquois visitors, both Bacon and Pickering fought back feelings of pessimism. He was 300 miles from home, Bacon wrote, and he "knew not when we should be at liberty to go." Pickering, watching the funeral of not one but two Oneida "antients" who were buried together in a single grave, covered the council fire for the day and told Emlen that "a dark cloud seems now gathering around us." The two dead men were escorted to their common grave by an Oneida who led the procession, with a three-gallon keg of rum under each arm and a bottle in his hands. The chiefs said a few words, and the warriors fired volleys.[14]

The Quakers awoke to find the snow seven or eight inches deep, Bacon believed, and with the news from Pickering that "an interpreter had come here from the British" at the invitation of some of the Senecas. Pickering was furious. He believed that the presence of the British "would obstruct our proceedings until he was dismissed, and he was determined not to permit" his attendance at the council.[15] The British interpreter, "a man named Johnson," appeared at the council later that day with the Senecas and, according to Savery, "seemed very intimate with them." Cornplanter rose to speak in defense of the British Indian department agent. He was surprised, he said, that "ever since the conclusion of the peace with the British nation, such an antipathy had existed that the United States and the British could not bear to sit side by side in treaties held with the Indians." Johnson had a message from Brant and others at Grand River. It invited the Six Nations to travel to a council at Sandusky in the next year to work out a peace with the western Indians.[16]

Pickering delivered a blistering reply, making it precisely clear why he would not allow a British agent at the treaty council. Johnson was a spy, Pickering said. Antipathy between the British and the United States did indeed exist. The United States and the Six Nations for several years had been attempting to work out a peace with the western Indians. It was the British, he said, who prevented them from arranging a peace. They had kept their posts on American soil, and they attempted to foment war. "You recollect the violent, inflammatory speech of Lord Dorchester which the British interpreted to you last spring, at Buffalo Creek," Pickering said. Dorchester, Pickering reminded them, "said that a war would probably take place between the British and the Americans; and then the settlements in all this country here, would be considered as encroachments on the rights of the King." Be clear, Pickering said. Lord Dorchester was trying to "prepare your minds for war, and to take up the hatchet against the United States."[17]

Pickering mentioned British attacks on American shipping, of their determination to enslave their former colonists. Pickering, replying to

Cornplanter, said that "We are a free and independent nation treating with the Six Nations, who also profess to be free and independent." If problems existed in that relationship, they could be handled by the United States and the Six Nations without British interference. Pickering would not continue the council in the presence of a British spy. "Brothers," he said, "it now remains with you to determine whether the great business for which we have met shall go on; or whether the Council Fire shall be extinguished." It was up to them. "You are a free and independent people, and as such you will determine this question."[18]

Pickering left the council. The Quakers departed with him. A half-hour later, Cornplanter called them back and apologized. He personally saw no reason why Johnson should not stay. Because the United States and Great Britain had worked out a peace, he believed that all animosity should have ceased as well. That is what Cornplanter said, but surely he knew better. The British had betrayed the western nations at Fallen Timbers, but they still lived close to the Six Nations on the Niagara frontier. Cornplanter and the rest of the Senecas especially had an interest in maintaining a relationship with the British in Canada. They hoped to be able to pass and repass through their lands, to make use of its waterways, and to maintain the paths that linked Iroquois people in New York to those who had settled at Grand River. Johnson's presence also allowed the British in Canada and Brant at Grand River a window into the proceedings in Canandaigua. The Seneca invitation to Johnson was a maneuver designed to improve the bargaining position of the Iroquois communities involved. It was also a maneuver that Pickering effectively checked. Johnson left on October 26, the next morning, carrying a letter from Cornplanter to Brant, explaining that they had no choice but to expel Johnson. The expulsion of Johnson left Pickering feeling more confident than before the "spy" arrived. "Of one thing I am well satisfied," he wrote to Knox, "that they have no thought of war."[19]

Pickering understood what the Iroquois needed in order for them to sign a treaty. He met on October 27 with small groups of chiefs, trying to nudge them down the path toward an agreement. He met with Cornplanter, and with others, distributing gifts and giving assurances. The weather warmed, and many of those gathered used the opportunity to drink. Pickering informed the Quakers that he was making progress and that he hoped to hold "a full and general council" the next day, "when he will cut the business short by decidedly opening the proposals to accommodation."[20]

This was welcome news to the homesick Quakers. They waited at their quarters. They met with Sayguaresy, or Sword Bearer, a chief of the Tuscaroras. He asked the Friends whether they might "send some white people amongst them for their instruction." It seemed to them a massive undertaking. The Senecas numbered in all about 1,900, the Tuscaroras 300, the Oneidas 600, the Cayugas 400, the Onondagas 500, and the Mohawks about 800. They had broken up. More Cayugas and Onondagas lived near Buffalo Creek than in their homeland. Still, both Savery and Emlen thought something might be done, "at least for the cause of humanity and justice, and for the sake of this poor declining people." The Quakers had none of "those heavy ecclesiastical expenses which are the effects of an hireling Ministry," Emlen wrote, and he believed that the resources existed to do a "substantial good . . . for the help & benefit of this greatly injured people," especially "if any religiously minded young men" could be persuaded to undertake the work.[21]

Pickering's meetings with Cornplanter, however, stirred up some resentment among other Senecas. "Many of the chiefs and warriors," Savery wrote, "were very uneasy at Corn-Planter's frequent private interviews with the commissioners." Little Billy berated Cornplanter. He told Cornplanter that "he should consider who he was; that he was only a war-chief, and it did not become him to be so forward as he appeared to be." Cornplanter confronted the legacy of the earlier treaties he had signed. It was, Little Billy continued, "the business of the sachems, more than his, to conduct the treaty." He did not trust Cornplanter to act in the best interest of all Iroquois, and he felt that Cornplanter should agree to nothing unless his Longhouse kin were present. Cornplanter replied. He had worked for years for the good of his nation, he said, "but if they had no further occasion for him, he would return home."[22]

This Pickering could not allow. Cornplanter was the most important leader from the Allegheny, a community that occupied too important a place in the difficulties among the Six Nations, the western tribes, the British, and the United States, to play no role in the final treaty. It was the Allegany Senecas who complained most fiercely about the occupation by Pennsylvania of the Erie Triangle. Pickering and Chapin persuaded him to stay. Then they met in council in the afternoon, a gathering from which Cornplanter absented himself. Pickering described his individual meetings and "what the substance of their business was." He apologized if his meeting with Cornplanter caused them uneasiness, but the fault was his, not Cornplanter's. Pickering had invited Cornplanter to come see him.[23]

It seemed that this allayed their concerns. Pickering wanted to move past the problems raised by distrust of Cornplanter. The business already having been "retarded so long," Pickering told the Six Nations that "he was now determined to open to them fully and candidly, the terms upon which the chain of friendship would be brightened, and the extent of what he intended to do towards it." He asked Savery to read to the gathered Indians his commission in order to assure them that he had been granted by the president the power to set things right.[24]

He mentioned briefly to the Indians the treaties they had entered into with the United States and with the state of New York. These were real agreements, and they could not be undone. The Erie Triangle had been twice paid for by the Pennsylvanians, and there was no way that they were going to give that up. Some of the principal grievances of the Indians, in other words, were problems Pickering claimed he could not solve. But he did have $10,000 worth of gifts he could distribute to the Iroquois, and he could increase the annuity of $1,500 guaranteed to them in 1792 to $4,500. He would obtain life annuities for some of the Seneca leaders who helped secure the treaty. He could also return to them some of the lands along the Niagara River, eliminating one of the barriers that had hemmed them in. He hoped that the Six Nations would consider these offers and "cheerfully comply, and join him in digging a deep pit to bury all former differences, and take hold of the chain of friendship." He asked the Iroquois to think things over, and to come back to him when they had an answer.[25]

Older brothers, younger brothers: The leaders of the Six Nations met on their own and discussed their options. They confronted difficult issues, but Haudenosaunee leaders directed their councils toward finding consensus, slowly, steadily, and deliberately agreeing on principles to guide their conduct in their meetings with Pickering.

These meetings took place out of Pickering's sight, away from the Friends. As a result, we do not know what these councils looked like, but it was at meetings like these—Senecas on one side, Cayugas and Oneidas on the other, with Onondagas moving between—where a critical part of the treaty-making process took place. It would take several days for the leaders of the Six Nations to decide their course. In the interim, a period of warm weather descended on Canandaigua. It was "a fine, warm day," Savery wrote, with "the Indians almost all turned out of their cabins; some of the young warriors having good horses, were running races all day with the white people; others engaged in different sports, dancing, &c., which is almost a daily exercise." Bacon visited one of the camps. It was to him "admirable to see how soon those people can build a town so as for them to live in comfortably in their way." He saw the women "at worke at several branches of business, some making Mogasons others Belt & shifts &c baskets cooking venison."[26]

The Iroquois still distrusted Cornplanter, but that did not keep them from considering Pickering's proposal. On the last day of October, representatives from four of the Six Nations visited the Quakers: Red Jacket from the Senecas, Clear Sky from the Onondagas, Sword Bearer of the Tuscaroras, and an unnamed Cayuga, quite likely Fish Carrier. They wanted to speak to the Quakers in confidence. The Quakers asked several "Indians and white people being in the room with us" when they arrived to depart. But it was not enough, and "apprehending that we should be interrupted in the house, we retired to a distance and sat down upon some logs." Red Jacket spoke for the four leaders.[27]

Red Jacket told the Quakers that he trusted them. He wanted their advice. "Brothers, You all know the proposals that have been made by Cunnitsutty (Colonel Pickering, the commissioner) as well as the offers made by us to him," Red Jacket said. "We are all now in the presence of the Great Spirit, and we place more confidence in you than in any other people." You offered to help, he said. Give us advice. "We hope you will not deceive us; for if you should do so, we shall no more place any confidence in mankind."[28]

Red Jacket wanted everything they discussed to be kept secret. "We are now willing to give up the four-mile path, from Johnson's landing-place to Cayuga Creek, agreeably to our compact with Sir

William Johnson, long ago," Red Jacket said. He spoke of the 1764 cession of Grand and other islands in the Niagara River in recompense for the Devil's Hole attack. "The other part proposed by Colonel Pickering to be relinquished by us, that is, from Cayuga to Buffalo Creek, we wish to reserve on account of the fisheries; that our women and children may have the use of it for that purpose." He wanted to know "if you can inform us, why the triangle on Lake Erie cannot be given up." After all, those who signed the treaty at Fort Stanwix, notably Brant and Cornplanter, were supposed to report on the proceedings before consenting to anything. They were supposed to consult with the sachems, but "they were threatened into a compliance" by the commissioners.[29]

Savery replied the next day. It is not precisely clear what he said, but Red Jacket thanked the Quakers for their advice. Savery recognized the weightiness of the issues. He and Parrish rode over to Farmer's Brother's camp, where nearly 500 Senecas from the Genesee stayed. They had built together between seventy and eighty houses from bark and the boughs of trees, "by far the most commodious and ingeniously made of any that I have seen." Savery noticed that the men and women in the camp seemed to him busy, active, and industrious. There were in the camp as well a "large number of pretty children, who, in all the activity and buoyancy of health, were diverting themselves according to their fancy." They had plenty of food: Savery saw that they had received rations of beef from Chapin, and the venison drying seemingly everywhere in camp. "The ease and cheerfulness of every countenance, and the delightfulness of the afternoon, which these inhabitants of the woods seemed to enjoy, with a relish far superior to those who are pent up in crowded and populous cities, all combined to make this the most pleasant visit I have paid to the Indians." Savery thought about what he saw, and he was a sensitive observer. He believed "that before they became acquainted with white people and were infected with their vices, they must have been as happy a people as any in the world."[30]

The Quakers headed over to the council on Sunday, November 2, after attending meeting at the school house. The Onondaga Clear Sky opened the gathering, expressing the hope that the days they spent deliberating on a response to Pickering occasioned no hard feelings. Red Jacket then rose. He restated what had been covered over the previous meetings. "We told you before of the two rusty places on the chain," but "instead of complying with our request, respecting the places where we told you the chain was rusty, you offered to relinquish the land on Lake Erie, eastward of the triangular piece sold by Congress to Pennsylvania, and to retain the four-mile path between Cayuga and Buffalo Creek, by which you expect to brighten the chain."[31]

Red Jacket expressed his reservations. "With respect to the four-mile path, we are in want of it on account of the fisheries; although we are but children, we are sharp sighted, and we see that you want that strip of land for a road, that when you have vessels on the lakes, you may have harbors, &c." Red Jacket thought that Pickering asked for too much, that his compromise did not go far enough. "We wish," Red Jacket said, "that in respect to that land, the treaty at Fort Stanwix may be broken." The white population was increasing rapidly, and they were taking the lands that had been given to the Indians by the Great Spirit. "We are now become a small people," he said, "and you are cutting off our lands, piece after piece—you are a very hard-hearted people, seeking your own advantages."[32]

Red Jacket did not mention the Erie Triangle. But he did persist in requesting the four-mile strip. "We are tender-hearted, and desirous of peace," Red Jacket said, and "if you will relinquish that piece of land we have mentioned, our friendship will be strong." It was in his view a reasonable request. "We have told you of the rusty part, which the file passed over without brightening it, and we wish you to take up the file again, and rub it very hard; you told us," Red Jacket argued, "if it would not do without, you would apply oil."[33]

Pickering saw room for compromise. He told the Six Nations that the United States desired peace as earnestly as they did. He emphasized that the United States needed a road that ran between Lakes Erie and Ontario. Pickering wanted to be sure that the Iroquois "should have no objection, if the land remains yours, to our cutting a road, and if we do so, it will be very inconvenient, unless we can have taverns to accommodate travellers, as the distance is great." Furthermore, Pickering accepted Red Jacket's observation that the United States might like to build a harbor along the waterway, and that "they can have no benefit from a harbor unless they have the privilege of building houses and stores." The tract, in this sense, would have to be shared, "but if this is all the difficulty between us, I trust we shall not be long in coming to conclusion." Would they accept the necessity of allowing roads, houses, and harbors in the tract?[34]

Pickering would give them back the land along the Niagara, and wanted to know whether the Senecas were ready to conclude the business. Red Jacket said that they wanted to talk it over further, so Pickering asked them to meet him tomorrow. He hoped to see some of the chiefs prior to the meeting of the council in his private quarters, which "he thought would expedite the business."[35]

It took more than a day. Some of the chiefs were so "much intoxicated," Savery said, that no council could be held. The Quakers met with several Oneidas about the Hopewell lands. They had heard from the Senecas, but they wanted to hear from others as well. Big Beard, their spokesman, said "it was beyond a doubt, that the original proprietors were incorporated with the Six Nations, yet they were so mixed and intermarried among the different tribes, that it would be difficult to point them out." They suggested that the Friends distribute a payment for the lands among the Six Nations at large.

On November 4, the council reconvened. Red Jacket again addressed Pickering. He restated Pickering's position. The Six Nations gave his proposals serious consideration. "If we consent to your proposals," Red Jacket said, "we know it will injure us." Red Jacket explained precisely what he meant:

> If these houses should be built, they will tend to scatter us and make us fall in the streets, meaning, by drinking to excess, instead of benefitting us: you want land to raise provisions, hay, &c.; but as soon as the white people settle there, they would think the land theirs, for this is the way of the white people. You mentioned that when you got possession of the garrisons, you would want landing-places, stores, fields to plant on, &c.; but we wish to be the sole owners of this land ourselves; and when you settle with the British, the Great Spirit has made a road for you, you can pass and repass by water; what you want to reserve is entirely in your own favor.[36]

Red Jacket said that the matters preventing an agreement were small ones. The chain might easily be brightened, he said. "If you will consent to give up this small piece and have no houses on it," he said, "the chain will be made bright." The white people already coveted the

Senecas' lands, Red Jacket said. They sat at the council, watching the proceedings, "with their mouth open to take up this land." Red Jacket asked Pickering, "if you are a friend to us," to "disappoint them."[37]

Pickering thought about what Red Jacket said. Allow us the right to pass through your country, Pickering said. As for the road along the Niagara River, Pickering pointed out that a path already existed. "I only ask liberty to make a better path," he said, "to clear the stumps and logs out of the way." Think it over, Pickering said. He would wait for their answer. The agent, Israel Chapin, a man many of the Iroquois trusted, would oversee the opening of the road and would "take care to have it done so as to be as little injurious as possible to the Indians."[38]

A half-hour later Red Jacket replied. He thanked Pickering for "complying with our request, in giving up the particular spot in dispute." As for the road running through the Senecas' country, Red Jacket asked Pickering to "remember your old agreement, that you were to pass along the lake by water." Pickering was not listening, it seemed to Red Jacket. He was writing. And Red Jacket paused until Pickering looked him in the eye. He would grant to Pickering and the United States a road running from Fort Schlosser to Buffalo Creek, but not "from Buffalo-creek down this way at all." Pickering could live with this, and he told the Iroquois that a few small matters needed to be discussed before he prepared the treaty. He needed to determine a mode for distributing the annuity, and "as there are bad people both amongst you and us, it would be well to fix some modes of settling disputes, when they arise between individuals of your nations and ours."[39]

The Quakers spent the following days discussing the Hopewell lands. Chapin told them that the Tuscaroras were most likely the original proprietors. Pickering, meanwhile, met with small groups of chiefs, trying to iron out the details for an agreement. Much dissatisfaction remained. Pickering was exasperated. He felt the need to extract from the Iroquois an explicit affirmation of those parts of the Fort Stanwix and Fort Harmar treaties not specifically reversed by Canandaigua. But the Six Nations delegates would not explicitly affirm those transactions. They "were unwilling to *relinquish* or *give up* or use any words of that import, respecting the lands ceded by former treaties to the United States." The chiefs were drunk, Pickering wrote, and they seemed reluctant to come to a final agreement. They were, he said, "perverse and shifting, thro' fear of offending the

British and the Western Indians." Pickering confided to Knox that he had never been "more weary" of negotiations, and that "more than the patience of Job is requisite, to endure their delays, their trifling, and their drunkenness."[40]

Pickering and Chapin cut off the alcohol on the morning of November 8: no more liquor until the treaty had concluded. Meeting with the sober chiefs, Pickering moved forward, spending most of the day in close negotiations. Around three in the afternoon, Savery noted, Pickering and the Six Nations delegates "agreed on all the articles of [the] treaty to be engrossed on parchment and signed tomorrow." It seemed the work was nearly finished. The Quakers met after the council adjourned with Cornplanter, Red Jacket, "two ancient Conestogas," and a number of Tuscaroras to consider again the Hopewell lands. A Tuscarora man claimed that "he had papers at home that would, as he thought, confirm their claim to" the Hopewell lands. There was nothing more to do until those documents arrived, and Chapin would forward them to Philadelphia if he thought them worthwhile. It rained all day, and everyone wanted to get home.[41]

The Quakers went to meeting on the ninth and then headed to the council "in order to finally finish the treaty & have the articles signed." Pickering had the documents ready, but in the afternoon, Cornplanter rose and objected to the agreement. "I consider the conduct of the United States, since the war, to have been very bad," he said, and "I conceive they do not do justice." The United States had deceived warriors like himself at Fort Stanwix, and now it was deceiving the sachems. He would not sign the treaty, and he urged other warriors to join him. He would honor whatever agreement the sachems entered into, but he would not take part.[42]

Pickering needed to act. He could not accept a treaty that the warriors did not sign. He reminded all who had gathered of the great pains that had gone into negotiating the agreement that he hoped they soon would sign. He reminded them that both warriors and sachems had been present for those negotiations, and that no objection had then been raised. Pickering could not accept the agreement as a firm peace unless the sachems and the warriors remained united. He asked them to consider their actions and give an answer tomorrow. "If the warriors expect to live in peace with the United States as well as the sachems; if they desire to brighten the chain of friendship;

if they wish to act for the advantage of themselves and their children, I am sure they will sign this treaty." Without their signatures, Pickering could not consider the agreement upon which he had expended so much labor to be of any value.[43]

There was more drinking the next day. Savery expected a council to be held, "but several of the principal sachems being intoxicated," no meeting occurred. The Quakers met with Captain Printup of the Tuscaroras to discuss once again the Hopewell lands. He asked that whatever they might pay for the lands, they pay it all at once. Savery told him that before they could pay out any amount, they needed to consult with "our brethren at home." Finally, around two in the afternoon on November 11, Savery wrote, "we were sent for to the council, where a great number were assembled." The Eel, an Onondaga, spoke of the importance of unanimity, that the chiefs and the warriors must come together to sign this important document. They must achieve a good mind. It was significant that this appeal came from the Onondagas, the keepers of the League's central council fire. Pickering held up two copies of the treaty. He asked the members of the Six Nations if they were prepared to sign. Pickering gave one copy of the document to Savery, as he read aloud the other. Savery announced that the two "were word for word alike." The gathered sachems and warriors then agreed to sign the treaty. Two head warriors, Savery wrote, "who, though they were young men, were by some custom in their nation, the persons who were to stand foremost in ratifying contracts," signed the treaties first, and they were followed by "the chiefs and warriors, some of the most eminent in each nation, being in all upwards of fifty."[44]

Twenty-six Senecas signed the treaty. Their signatures filled the two right-hand columns. Six Onondagas, headed by Clear Sky, headed the third column from the right, followed by the marks of Fish Carrier and six more Cayugas. Six Oneidas made their marks in the fourth column from the right, followed by a pair of Munsees, Captain Printup and another Tuscarora, an additional Seneca, and Henry Young Brant, Joseph Brant's nephew and the only Mohawk to sign. In the fifth column two Onondagas, two Cayugas, two Mahicans, including Hendrick Aupaumut, and two more Tuscaroras signed. Pickering signed, as did the witnesses and the interpreters. The four Quakers did not sign the treaty. That nearly half the signatures came from

Senecas reveals the extent to which the treaty focused on matters of concern most to the Senecas at Buffalo Creek and Allegany.[45]

Farmer's Brother spoke to the four Quakers. He thanked them for attending the council. He wanted them to look once again at the treaty, and he desired "to know your opinion whether we have made a good peace or not, as we cannot read, we are liable to be deceived, as you have no doubt considered them we wish to know your minds whether there be any flaw . . . which might hereafter occation uneasiness." The Quakers met thereafter with about forty chiefs in their quarters, gathered by Farmer's Brother and Red Jacket. The Quakers assured the Indians that the treaty they had signed was a good one. The Friends then gave to them the gifts they had brought to the council.[46]

And that was it. The Quakers departed the next morning, making their way back toward Philadelphia, through weather that "was very cold," along "roads exceedingly bad." At times, Savery wrote, "we felt like poor, forlorn pilgrims." The conditions made "the traveling truly hard." It took them two weeks. On November 27, Bacon recorded that he had arrived home safely in Philadelphia, "thankfull for the favours of healthy preservation through a trying & long journey."[47]

Pickering did not follow the Quakers. He headed east, toward Oneida Castle and New Stockbridge, to take care of business there. Pickering convened a council and entered into a treaty with the Oneidas and Tuscaroras, who had suffered for their adherence to the United States during the Revolution. Pickering drew up a treaty in which the United States agreed to pay $5,000 to the Tuscaroras and Oneidas "as a compensation for their individual losses and services" during the war, and to construct grist and saw mills in Oneida territory. The United States, as well, would pay $1,000 to build a church to replace the one burned during the war. His work completed, Pickering left the Oneida Country early in December and reached Albany and the Hudson River on the twelfth. It was cold and it snowed a lot. He reached Philadelphia on December 20, more than 100 days after he had left home.[48]

CHAPTER 8

"All Causes of Complaint"

On January 2, 1795, President Washington transmitted to the U.S. Senate the treaty Pickering negotiated at Canandaigua with the Six Nations "for the purpose of removing from their minds all causes of complaint, and establishing a firm and permanent friendship with them." Washington saw the treaty in limited terms. For him it addressed and resolved a specific set of problems the United States confronted along one portion of its frontier and in its military and diplomatic relationship with the Six Nations. He also on that day nominated Pickering to replace Henry Knox as secretary of war. Neither item was controversial: The Senate quickly confirmed Pickering that day and offered its approval of the treaty one week later.[1]

The Treaty of Canandaigua consisted of seven articles. In the first, Pickering and the "Sachems and Warriors of the Six Nations" agreed that "peace and friendship are hereby firmly established, and shall be perpetual, between the United States and the Six Nations." Pickering thought of this as much more than a mere formality. The Six Nations still possessed a considerable number of warriors. Early in January, in a report informing Congress of the state of negotiations in the west, Pickering emphasized that significant threats still existed. Wayne had triumphed at Fallen Timbers. His forces burned Indian villages. Still, to Pickering it did not "appear that these events have produced amongst them a general disposition to make peace." Pickering envisioned a program of fort construction in the Northwest Territory, and he felt that "the hostile nations may yet embody in numbers equal to those which opposed our arms in the last campaign." The treaty with the Six Nations, Pickering believed, effectively removed a prop that the western nations may have hoped still to lean on, and brought significant comfort to the New York frontier.[2]

In the second article, the United States acknowledged that "the lands reserved to the Oneida, Onondaga, and Cayuga nations, in their respective treaties with the state of New-York, and called their reservations" were their property, and that the United States "would never claim the same, nor disturb them or either of the Six Nations, nor their Indian friends residing thereon and united with them, in the free use and enjoyment thereof." Pickering understood very well that groups like the Brothertowns and Stockbridges lived on Oneida land, and he viewed these communities as having rights the United States must recognize. The second article also recognized that the state had purchased an enormous sum of Haudenosaunee land in the years after the Fort Stanwix treaty. Although some of those transactions may have violated the provisions of the Trade and Intercourse Act and according to that law ought to have been rendered null and void and of no effect, Pickering viewed them as an accomplished fact that he would not reverse. The damage could not be undone, but he could promise that the Cayugas, Onondagas, and Oneidas could rest secure in the possession of their remaining lands until they sold them to "the people of the United States, who have the right to purchase." By recognizing the Oneidas', Onondagas', and Cayugas' right to the "free use and enjoyment" of their remaining lands, the treaty endorsed their status as separate political communities, able to regulate and oversee their own affairs on their own lands.[3]

The third article of the treaty defined the boundaries of the lands belonging to the "Seneka nation." The treaty did nothing about the Erie Triangle, but it did restore the Six Nations' access to the Niagara River. Doing so involved the return of a tract for which the Iroquois argued in an "extremely tenacious" manner, but which cost Pickering little. He expected that when the British surrendered Fort Niagara, the Senecas would cede the lands along the river. These lands the United States acknowledged to be the property of the Senecas, and the United States promised to "never claim the same, nor disturb the Seneka nation, nor any of the Six Nations, or of their Indian friends residing thereon and united with them, in the free use and enjoyment thereof; but it shall remain theirs, until they choose to sell the same to the people of the United States, who have the right to purchase."[4]

Pickering had found the Erie Triangle question a frustrating one during the negotiations. The land in question had been paid for on two previous occasions by the state of Pennsylvania, he pointed out. Pickering wanted to preclude for the future any additional instances where members of the Six Nations claimed lands that the United States viewed as lawfully ceded. He wanted to hear no more about the massive cession at Fort Stanwix in 1784, reaffirmed four and a half years later at Fort Harmar. Therefore, the fourth article of the treaty stated that the Six Nations would "never claim any other lands within the boundaries of the United States; nor never disturb the people of the United States in the free use and enjoyment thereof." Iroquoia was finite, the treaty showed. Gradually, the land belonging to the Six Nations would become part of the United States. Ultimately, he believed, they would sell their lands. The new nation would expand, but the Six Nations would not. It was important to Pickering that the federal government oversee this process—that was the purpose of the Trade and Intercourse Act—but for him the Haudenosaunee estate would never grow, and never increase in size again.[5] Further, the United States secured for itself the right to move through Seneca land, and to construct "a wagon road from Fort Schlosser to Lake Erie, as far south as Buffalo Creek." The fifth article of the treaty granted to American citizens "the free and undisturbed use of this road, for the purposes of travelling and transportation."[6]

Timothy Pickering long had hoped to advance civility among the Six Nations, a goal shared by Washington and Knox as well. In return for signing the treaty, and "in consideration of the peace and friendship hereby established," the United States agreed to pay to the Six Nations "a quantity of goods of the value of ten thousand dollars." Further, the government would increase the annuity it allocated for the Six Nations from $1,500 to $4,500, "which shall be expended yearly forever, in purchasing clothing, domestic animals, implements of husbandry, and other utensils suited to their circumstances, and in compensating useful artificers, who shall reside with or near them, and be employed for their benefit." Pickering thus advanced with the Canandaigua treaty the government's civilization program, and the Six Nations obtained access to the material goods and instruction they needed to adjust to life in a state where the settler population increased every year.[7]

Because one source of the troubles between Iroquois peoples and the United States had been acts of violence committed by settlers on Indians, the seventh article contained a provision intended to reduce the likelihood of conflict by spelling out, in the most general terms, a method for their resolution. Private revenge and retaliation were expressly prohibited, and when acts of violence occurred, "complaint shall be made by the party injured to the other: By the Six Nations or any of them, to the President of the United States, or the Superintendent by him appointed: and by the Superintendent, or other person appointed by the President, to the principal chiefs of the Six Nations, or of the nation to which the offender belongs."[8]

The Treaty of Canandaigua helped bring order to the borderlands of the American republic, but its impact cannot be understood entirely apart from two other treaties that the United States concluded at nearly the same time. While Pickering met with the Six Nations, Supreme Court Chief Justice John Jay met with officials from the British government in London. Pickering knew of Jay's mission, but he knew little of the progress of the negotiations, and word of the treaty's contents did not reach the United States until early in 1795.

Jay had little bargaining power. The British did not respect the Americans as an enemy, nor could the young republic offer much to compel their former rulers to negotiate in good faith. But the British did not want to fight a war on two fronts and did not want to dilute their war effort against France with an open conflict in North America. While the British refused to abdicate their claimed right to search for and recover deserters from the Royal Navy, a justification for its impressment of American sailors, it did enter into a treaty on November 19, 1794, in which the Americans received trading privileges in the British West Indies and a pledge to abandon, at long last, the British posts on American soil within one year. Jay's Treaty thus eliminated a critical cog in the machinery that threatened the security of the United States. Jay extracted from the British a concession that limited their abilities to arm and equip Indian allies living within the boundaries of the United States.[9]

But there was much more to the treaty, including a provision that over time took on a life of its own for Haudenosaunee peoples. In the Jay treaty's third article, the United States and Great Britain agreed

"That it shall at all times be free to His Majesty's Subjects and to Citizens of the United States, and also to Indians dwelling on either side of the said Boundary Line freely to pass and repass by Land, or Inland Navigation, into the respective Territories and Countries of the Two Parties . . . and to navigate all the Lakes, Rivers, and waters thereof, and freely to carry on trade and commerce with each other." Furthermore, the parties agreed that Indians "passing or repassing with their own proper goods and effects of whatever nature" would never "pay for the same any Impost or Duty whatever." The precise definition of Indian goods in the treaty remained imprecise, defined more for what they were not than for what they were: "goods in bales, or other large packages unusual among Indians shall not be considered as Goods belonging bona fide to Indians."[10] An "Explanatory Article" agreed to at Philadelphia in May 1796 (Timothy Pickering represented the United States at this negotiation) stated that "no stipulation in any treaties subsequently concluded by either of the contracting parties with any other State or Nation or with any Indian tribe, can be understood to derogate in any manner from the rights of free intercourse and commerce secured by the aforesaid third Article of the Treaty of Amity, commerce and navigation." Specifically, despite treaties like that negotiated at Greenville in 1795, which put an end to all Indian warfare in the American northwest, and legislative enactments like the federal Indian Trade and Intercourse Act, which required all traders in Indian country to possess a government-issued license, the United States and Great Britain affirmed that all persons, British, American, or Indian, "shall remain at full liberty to pass and repass by land or inland navigation, into the respective territories and countries of the contracting parties, on either side of the said boundary-line."[11]

These terms the United States and Great Britain reaffirmed at the Treaty of Ghent, negotiated in 1814 to put an end to the conflict between them that began two years earlier and that was waged along the frontiers of Iroquoia in New York state. In the treaty's ninth article, the United States agreed "forthwith to restore to such Tribes or Nations" with whom they had been at war "all the possessions, rights, and privileges which they may have enjoyed or been entitled to in one thousand eight hundred and eleven previous to such hostilities." The British agreed to similar terms, restoring the *status quo ante bellum*.[12]

Native peoples were not parties to Jay's Treaty. They played no role in the negotiation of the Explanatory Article in 1796 or, for that matter, in the negotiation of the peace treaty at Ghent. The British and the United States engaged in diplomacy to advance their own respective interests, not those of Indians. Nonetheless, an important historical point can be made about Jay's Treaty and the subsequent restatements. Haudenosaunee people, in the 1790s and thereafter, continued to cross the international boundary and move between Iroquois communities in Canada and the United States, and both countries agreed through formal diplomatic agreements that the Iroquois had the right to do so. The significance of the Jay Treaty is thus twofold: It resolved a threat that had menaced American settlements since the end of the Revolutionary War, but it also contained language that effectively validated and recognized the importance of mobility and the capacity to move through a greater Iroquoia that had long been a focal concern of Haudenosaunee interactions with their neighbors.[13]

Jay's Treaty became a deeply divisive political issue in the United States. Federalists and Democratic-Republicans argued feverishly over its contents. The debate over its ratification played a critical role in the formation of what historians call the First American Party System.[14] The treaty Anthony Wayne negotiated with the Northwestern confederates in 1795 was not nearly as controversial. Pickering drew up instructions for Wayne. He would insist on the Fort Harmar treaty line, with provision for additional American posts and land grants beyond that line. The Indians who signed the treaty would receive an annuity from the United States and pledge themselves to keep the peace. Recognizing the central government's lack of control over affairs in the west, Pickering told Wayne that "a provision for their delivering up murderers *to be punished by our laws* is purposely omitted: because experience has too long shown that, regardless of our stipulations, *we cannot punish our own.* It is a maxim with the frontier people not to hang a White Man who murders an Indian."[15]

Many Shawnees refused to attend the council. Those who met Wayne at Greenville late in the summer of 1795 agreed "to put an end to a destructive war, to settle all controversies, and to restore harmony and a friendly intercourse between" them and the United States. The price of peace was steep: The chiefs present signed a treaty deeding to the United States roughly the eastern two thirds of Ohio and a small portion of land in what is today the state of Indiana.[16]

When Timothy Pickering notified the Six Nations that the president had ratified the Treaty of Canandaigua with the advice and consent of the Senate, he informed them that they may "rely on the complete performance of every article of the treaty on the part of the United States, and we rely with confidence on the faithful execution on your part of a treaty so entirely calculated to promote your best interests." After the death of Israel Chapin in the spring of 1795, Pickering appointed his son, Israel Chapin, Jr., to take his place as agent to the Iroquois. In the instructions he issued, Pickering told the younger Chapin that "the affairs of the Six Nations, I expect," will "henceforward be managed with much less trouble than formerly." The Canandaigua treaty, he wrote, "superseded all pre-existing causes of complaint," and the Jay Treaty "will, I trust, rid you of all such embarrassments as heretofore have sprung from British influence." All Chapin needed to do was "protect the tribes under your superintendence from injury and imposition, which too many of our own people are disposed to practice upon them; diligently to employ all means under your direction, to promote their comfort and improvement, and to apply the public money and goods placed in your hands with inviolable integrity and prudent economy." Much indeed had been accomplished the previous autumn.[17]

Scholars have emphasized the importance of the Treaty of Canandaigua. It was, one wrote, "an amazing accomplishment" and "something that both parties might view with awe." Another asserted that "the Treaty of Canandaigua is clearly a treaty between sovereigns," in that it recognized the right of Haudenosaunee peoples to govern their communities in their own way without interference. Another, looking at the successful suppression of the Whiskey Rebellion in western Pennsylvania and the success of Wayne's campaign, saw Canandaigua as part of a trio of events in 1794 that established "firm federal supremacy over the states." The treaty, in this sense, "was deeply embedded in the creation of a broader system of political power that, for better or worse, has shaped the lives of both Native and Euro-Americans ever since."[18]

Yet the legacy of the treaty for the Six Nations is far more ambivalent than these statements might lead one to believe. Take, for instance, the treaty's recognition of the right of the Iroquois to retain their reserved lands until they chose to sell them. In the light of the Trade and Intercourse Act, and all that Pickering, Knox, and Washington had told Six Nations people with whom they spoke or corresponded since 1790, the process of purchasing Iroquois land was one that the federal government would oversee. Yet officials in the New York state government never relented in their efforts to acquire every acre of Iroquois land they could, and the federal government seemed power-less to stop them.

Israel Chapin, Jr., told Pickering after he had received his ap-pointment that it would be difficult from his base at Canandaigua to oversee the affairs of all the Six Nations. Chapin, nonetheless, ap-pears at least to have tried to do his job, although it also appears that he was in well over his head and was not a competent representative of the U.S. Government. When he learned that the state of New York intended to hold treaties with the Cayugas and Onondagas in the summer of 1795, he informed Pickering. The new secretary of war instructed his agent to halt the proceedings and obtained from the U.S. Attorney-General, William Bradford, an opinion declaring that New York's actions violated the Trade and Intercourse Act. Bradford stated clearly that New York could not legally purchase Indian lands "but by a treaty holden under the authority of the United States, and in the manner prescribed by Congress." Pickering demanded that Chapin give "no countenance to this unlawful design . . . as it is repugnant to the law of the United States to regulate trade and Intercourse with the Indian tribes."[19]

Before Pickering's letter and Bradford's opinion could arrive at Canandaigua, Chapin departed to accompany the Onondagas and Cayugas to their meetings with the state commissioners, led now by Philip Schuyler. Chapin, in a letter written on the last day of July upon his return to Canandaigua, informed Pickering of what had happened. A young man alone against the state's determined com-missioners, Chapin "inquired of Genl. Schuyler how he construed the laws of Congress in regard to holding treaties with the Indian tribes?" Schuyler "made very little reply by saying it was very well where it would correspond with that of the individual states." Chapin did not know what to do. Had he then knowledge of the contents of Pickering's letter and the attorney-general's opinion, he wrote,

"I could have managed the business more to your mind but as I had supposed the Government of the State of New York had applied to the General Government and had obtained sufficient power to call the Indians to the treaty," Chapin did nothing. He pledged to Pickering to leave at once for Oneida to try to "engage the treaty will not take place then under the present commissioners."[20]

Pickering seems to have recognized that Chapin had little chance of succeeding against the force of a determined state. "Seeing that the Commissioners" of the state "were acting in defiance of the law of the United States," he wrote back to Chapin, "it was certainly proper not to give them a countenance; and as the law declares such purchases of the Indians as those Commissioners were attempting to make invalid, it was also right to inform the Indians of the law and of the illegality of the purchase." Go to Oneida, Pickering said, but "the negotiation is probably finished ere now." Philip Schuyler rejected the federal government's interpretation of the Trade and Intercourse Act and proceeded with the treaty. He learned from Chapin that the United States viewed the state's actions as illegal, but he acquired for the state nonetheless nearly 100,000 acres of the Oneida homeland.[21]

Why did the government that Timothy Pickering pledged to protect the lands of the Iroquois prove so impotent in the face of a determined state government? The young national government, despite the fears of the Antifederalists who dominated New York politics in 1787 and 1788, was indeed a tiny entity. The 1790s was no era of big government. The total number of nonuniformed employees of the federal government in 1801, the first year for which we have good figures, was less than 3,000, and the vast majority of these worked in customs or other revenue-related functions, or for the postal service. Only 214 federal employees resided in all of New York state, nearly all of them in the immediate vicinity of New York City, and almost all of them employed in customs.[22]

Chapin was on his own. The Trade and Intercourse Act, the law Congress charged him with enforcing, was not strictly speaking an "Indian law." Rather, Congress intended the law, first passed in 1790 and revised periodically thereafter until 1834, to curb the long list of abuses Indians historically had suffered from their white neighbors. In enacting and then revising the Trade and Intercourse Acts, Congress assumed that white settlement would advance and Indians retreat, and its intent through the laws was to ensure that the process avoided as much disorder and violence as possible. But agents simply lacked the power to secure order on the frontier and compliance with federal law. It is, sadly, an old and blood-drenched story.[23]

Thus, despite the language of the Treaty of Canandaigua, Iroquois land holding in New York state remained insecure. The state, whose leaders only occasionally felt themselves bound by federal law, continued to purchase land from the Oneidas, Cayugas, Tuscaroras, Mohawks, and Onondagas in the late 1790s and beyond. And the state was not alone in purchasing Iroquois land.[24]

Robert Morris, for example, the financier of the American Revolution, had purchased the right of pre-emption, or first purchase, to those lands remaining with the Senecas after the failed Phelps and Gorham enterprise. He in turn sold these rights to the Holland Land Company in December 1792. A well-financed syndicate of Dutch merchants and bankers, the Holland Land Company was much better equipped than Morris to oversee the actual opening up of the Seneca homeland to white settlement—a massive undertaking that involved administering an enormous territory and absorbing the costs associated with surveying, building roads, and laying out towns. Before they would pay, however, the Holland investors insisted that Morris extinguish the Senecas' possessory right, or aboriginal title, to the lands in question.[25]

The warfare in the northwest delayed Morris's plans for several years. In the meantime, Morris fell upon hard times. His finances stood in ruins, and he needed to part with the pre-emption rights he had acquired. Finally, in 1797, he began to lay plans for a treaty council to acquire the Senecas' lands. Because Morris was ill and because he feared prosecution for debt should he leave his home in Philadelphia, his son Thomas traveled to Big Tree on the Genesee River to conduct the treaty.[26]

At Big Tree, the Senecas parted with all of their land, save for 200,000 acres distributed across eleven reservations. With white settlers beginning to overrun their lands, and with acts of violence continuing to occur, as well as other crimes against Seneca persons and property, Red Jacket ceded the bulk of the Seneca estate while preserving eleven key sites of settlement. In exchange for this massive cession of lands, Morris, who acted under the oversight of a federal commissioner and who obeyed the letter, if not the spirit, of the

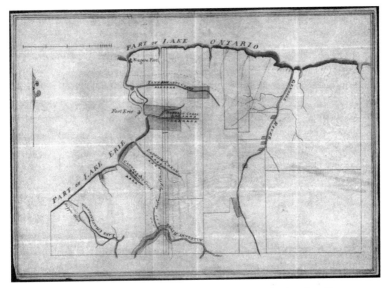

The eleven Seneca Reservations, that remained after the Big Tree Treaty
of 1797.
*Archives of the Holland Land Company, Archives and Special Collections, Daniel A. Reed
Library, SUNY Fredonia*

Indian Trade and Intercourse Acts, agreed to pay "the sum of one
hundred thousand dollars, to be by the said Robert Morris vested in
the stock of the bank of the United States, and held in the name of
the President of the United States, for the use and behoof of the said
nation of Indians." The Senecas would receive as a payment, each
year, the interest earned on this investment.[27]

It is difficult to look at the Treaty of Canandaigua, then, and see
that it provided immediate benefits in protecting the lands of the Six
Nations. The Big Tree purchase, which followed it by only three years,
resulted in the Senecas' losing much of their land, and additional sales
followed. By the end of the eighteenth century, Iroquois people owned
only a tiny fraction of the land they controlled a quarter-century before.
At a treaty held in Albany in August 1802, for instance, the Senecas
agreed to cede to the state of New York "all that tract of land, one mile
wide, on Niagara River, extending from Buffalo creek to Stedman's
farm, including Black Rock, and bounded to the westward by the shore

or waters of said river." The Senecas preserved the right to fish on the river, and free ferriage across the Niagara. In exchange, Governor Clinton agreed to pay to the Senecas "the sum of two hundred dollars; and doth grant to the said Indians, that the People of the said State of New York shall pay to them, or their order, at the city of Albany, the further sum of five thousand three hundred dollars; and also, to the value of five hundred dollars in chintz, calico, and other goods, suitable for their women, on the fifteenth day of February," 1803. In 1815, the state purchased the islands in the Niagara River from the Senecas. And in 1826, a further agreement reduced the size of the Buffalo Creek, Tonawanda, and Cattaraugus reservations significantly. All told, the Seneca estate had been reduced by more than a third.[28]

The Senecas and their supporters immediately challenged and contested the legality and the morality of the treaty. Some Senecas opposed the treaty, while others sent petitions and memorials to Washington supporting it. To sort all this out took some time. Those who signed the treaty, according to the author of the best account of the period, did so because they feared that if they did not sell, they would lose their lands outright to the squatters whom nobody seemed able to control. The U.S. Senate finally voted on the treaty in late February 1828, but the vote was a 20–20 tie. John C. Calhoun, the vice president, was not in attendance to break the tie. The agreement thus did not receive the two-thirds vote required by the Constitution for ratification.[29]

Protests from Red Jacket, from the Quakers, and from others continued, however, and they finally had an effect on President John Quincy Adams. He ordered his secretary of war to conduct an investigation. Richard Livingston undertook the task. He found evidence of considerable corruption and fraud at the treaty council. According to Seneca informants, the interpreters at the council threatened the gathered Indians with removal if they refused to sell. Jasper Parrish reportedly offered bribes to certain Senecas in return for their signatures. As a result, the flawed treaty was never resubmitted to the Senate, and it never received proper ratification. Still, the damage had been done, and by doing nothing, the U.S. Government in effect acquiesced in a fraudulent, unethical, and illegal treaty that carved a huge gash of territory out of the Seneca estate.

CHAPTER 9

....

The Long Life of the Treaty of Canandaigua

What, then, are we left with? The Treaty of Canandaigua brought few immediate benefits to the Six Nations. The lands the Senecas lost in its aftermath represented a massive share of their homeland. The state of New York, meanwhile, took every opportunity it could, fair or foul, to acquire lands belonging to the Cayugas, Oneidas, Onondagas, Mohawks, and Tuscaroras, and the national government seemed unable and unwilling to oversee the process as spelled out in federal law. But it was not all a tale of victimization and loss, although plenty of both characterized the story. There were other resources upon which Iroquois people drew to protect their remaining lands, their autonomy, and their culture.

Six Nations people never relied solely upon the Treaty of Canandaigua to solve their problems and protect their interests. Some, like the Onondagas, developed a rugged and determined sense of self-reliance: they turned their back on the state of New York as much as they could, ignored the federal government entirely, and went about their ways on their territory south of today's city of Syracuse. Others moved. Oneidas in central New York, their lands pressed upon endlessly by the state and its citizens, and with no significant protection offered by a federal government that seldom seemed aware that illegal land sales had taken place until well after the fact, decided to relocate to new homes in Wisconsin. Indian removal is often described as something done to Indians, a notorious policy most often associated with Andrew Jackson. But Indians like the Oneidas worked with the policy and bent it to serve their interests. It left a mixed and painful legacy, to be sure, but the determination of New York Indians to find new homes in the west ought to be viewed at least in part as an attempt to preserve their cultural autonomy, to secure their persons and property, and to avoid the continued lawlessness of the New York frontier.[1]

As for the Senecas, the most numerous of the Six Nations, and the nation whose interests most closely intertwined with the success or failure of the Treaty of Canandaigua, they drew first upon a revitalization movement led by the Seneca Handsome Lake, a religious message that became a social gospel consonant with the preservation of Seneca lands. Next they drew upon the assistance offered by missionaries and instructors from the Philadelphia Yearly Meeting of the Society of Friends, the organization that sponsored Savery, Emlen, Bacon, and Parrish. With Quaker assistance, the Senecas adopted selectively changes in their ways of living that aided them in their desire to preserve their lands and the core of their culture.[2]

Late in 1799, the Seneca leader Handsome Lake experienced the first of several visions that became the core of the *Gaiwiio*, which he began to preach in longhouses across Iroquoia. Unlike contemporary prophetic figures in the western Great Lakes, Handsome Lake did not call for armed resistance against the growing numbers of white people enveloping Iroquois land: He recognized that the geographic realities of New York state made armed resistance futile. He and his followers did, however, assemble a rich gospel that defined sin and what one must do to achieve salvation. He defined heaven and hell and gave guidance to Senecas and their neighbors on how to live well in a world increasingly dominated by white people who were different and who threatened fundamentally native ways of living.[3]

Handsome Lake looked past tribal and geographic boundaries. He described his followers as *Indians*, people who had something in common that distinguished them from "the white-skinned race" despite their tribal differences. The Indians, Handsome Lake believed, "were entitled to a different religion, a religion adapted to their customs, manners and way of thinking." They must sin no more, reform their ways, and restore rituals that he described. Handsome Lake denounced the sin of drunkenness. Those who drank destroyed their communities, or their own lives, or were "thrown into houses of confinement by the pale faces." The Great Spirit, Handsome Lake preached, commanded followers to abandon the drinking of alcohol.[4]

Drunkenness brought great destruction to the Senecas, but so, too, did the sale of their lands. Handsome Lake told his followers that "your chiefs have violated and betrayed your trust by selling lands." All should enjoy the land equally; nobody had a right to sell it. Any sale of land, Handsome Lake said, was a sin that offended the Great Spirit. The Senecas must preserve their lands. But Handsome Lake recognized that his followers lived in the midst of white people. Compromises had to be made. The Creator intended for the Senecas to live off animals they hunted, but, because of the presence of the Americans, soon "there will be no more game for the Indian to use in his feasts." The Senecas, Handsome Lake taught, could thus raise domestic animals. "The pale-faces are pressing you upon every side." Senecas could tend cattle and other livestock and build comfortable houses. This was "all you can safely adopt of the customs of the pale-faces."[5]

Some of those customs were the source of pain and misery for the Senecas. Handsome Lake's religion, which still is practiced, institutionalized these concerns. Handsome Lake journeyed in one of his visions along a road until he reached a fork. One path led to the House of the Great Spirit. The other led to the House of Torment, a hell reserved for Indian sinners. Handsome Lake visited this hell. He looked down on the many rooms in a dark, soot-stained mansion. In one chamber, he saw a drunkard, forced by a malevolent figure named "The Punisher" to drink molten metal, which he spewed from his mouth in a blaze of fire. Handsome Lake saw a husband and a wife. They began to argue and their tongues and eyes became so distorted that they could neither see nor speak. It was a frightening place, with card players burning; wife-beaters striking women as their arms exploded; alcohol vendors with their flesh rotting away; fiddlers sawing off their arms for all eternity. These were the sins of white men and women, and through the *Gaiwiio*, Handsome Lake's followers learned to avoid them.[6]

Handsome Lake, like other prophets in Native America, borrowed much. Outside of the Iroquois heaven, Handsome Lake reported, George Washington resided. There, "dressed in his uniform, and in a state of perfect felicity, he is destined to remain through eternity in the solitary enjoyment of the celestial residence prepared for him by the Great Spirit." Washington occupied this reverenced position, despite the military damage he had called down upon the Senecas, for his explication of the Trade and Intercourse Act, a law that Senecas believed insulated their lands from illegal purchase, despite its evident shortcomings. Handsome Lake, like many of his critics in Iroquois society, hoped to develop and encourage a self-sufficient Seneca society with as little interaction with white people as possible. They would live with their white neighbors in peace, but each would stay out of the other's affairs. It was, in this sense, entirely consistent with the principle of *guswenta*: parallel lines, traveling the same stream but not crossing.[7]

While Handsome Lake and his followers developed his visions into a systematic religious outlook, his half-brother Cornplanter also considered the best way for the Senecas to live in the midst of growing numbers of white people. Cornplanter believed that "the Great Spirit intended they should not continue to live by hunting," but by learning how to "till the ground with the plow, as the white people do." To that end, he invited the Quakers to come to join the Senecas. He asked them, in 1798, to teach the Senecas so that "we should cease pursuing after the wild beasts of the forest, and turn from the ways of our forefathers, to be tillers of the Ground and keepers of flocks and of herds." They needed instruction, but they also needed livestock and tools, which Cornplanter hoped the Quakers could provide.[8]

Most Senecas welcomed the Quakers, who offered to teach the Indians "some of our useful trades such as Blacksmiths, Millwrights, Wheel-wrights, and Carpenters: that you may build houses, Mills and do other necessary things to make your lives more comfortable." Seneca leaders like Red Jacket who "were not able to discover any benefit to be derived from" the Quakers' religious instruction, still highly approved "of the measures adopted by you in the art of cultivating the land."[9] And the Quakers understood this. As Timothy Pickering explained to Jasper Parrish, the Friends' "great object is, not to teach peculiar *doctrines* but useful *practices*: to instruct the Indians in husbandry and the plain mechanical arts and manufactures directly connected with it." This was the critical first step, he believed, entirely consistent with the sixth article of the Canandaigua treaty. Other changes to Seneca beliefs, Quakers believed, would follow this broader cultural transformation.[10]

The Quakers sought to effect this cultural transformation through isolation. Seneca women, who traditionally had conducted agricultural work, would move into the home, conforming to emerging American definitions of domesticity. They would learn to spin and weave and manage their households. Seneca men, meanwhile, would remain close to home as well if the Quakers had their way. They would no longer travel the woods as hunters and traders. Rather, they would transform their lands into farms on the American model where men performed the bulk of the fieldwork. Seneca men, in a manner consistent with yet another American ideal, would own their lands as individuals, and communal ownership of the land would disappear.[11]

The Senecas welcomed Quaker assistance. One year after the commencement of their mission, the Friends recorded their pleasure "that some of the Indian men are beginning to help their women to work and raise corn, and make fence." With a commitment to agriculture, the Friends told Cornplanter in 1801, the Senecas will see "that your ground is good, that you may raise a great deal of wheat, rye, corn, potatoes, and other good things, like the white people." Nearly every year, in nearly every report written by the members of the Society of Friends, they remarked upon the progress: evidence that the Senecas "have much declined the use of strong drink;" "an encouraging improvement in agriculture and some of the mechanic arts as also in the regularity of their lives and manners;" evidence that they have built 100 houses, "most of them well put up, of hewn logs many of them two stories high, and covered with shingles." By 1810, the Friends reported that "the condition of this people is already in various respects, considerably ameliorated, and as a liberal and steady perseverance is maintained on our part a hope is cherished that they will be enabled to overcome the difficulties attendant on the former mode of life, and to acquire a comfortable living by their own labour."[12]

The Senecas made selective changes to their culture with the assistance of the Society of Friends because they believed that doing so would benefit them in ways that the Quakers did not always recognize. If the Quakers hoped to preserve the Senecas by isolating them from corrupting outside forces and transforming them into a nation of self-sufficient subsistence farmers, the Senecas made choices designed to preserve their independence through a selective engagement with the market economy. As in other rural communities, engagement with the market economy could and did provoke divisions among the Senecas. Like their rural neighbors, the Senecas faced difficult choices when they transformed woodlands into farmlands, enclosed fields, and built roads. In this sense, the changes Senecas faced were not dissimilar to those other rural Americans faced. The fundamental distinction was that while their white neighbors moved into the vicinity to obtain land from the land companies, the Senecas sought to retain the land they already possessed.[13]

To make a living and to acquire cash, some Senecas sold alcohol in western New York that they acquired downstream in Pittsburgh. Others continued to hunt. Even as the white population in western New York increased, Seneca hunters still found deer plentiful, as well as raccoon, mink, and muskrats, all of which seemed to thrive as the white population increased. According to the Mohawk John Norton, who visited the Senecas in 1809, they could "conveniently take skins, meat and timber to Pittsburgh, where they generally get a good price for these articles." The trip downriver took only two or three days.[14]

Seneca farmers found markets for their crops. The flax Seneca farmers planted they sold to whites rather than use it for themselves or their families. Seneca farmers found outlets for their food crops and for their livestock as well. During the War of 1812, a time of scarcity in western New York, settlers bought corn from Indian women. The Senecas used their land, one observer noted, "not only for their own subsistence but sell considerable to white people." At Allegany, eighty Seneca families consisting of 439 individuals possessed 479 cattle, 58 horses, 350 hogs, and 699 acres "of improved land in which 70 acres of meadow is included." From this, Seneca farmers produced a surplus that they sold to their non-Indian neighbors.[15]

Some of the swine kept by Senecas they butchered and salted for family consumption, but much of the rest they sold for cash. The Quakers encouraged the Senecas to acquire livestock, for food and as draft animals. But the Senecas, much to the concern of at least some members of the Society of Friends, seemed more interested in acquiring horses than oxen. The Senecas' white neighbors used horses for labor and transport in their lumbering activities; the Quakers, who were concerned about the Senecas' participation in the timber economy, thus viewed the growth of the Senecas' horse herds as a potential problem.[16]

Indeed, the Quakers complained in 1818 that progress in agriculture, although considerable, was less than they would have hoped for because more and more Senecas at sites like Tunesassah had been "much drawn to the cutting and rafting of pine timber." Senecas could sell stands of trees for harvesting and cutting by white lumbermen, an activity that allowed the elderly and infirm to derive an income from lands they may have lacked the physical capacity to work on their own. Although the Ogden Company tried to oppose this activity, millions of board-feet of cut timber were produced from stands of trees opened to outsiders by the Senecas.[17]

Senecas frequently asked the Quakers to assist them in erecting their own sawmills. Cornplanter operated the first sawmill on the Allegheny as early as 1795. Friends helped the Senecas operate their own mills, where they cut their timber, formed them into rafts, and floated "them down to Pittsburgh, at the time of high water." The Senecas carried with them "their Peltry, furrs, and good canoes, to push up their return cargoes." The Senecas' interest in clearing land, which the Quakers mentioned frequently, was less about readying fields for the plow than it was about selling timber for a profit. The Quakers could not curb the Senecas' enthusiasm and could only appeal to them and ask them to consider "whether you would not have been in a better situation generally if you had employed the same time which you have spent in cutting and rafting timber in cultivating your good land."[18]

By the 1820s, Senecas interested in participating in the timber trade cut trees, hauled the logs to the Allegheny, and rafted the logs downstream to Warren, Franklin, and Pittsburgh, in Pennsylvania. Some Senecas earned reputations as skilled pilots, a talent for which they were well paid. As with the sale of their agricultural produce, Seneca timbermen, floating downriver with their logs and other items, participated in a complex regional economy. Senecas traveled widely to exchange raw materials in the form of unmilled logs, processed items like furs and salted pork, and finished goods like moccasins, shingles, and finished lumber, for cash and goods unavailable to them locally.[19]

There are important lessons to be drawn from this discussion of the relationship between the Senecas and the Society of Friends. It is difficult to overestimate the importance of the Quakers' contributions, but the Senecas always engaged with the missionaries on their own terms. They accepted elements of the Friends' technology and advice and much of the economic change they advocated, but they did not become Quakers. They did not alter their religion. They engaged selectively with the market economy, preserving much of their freedom of movement, a significant degree of their autonomy, and their connections to Iroquois people living on their reservations and elsewhere.

They certainly faced continuing efforts to purchase their lands, the most notorious of which culminated in the Buffalo Creek Treaty of 1838. In what is arguably one of the most corrupt treaties ever negotiated under the superintendence of the United States, representatives from the federal government, land companies, and the state bribed some Seneca leaders, coerced others, and defrauded still more to obtain enough signatures to claim that the Senecas had ceded all their remaining lands. A protest movement, led by Senecas and their Quaker allies, succeeded in delaying the implementation of the treaty, and a compromise was worked out in 1842 between the Quakers and the United States where the Senecas were allowed to keep the Allegany and Cattaraugus reservations if they ceded Buffalo Creek and Tonawanda, but many Senecas were deeply dissatisfied. The Senecas at Tonawanda reacquired their reservation fifteen years later.[20]

To many Senecas, their traditional chiefs had failed them during the Buffalo Creek crisis. Since the treaty, they had misused the Senecas' annuity funds. According to the Quakers, "*there does not appear to have been any law or laws of sufficient force to ensure the keeping or rendering proper accounts, by the chiefs, or a due administration of the funds.*" As a result, "the people, the mass of the population on one side, as the receiving interest, have *for a long time* been fomenting, and *consolidating as an opposition to the chiefs* as receivers and holders of the national funds." When a critical mass of Senecas suspected that their chiefs had betrayed that trust, misappropriated the funds, and failed to use them to benefit the people, they organized to overthrow the traditional leadership structure. [21]

The New York state legislature enacted a law in May 1845 "for the protection and improvement of the Seneca Indians." The law set in place a revision of the tribe's traditional manner for governing community life. The Senecas began to organize into "Law" and "Anti-Law" factions. The conflict lasted until 1847, when the state amended the law to allow for the popular election of the officers it identified in the 1845 enactment. In the meantime, the U.S. Congress amended the Trade and Intercourse Act to allow for the payment, at the discretion of the president, of all annuities "to the heads of families and other individuals entitled to participate therein."[22]

These legislative enactments would provide the backdrop against which the Senecas acted out their revolution in 1848. The chiefs resisted change in the manner of distributing annuities. As the Society of Friends' Joint Committee argued, "to be deprived of the power to handle the people's money was more than they could bear." The majority of the nation, however, was angry and willing to change traditional forms of community government in order to more effectively manage their remaining lands and resources for the good of the community. They "became convinced, that neither peace nor security could be enjoyed by the people, until the chiefs should be shorn or every vestige of their official power." Thus a national council held at Cattaraugus late in 1848 declared itself a constitutional convention and declared the creation and founding of the Seneca Nation of Indians, a new and innovative framework of government, quite different from what had existed before. The constitution described the failure of the chiefs, and the delegates present declared that "we cannot enumerate the evils growing out of a system so defective, nor calculate its overpowering weight on the progress of improvement." In particular, the chiefs had withheld portions of the annuity for the purposes of government, calling the withholding of the annuity a "tax."[23]

The new constitution, which both the state of New York and the United States recognized, established a government consisting of an elected council of eighteen members, presided over by an executive department led by a president, a clerk, and a treasurer. Senecas split into two parties with regard to the new form of government. The New Government Party favored the constitution, while the Old Chiefs Party opposed the new framework. Both groups had talented and able leaders. Over time, the Old Chiefs Party, recognizing its near-equality in strength and its ability to successfully contest elections and to control the new frame of government, began to act like a political party. By the mid-1850s, the Seneca constitution had achieved what political scientists call "legitimacy." Although political contests could be as partisan and competitive as those in the surrounding non-Indian communities, and although the two parties might disagree deeply over the course the Seneca Nation should follow, both sides grew to accept a constitution that Seneca leaders recognized as consistent with the Seneca Nation's interpretation of the Treaty of Canandaigua, an agreement that grew in importance to Haudenosaunee peoples as time passed by.

The leaders of the Seneca Nation of Indians insisted upon respect for their new constitution. Seneca Nation President Zecheriah Jimerson told the U.S. Secretary of the Interior in November 1850 that the United States guaranteed to the Senecas "the peaceable possession and enjoyment of all their reservations." Constitution making, he asserted, was consistent with the "free use and enjoyment" of their lands. "The United States," wrote the Seneca Nation's Committee of Safety one year later, "have, by solemn treaties guaranteed to us our freedom and independence and that they will never interfere in our political matters." The Treaty of Canandaigua factored largely into these discussions. As the Seneca leader Ely Parker noted in the summer of 1853, his people wished the U.S. president to reassure them "of his continued intention to faithfully carry out and observe the sacred guarantees of all Treaties made with the Six Nations of New York."[24]

The Seneca Nation of Indians conducted its business in a manner consistent with and conscious of the Treaty of Canandaigua. They opposed proposed federal legislation in 1878, for instance, that would have made Indians citizens of the United States, on the grounds that "the passage of such a bill would tend to break up such tribal relation and would violate the treaty of the United States with the Six Nations of New York and Seneca Nation concluded Oct. 22, 1784" in which the United States "solemnly covenanted & guaranteed the Seneca Nation in the quiet and peaceable possession of their remaining lands."[25] Similarly, the Senecas opposed the push from both state and federal authorities to allot the Senecas' remaining reservations. Allotment, the breaking up of communally held native lands into individual parcels, they said, was a bad policy that would lead to dispossession and violate the Canandaigua treaty. The Senecas opposed any effort to transfer criminal and civil jurisdiction over their lands to the state of New York. They opposed, as well, New York's comprehensive "Indian Law" of 1892 on the grounds that the state legislature enacted it "without any consultation with our people, whose interests are so largely affected by it." Such far-reaching changes certainly threatened the Senecas' peaceful enjoyment of their lands. The Treaty of Canandaigua provided the lens through which the Seneca Nation interpreted the state's expansive law.[26]

The Seneca Nation's government also enacted policies and took steps to ensure that they preserved the "free use and enjoyment" of their lands. On occasion, they challenged the legality of agreements through which the Seneca Nation had earlier lost lands on the grounds that the United States had pledged itself to protect the Seneca Nation's land holdings. They sought to protect themselves against the damage that could result from the unauthorized encroachment of white people upon their lands. By a vote of 7–3, to cite one example, the Seneca Nation council voted in favor of a resolution in 1858 authorizing Senecas to remove from the reservation anyone selling alcohol. Senecas demanded that the United States enforce effectively the second section of the 1834 Trade and Intercourse Act prohibiting the unlicensed sale of alcohol.[27]

The Seneca Nation's government tried to protect its land and resources. As early as 1863, the Seneca Nation resolved that "white people be restrained from going into the Indian Reservation for the purpose of cutting & drawing off any kind of timber." They called upon federal authorities to remove intruders. They also asked for the appointment of a federal agent who would more energetically protect their lands from trespassers. They continued to enact resolutions of their own forbidding the unauthorized cutting of Seneca timber.[28]

In all of their economic activities, the Seneca Nation of Indians acted upon an understanding of their culture and their interactions with the outside world that they believed had been ratified at Canandaigua in 1794. The Senecas and their Indian friends continued to act autonomously to protect the "free use and enjoyment" of their lands. They continued to move throughout Iroquoia to discuss affairs of concern to Haudenosaunee people, even if formal Seneca involvement in the traditional league no longer occurred after the Revolution of 1848 and the overthrow of the traditional chiefs. The Seneca Nation, for instance, sent delegates to Onondaga, the seat of the Iroquois League, to meet with others of the Six Nations to discuss matters that might affect Haudenosaunee peoples across New York state.

The Seneca Nation asserted its right to determine who, in fact, was Seneca, and the rights of those "Indian friends" who lived on their remaining reservations. At the time of the Canandaigua treaty, the meaning of this phrase was relatively clear. In the aftermath of the American Revolution large numbers of Iroquois people had settled as refugees in Seneca territory. In 1838, when the United States met with the Six Nations at Buffalo Creek, a census indicated that 194 Onondagas and 130 Cayugas still resided on the Seneca reservations.[29]

Tensions among the Senecas, Onondagas, and Cayugas at Allegany and Cattaraugus raised issues that frequently drew the attention of the Seneca Nation government and federal authorities throughout the nineteenth century. In the summer of 1858, for instance, the Seneca Nation council rescinded a resolution enacted the year before ejecting the Onondagas from the Allegany and Cattaraugus reservations. Onondagas frequently raised the issue of their status on Seneca land, both with the Senecas and federal authorities. Daniel Sherman, the federal agent appointed to oversee New York's Indian reservations, noted the complications that emerged from intermarriage as children inherited their tribal identity through their mothers, leaving many men and women born at Allegany and Cattaraugus with no say in how their respective communities were governed.[30]

As whites encroached on reservations and resources became more scarce, these conflicts became more common. Charles Halftown, a Seneca Nation councilor, resolved in 1877 that no Cayuga or Onondaga could stand for election in the Seneca Nation. Two weeks later, the council resolved that "Cayugas, Onondagas, Half-breeds," and African-Americans should be prohibited from cutting timber on the reservations.[31] When a motion was introduced in the council in November 1884 that Onondagas resident on Seneca land should receive a share of Seneca Nation annuities, the council voted to reject the proposal. Moneys derived from the sale and leasing of Seneca lands should only benefit Senecas, and not members of other Haudenosaunee nations resident at the western door of the Longhouse. Six months later, Seneca Nation council member Jacob Halftown resolved that "whenever any woman or man of the Senecas continue to reside in Canada or intermarry with any of the Canucks or rather the Canadians, [they] shall not be included in our census and shall not be entitled to their annuities." The money should stay in Seneca Country. And in April 1889, when a white man married to a Seneca woman told the council that he had lived on the reservation for more than twenty-five years and wanted his "rights" and "would like to draw annuity and be as one of your nation," the council refused his request. Federal officials expressed their wish on more than one occasion that the Onondagas or Cayugas receive the same rights and privileges as the Senecas, but only occasionally, and never successfully, did they interfere in this part of the Seneca Nation's internal affairs.[32]

In the twentieth century, Haudenosaunee peoples continued to assert powerfully their right to move freely among and between Iroquois communities in Wisconsin, New York, and Canada that made up a broader Iroquoia. They continued to assert the importance of the connections linking Haudenosaunee over this broad expanse of territory and the continuing vitality of their culture and autonomy. And they worked to guarantee for future generations the "free use and enjoyment" of their lands.

Deskaheh, or Levi General, for instance, traveled to Geneva in 1923 to present the grievances of Six Nations people against the Canadian government before the League of Nations. Using language similar to that expressed in the Canandaigua treaty, and basing his argument on the notion that the Six Nations preserved the right to the "free use and enjoyment" of their lands, Deskaheh appealed to the queen of the Netherlands. "We are an organized and self-governing people who, on the coming of the Dutch to the valley of the Hudson in North America, entered into treaties with them and faithfully observed our promise of friendship," he wrote. The British followed and entered into the Covenant Chain alliance with the Six Nations. After the American Revolution, "We, through our great Chief, Joseph Brant," accepted lands along the Grand River, which the English king "bestowed upon us and our posterity for ever, under the express condition that we should enjoy them for ever as the separate people we had ever been."[33] Deskaheh failed in his efforts to secure justice before the League of Nations. That fact, however, should not obscure the importance of his powerful assertion of Iroquois nationhood.[34]

Deskaheh died in 1925 at the Tuscarora home of Clinton Rickard, who later founded the Indian Defense League of America. Rickard and his colleagues protested the disavowal of treaty rights by both the governments of Canada and the United States, particularly so with the refusal of both countries to allow the free passage back and forth between Canada and the United States established in Jay's Treaty and reaffirmed at Ghent.[35] Meanwhile, a Kanawake Mohawk steel-worker named Paul Diabo, who resided in Philadelphia while working on bridges there, protested his arrest and deportation to Canada as an unjust restraint on that freedom of movement that Iroquois people so richly valued and that was recognized in Jay's Treaty. After a legal fight lasting three years, in which he received assistance from Iroquois communities in New York and Canada, the Third Circuit Court in Philadelphia at last ruled in Diabo's favor, recognizing in effect the right of Haudenosaunee people to free passage across the international border.[36]

The Iroquois nations in New York rejected overwhelmingly the Indian Reorganization Act of 1934, the pinnacle of Commissioner of Indian Affairs John Collier's "Indian New Deal." The Six Nations fiercely asserted their sovereignty in the twentieth century and did not need the types of reorganization advocated by Collier because they already possessed functional governing systems. A Tonawanda Seneca said in 1935, for instance, that "we are a nation, living on land of our own." Despite the passage of a federal law in 1924 that made native peoples citizens, he said that "we are not citizens of the United States and I hope we never will be. We must insist on our rights as a separate territory not responsible to any other government. We must rule ourselves. We must not pay taxes to the United States or we will lose our status as a separate nation." *Guswenta*, the principle enshrined at Canandaigua, appeared again. Although the state of New York influenced Iroquois life in a number of ways, the Tonawanda spokesperson insisted on Iroquois autonomy. They wanted less, not more, interference in their internal affairs, and they feared that the Indian Reorganization Act would bring complete control by outsiders over Iroquois communities.[37]

Some Senecas feared, moreover, that the definition of Indians in the act could undermine the Seneca Nation's government and its own beliefs about who qualified for membership in the community.

The IRA defined as an Indian, for purpose of the act, members of recognized tribes and "all other persons of one-half or more Indian blood." Cayugas, Onondagas, Mohawks, and Oneidas lived at Allegany and Cattaraugus, and they had the requisite "blood quantum," but they were not Senecas. There were also people who resided on the reservations who had white mothers and Indian fathers. These people, the eccentric Seneca activist Alice Lee Jemison pointed out, did not have the right to "hold lands and vote at tribal elections." Citizenship came through the mother in the matrilineal Seneca communities, and the inclusion of all these outsiders in a new Seneca Nation created and supported by the Interior Department raised the prospect that "our Seneca Nation will be entirely destroyed, because the new chartered community that will be set up will not be the Seneca Nation of Indians but will consist of other persons who on June 1, 1934, were living on our reservation." This was interference of the deepest dye.[38]

Iroquois people deeply distrusted the state and federal governments. They based their opposition to the act on an understanding of Seneca sovereignty and nationhood that many Iroquois people shared. The 1794 Treaty of Canandaigua allowed the Six Nations the "free use and enjoyment" of their lands without any interference. The Indian Reorganization Act, by requiring the approval of the Commissioner of Indian Affairs and the Interior Department for any contemplated action by the tribe, infringed directly upon the exercise of that right.

These powerful assertions of nationhood would continue. As the New Deal gave way to the Second World War, Senecas viewed the Selective Service Act as a threat to their sovereignty. In October 1940, the Seneca Nation's president, Wilfred Crouse, asserted that the United States had no right to draft Seneca young men for military service. According to the Canandaigua treaty, he said, "we are a distinct race, nation and people owning, occupying and governing the lands of our ancestors." When a federal court in 1942 ruled that Iroquois people were subject to conscription, the defiance of the Senecas and the rest of the Six Nations to the Selective Service Act ended. Still, they asserted their separate status. In June 1942 delegates from the Six Nations gathered to declare war on the Axis powers. "The New World's oldest democracy," an AP reporter wrote in the *New York Times*, declared "that a state of war exists between our Confederacy on the one part and Germany, Italy, Japan and their allies against whom the United States has declared war on the other part." Widely reported in the media, the Six Nations' declaration was cast in terms of propaganda, a sign that all Americans supported the war effort. They missed the significant point that the members of the Six Nations still believed strongly in and valued greatly their sovereignty, and that they would send their men to fight and die only in wars that they had declared themselves.[39]

Conclusion

Canandaigua Treaty Commemoration.
Michael Leroy Oberg

Every November 11, on the grounds of the Ontario County Courthouse, citizens of the Six Nations gather to commemorate the Treaty of Canandaigua. They march in a parade that begins at the Canandaigua Primary School, near where the Iroquois established their camps in 1794. Representatives from the Society of Friends attend, as does the occasional representative from federal, state, and local governments. Townspeople and, at times, students attend as well. They come to Canandaigua to celebrate a treaty that continues to retain its vitality and to serve as a symbol and assertion of the autonomy and nationhood of the Haudenosaunee.

There is indeed much worth celebrating. If any number of people had their way, the Iroquois would no longer reside in New York. They have endured epidemic disease, military invasion, dispossession, and policies intended to eradicate their culture, their autonomy, and their independence. Even their best friends in the first half of the nineteenth century looked forward to their relocation to new homes in the west, while, later, self-proclaimed allies looked forward to the allotment of their remaining reservation lands and their assimilation and disappearance into the American body politic. They endured boarding schools, in New York and elsewhere.[1] Assaults upon their lands continued throughout the twentieth century: along the Niagara River, on the St. Lawrence, and, notoriously, in Seneca Country, with the construction of the Kinzua Dam and the flooding of a large chunk of the Allegany Reservation. All, on their surface, were violations of the Canandaigua accord.[2]

Very few New Yorkers historically have looked forward to a future that included the people of the Longhouse on their own lands with their own culture in the Empire State. We are still here, the Haudenosaunee assert, and we are determined to benefit from the "free use and enjoyment" of our lands. *Guswenta*: They constantly assert the principle, whatever the historical and interpretive problems associated with the "Two Row" wampum. Two vessels, side by side, parallel lines: the Iroquois and their neighbors, pledged to non-interference in each other's affairs. The principle rested at the heart of the Treaty of Canandaigua and continues to rest at the heart of Haudenosaunee understandings of their relationship with state and federal governments in the United States.

In places like Niagara County in the state's northwest corner, or in Oneida and Madison counties in its center, Iroquois communities are significant players in the local economy. They are major employers. Gaming operations, on the Seneca reservations in Oneida Country and way up at Akwesasne on the St. Lawrence, provide employment and entertainment to many non-Indians. They are in places some of the only significant engines of local economic growth, whatever the real merits of casino gaming. New Yorkers travel to Indian communities to purchase cigarettes and gasoline that the state thus far has been prohibited from taxing. The Oneidas support local schools with generous donations. Even if poverty remains a challenge on Indian reservations, as it does in rural communities throughout New York state, smoke shops, casinos, gas stations, and a host of other enterprises have helped a fragile prosperity take root.

In the midst of New York state, Iroquois people remain committed to a culture, elements of which were old when the American patriots declared their independence from Great Britain. Much has changed, to be sure, but the Iroquois continue to play a large role in public life in New York state as they preserve a powerful commitment to their culture. They regularly remind New Yorkers of their autonomy and their nationhood, and the long history that upholds both.

But state and local officials have cast an avaricious eye toward economic prosperity in Iroquois communities. They look for means to tax Indian businesses or to allow non-Indian gaming operations to open in economically marginal parts of the state to spur economic growth and compete with native enterprises. These issues have been compromised, but still the state of New York looks for opportunities to benefit from this prosperity. It poses obstacles, erects barriers, and interferes. Many non-Indians express resentment for the special "benefits," imagined mostly, that they believe Iroquois people in the state receive. The Iroquois, in short, face continual threats to their autonomy and independence, considerable interference that impinges upon the "free use and enjoyment" of their lands. For these reasons and more, the Treaty of Canandaigua remains a critical safeguard for their rights.

There is a bumper sticker that often is seen in Indian Country. Its message is simple: "Honor Indian Treaties," it reads. Yet so many Indian treaties are little more than real-estate transactions, where American commissioners dictated cessions to militarily defeated native peoples and asserted control over their communities. They were, too often, instruments of colonial control, licenses for empire and subjugation. Canandaigua was different. At the time the treaty was negotiated in 1794, the Iroquois still retained the capacity, should they align themselves with the Northwestern confederates or the British, to pose an existential threat to settlements in the Pennsylvania and New York borderlands. And they used that considerable power, and their own powerful diplomatic skills, to secure the return of a key parcel of land and, more importantly, the recognition of their sovereign right to the "free use and enjoyment" of their lands.

Attempts to limit that sovereignty continue, and the ability of the Iroquois to recover the lands the state acquired in transactions that explicitly violated the terms of the Trade and Intercourse Act has recently been dealt a lethal blow by a U.S. Supreme Court that has proven itself increasingly hostile over the past forty years to the rights of native peoples. But the treaty remains a powerful symbol, and part of the "supreme law of the land," that recognizes and affirms the rights of the people of the Longhouse to their lands and their way of life.[3]

ABBREVIATIONS USED IN NOTES

ASPIA   *American State Papers. Documents, Legislative and Executive, of the Congress of the United States,* 38 vols. Class 2: *Indian Affairs,* 2 vols. (Washington, DC: Gales & Seaton, 1832).

IIM   *Iroquois Indians: A Documentary History of the Diplomacy of the Six Nations and Their League,* Microfilm, 50 reels. (Woodbridge, CT: Research Publications, 1984).

LR-OIA-6N   Correspondence of the Office of Indian Affairs. Letters Received, 1824–1881, M234, RG 75. Six Nations Agency, 1824–1834, National Archives, Washington, DC, Microfilm reel 832.

LR-OIA-NY   Correspondence of the Office of Indian Affairs, Letters Received, 1824–1881, M234, RG 75. New York Agency, 1829–1880, National Archives, Washington, DC, Microfilm reels 583–596.

NA   National Archives, Washington, DC

NYHS   New York Historical Society

NYSA   New York State Archives, Albany, New York

NYSL   New York State Library, Albany, New York

PYMIC   Philadelphia Yearly Meeting of the Society of Friends, Indian Committee

TPP   Timothy Pickering Papers, Massachusetts Historical Society, Boston, Massachusetts

NOTES

....

Introduction

1. There is no single monograph that focuses upon the Treaty of Canandaigua. For important treatments, see the essays in Peter Jemison and Anna M. Schien, eds., *Treaty of Canandaigua: 200 Years of Treaty Relations between the Iroquois Confederacy and the United States* (Santa Fe, NM: Clear Light Publishing, 2000), and William N. Fenton, *The Great Law and the Longhouse: A Political History of the Iroquois Confederacy* (Norman: University of Oklahoma Press, 1998).

2. The paradoxical connection of Iroquois culture to peace and war is best explained in Matthew Dennis, *Cultivating a Landscape of Peace: Iroquois-European Encounters in Seventeenth Century America* (Ithaca, NY: Cornell University Press, 1993), and Daniel K. Richter, "War and Culture: The Iroquois Experience," *William and Mary Quarterly*, 40 (October 1983), 528–559.

3. On treaties see Francis Paul Prucha, *American Indian Treaties: The History of a Political Anomaly* (Berkeley: University of California Press, 1994), and Colin G. Calloway, *Pen and Ink Witchcraft: Treaties and Treaty Making in American Indian History* (New York: Oxford University Press, 2013).

4. Stuart Banner, *How the Indians Lost Their Land: Law and Power on the Frontier* (Cambridge, MA: Harvard University Press, 2006).

5. *Cherokee Nation v. Georgia*, 5 Peters 1, (1831). The "plenary power" doctrine appeared in a number of cases, but in none more starkly than *Lone Wolf v. Hitchcock*, 187 U.S. 553, (1903).

Chapter 1

1. Jon Parmenter, *The Edge of the Woods: Iroquoia, 1534–1701* (Lansing: Michigan State University Press, 2010), xxxv–xxxvii.

2. Dennis, *Cultivating a Landscape of Peace*, 43–75; Daniel K. Richter, *The Ordeal of the Longhouse: The Peoples of the Iroquois League in the Era of European Colonization* (Chapel Hill: University of North Carolina Press, 1992), 30–32; Dean R. Snow, *The Iroquois* (Cambridge, MA: Blackwell, 1994), 38; James W. Bradley, *Evolution of the Onondaga Iroquois: Accommodating Change*, rev. ed. (Lincoln: University of Nebraska Press, 2005), 56–58.

3. Richter, *Ordeal of the Longhouse*, Chapter 3; Bradley, *Evolution*, 69–74; Snow, *Iroquois*, 77.

4. *The Jesuit Relations and Allied Documents*, ed. Reuben Gold Thwaites (Cleveland, 1896–1901), 10: 219; Lewis Henry Morgan, *League of the Iroquois*, reprint ed. (New York: Citadel Press, 1962), 164.

5. Zena Pearlstone Mathews, "Of Man and Beast: The Chronology of Effigy Pipes Among Ontario Iroquoians," *Ethnohistory*, 27 (Autumn 1980), 295; Anthony Wonderley, "Effigy Pipes, Diplomacy, and Myth: Exploring Interaction Between St. Lawrence Iroquoians and Eastern Iroquois in New York State," *American Antiquity*, 70 (April 2005), 213, 215, 232. See also Wonderley, "Mythic Imagery in Iroquoian Archaeology," in *At the Font of the Marvelous: Exploring Oral Narrative and Mythic Imagery of the Iroquois and Their Neighbors* (Syracuse, NY: Syracuse University Press, 2009), 115–149.

6. Robert D. Kuhn and Martha L. Sempowski, "A New Approach to Dating the League of the Iroquois," *American Antiquity*, 66 (April 2001), 301–314.

7. See the discussion of wampum in Snow, *Iroquois*, 66–67; Elizabeth Shapiro Peña, "Wampum Production in New Netherland and Colonial New York: The Historical and Archaeological Context" (Ph.D. diss., Boston University, 1990), and Neal Salisbury, *Manitou and Providence: Indians, Europeans and the Making of New England, 1500–1643* (New York: Oxford University Press, 1982).

8. See the account in Dennis, *Cultivating a Landscape of Peace*, 85–94.

9. Parmenter, *Edge of the Woods*, 16–17; William N. Fenton, *The Great Law and the Longhouse: A Political History of the Iroquois Confederacy* (Norman: University of Oklahoma Press, 1998), 51–65, 85–103.

10. William Howard Carter, "Chains of Consumption: The Iroquois and Consumer Goods, 1550–1800" (Ph.D. diss., Princeton University, 2008), 211–217. See also Martha L. Sempowski, "Early

Historic Exchange Between the Seneca and the Susquehannock," in *Archaeology of the Iroquois: Selected Readings and Research Sources*, ed. Jordan E. Kerber (Syracuse, NY: Syracuse University Press, 2007), 194–218; Salisbury, *Manitou and Providence*, 147–152.

11. Dennis, *Cultivating a Landscape of Peace*, 124–126.
12. Dennis, *Cultivating a Landscape of Peace*, 94.
13. Dennis, *Cultivating a Landscape of Peace*, 94–95, 97–105.
14. Mary A. Druke, "Linking Arms: The Structure of Iroquois Intertribal Diplomacy," in *Beyond the Covenant Chain: The Iroquois and Their Neighbors in Indian North America, 1600–1800*, eds. Daniel K. Richter and James H. Merrell (Syracuse, NY: Syracuse University Press, 1987), 33.
15. Gunther Michelson, "Iroquoian Terms for Wampum," *International Journal of American Linguistics*, 57 (January 1991), 108–116.
16. Parmenter, *Edge of the Woods*, 23–24; James W. Ransom and Kreg T. Ettenger, "Polishing the Kaswentha: A Haudenosaunee View of Environmental Cooperation," *Environmental Science and Policy*, 4 (2001), 219–228; Richard Hill, Sr., "Oral Memory of the Haudenosaunee: Views of the Two Row Wampum," *Northeast Indian Quarterly*, 7 (Spring 1990), 21–30; Doug George-Kanentiio, *Iroquois Culture and Commentary* (Santa Fe, NM: Clear Light, 2000), 118–121. For the concept of *guswenta* (also *kaswentha*) see Jon Parmenter, "L'Arpe de Paix," *French Colonial History*, 4 (2003), 65, 68.
17. For the "Two Row" belt, see Jon Parmenter, "The Meaning of Kaswentha and the Two Row Wampum Belt in Haudenosaunee (Iroquois) History: Can Indigenous Oral Tradition be Reconciled with the Documentary Record?" *Journal of Early American History*, 3 (No. 1, 2013), 82–109. L. G. Van Loon, "Tawagonshi: Beginning of the Treaty Era," *Indian Historian*, 1 (1968), 23–26, claimed to have discovered the treaty in question, but Van Loon's work has been entirely discredited. On why Van Loon cannot be trusted, see Jaap Jacobs, "Early Dutch Explorations in North America," *Journal of Early American History*, 3 (no. 1, 2013), 59–81, and Charles T. Gehring, William A. Starna, and William N. Fenton, "The Tawagonshi Treaty of 1613: The Final Chapter," *New York History*, 68 (October 1987), 373–392. On the modern history of the Two Row wampum belt, see Kathryn Muller, "The Two Row Wampum: Historic Fiction, Modern Reality" (M.A. thesis, Université Laval, 2004). For a retelling of the *guswenta* story that focuses on a 1664 agreement with the English rather than the 1613 agreement with the Dutch, see Michael Mitchell, "Akwesasne:

The Unbroken Assertion of Sovereignty," in *Drumbeat: Anger and Renewal in Indian Country*, ed. Boyd Richardson (Toronto: Assembly of First Nations, 1989), 109.

18. Harmen Van den Bogaert's account in *In Mohawk Country: Early Narratives about a Native People*, eds. Dean Snow, Charles T. Gehring, and William A. Starna (Syracuse, NY: Syracuse University Press, 1996), 4.

19. Michael Leroy Oberg, *Dominion and Civility: English Imperialism and Native America* (Ithaca, NY: Cornell University Press, 1999), 142; Dennis, *Cultivating a Landscape of Peace*, 157–163.

20. "Articles Made and Agreed upon the 24th Day of September 1664," NYCD 3: 67–68.

21. Oberg, *Dominion and Civility*, 150; Charles Z. Lincoln, ed., *The Colonial Laws of New York from the Year 1664 to the Revolution* (Albany, 1894), 1: 40–41.

22. On alcohol in Indian communities in early America, see Peter Mancall, *Deadly Medicine: Indians and Alcohol in Early America* (Ithaca, NY: Cornell University Press, 1995). On Iroquois drinking, see Maia Conrad, "Disorderly Drinking: Reconsidering Seventeenth-Century Iroquois Alcohol Abuse," *American Indian Quarterly*, 23 (1999), 1–12; Richter, *Ordeal*, 120–132. The turmoil in the Mohawk Valley communities can be traced in Thwaites, ed., *Jesuit Relations*, 62: 166–187. On the founding of Kahnawake, see David Preston, *The Texture of Contact: European and Indian Settler Communities on the Frontiers of Iroquoia, 1667–1783* (Lincoln: University of Nebraska Press, 2009), 28–30; Allan Greer, *Mohawk Saint: Catherine Tekakwitha and the Jesuits* (New York: Oxford University Press, 2005).

23. Gerald F. Reid, *Kahnawake: Factionalism, Traditionalism and Nationalism in a Mohawk Community* (Lincoln: University of Nebraska Press, 2004), 12; David Blanchard, "The Seven Nations of Canada: An Alliance and a Treaty," *American Indian Culture and Research Journal*, 7 (no. 2, 1983), 6.

24. Richter, "War and Culture," 528–559.

25. Ibid.

26. On the Covenant Chain alliance, see Stephen Saunders Webb, *1676: The End of American Independence* (New York: Knopf, 1984), 355–406, and Francis Jennings, *The Ambiguous Iroquois Empire: The Covenant Chain Confederation of Indian Tribes with English Colonists from its Beginning to the Lancaster Treaty of 1744* (New York: Norton, 1984).

27. "Proposition or Oration of the Onnondages and Cayouges Sacheims made in Town Hall Albany Before the Right Honble the Lord Howard of Effingham, Governor of Virginia, and Col. Thomas Dungan of New York upon the 2nd day of August 1684," NYCD 3: 418, 417.

28. Fletcher speech to the Five Nations, July 3, 1693, NYCD 4: 41.

29. NYCD 5: 222, 229; Richard Aquila, *The Iroquois Restoration: Iroquois Diplomacy on the Colonial Frontier, 1701–1754* (Detroit: Wayne State University Press, 1983), 112–113, 119; De Canasora, Speech, September 21, 1713, NYCD 5: 375; Propositions made by the Sachims of the Five Nations of Indians in Albany, August 27, 1715, NYCD 5: 438.

30. Richter, *Ordeal of the Longhouse,* 249–254, 262–270.

31. Kurt Jordan, *The Seneca Restoration, 1715–1754: An Iroquois Local Political Economy* (Gainesville: University Press of Florida, 2008), 338–356.

32. Ibid.

33. The Mohawks also seem to have moved into smaller houses during these years, a shift that was accompanied by a growing awareness of private property, the adoption of European-styled surnames, and descent being traced through the father's side of the family. See Gail D. MacLeitch, *Imperial Entanglements: Iroquois Change and Persistence on the Frontiers of Empire* (Philadelphia: University of Pennsylvania Press, 2011), 223.

34. Gansevoort is quoted in Barbara Graymont, *The Iroquois and the American Revolution* (Syracuse: Syracuse University Press, 1972), 181; MacLeitch, *Imperial Entanglements,* 85, 196–197.

35. Richard Smith is quoted in Carter, "Chains," 315–318; MacLeitch, *Imperial Entanglements,* 85.

36. Preston, *Texture of Contact,* 61–115.

37. Ibid.

38. Preston, *Texture of Contact,* 37, 57, 103.

39. MacLeitch, *Imperial Entanglements,* 198, 209–210.

40. Timothy J. Shannon, *Indians and Colonists at the Crossroads of Empire: The Albany Congress of 1754* (Ithaca: Cornell University Press, 2000), 73–75.

41. Sir William Johnson to William Denny, July 21, 1758, in *Papers of Sir William Johnson,* ed. James Sullivan (Albany, 1921), 2: 879.

42. These movements are best described by Gregory Evans Dowd, *A Spirited Resistance: The North American Indian Struggle for Unity, 1745–1815* (Baltimore, MD: Johns Hopkins University Press, 1992); Carter, "Chains," 327.

43. Peter Wraxall, *An Abridgment of the Indian Affairs*, ed. Charles Howard McIlwaine (Cambridge, MA: Harvard University Press, 1915), xl; Fenton, *Great Law and the Longhouse*, 269.

Chapter 2

1. Dowd, Spirited Resistance, 32–40.
2. Jon Parmenter, "Forging New Links in the Anglo-Iroquois Covenant Chain, 1758–1766," Ethnohistory 44 (Autumn 1997), 617–654; Michael J. Mullin, "Sir William Johnson's Reliance on the Six Nations at the Conclusion of the Anglo-Indian war of 1763–1765," American Indian Culture and Research Journal, 17 (no. 4, 1993), 69–90; Laurence M. Hauptman, "Who Owns Grand Island (Erie County, NY)?" in *Treaty of Canandaigua 1794*, eds. Jemison and Schein, 129–130.
3. See the discussion in Woody Holton, *Forced Founders: Indians, Debtors, Slaves and the Making of the American Revolution in Virginia* (Chapel Hill: University of North Carolina Press, 1999), 4–29; Louis De Vorsey, Jr., *The Indian Boundary in the Southern Colonies, 1763–1775* (Chapel Hill: University of North Carolina Press, 1961), 64–78; William J. Campbell, *Speculators in Empire: Iroquoia and the 1768 Treaty of Fort Stanwix* (Norman: University of Oklahoma Press, 2012).
4. Graymont, *Iroquois and the American Revolution*, 26–47.
5. Karim M. Tiro, *The People of the Standing Stone: The Oneida Nation from the Revolution through the Era of Removal* (Amherst: University of Massachusetts Press, 2011), 40.
6. Graymont, *Iroquois and the American Revolution*, 48–85.
7. James E. Seaver, *The Life of Mary Jemison: Deh-He-wa-Mis* (New York: Miller, Orton and Mulligan, 1856), 117.
8. Seaver, *Mary Jemison*, 92–96.
9. Tiro, *People of the Standing Stone*, 48–61.
10. Seaver, *Mary Jemison*, 118; Joseph R. Fischer, *A Well-Executed Failure: The Sullivan Campaign Against the Iroquois, July–September, 1779* (Columbia: University of South Carolina Press, 1997); Anthony F. C. Wallace, *Death and Rebirth of the Seneca* (New York: Knopf, 1970), 194.
11. Colin G. Calloway, *The American Revolution in Indian Country: Crisis and Diversity in Native American Communities* (Cambridge: Cambridge University Press, 1995), 290; Wallace, *Death and Rebirth*, 195–196.
12. Shelburne, quoted in Alan Taylor, *The Divided Ground: Indians, Settlers and the Northern Borderland of the American Revolution*

(New York: Knopf, 2005), 112; Colin G. Calloway, *Crown and Calumet: British–Indian Relations* (Norman: University of Oklahoma Press, 1987), 8–10.

13. Thomas S. Abler, *Cornplanter: Chief Warrior of the Allegany Senecas* (Syracuse, NY: Syracuse University Press, 2007), 153.

14. J. David Lehman, "The End of the Iroquois Mystique: The Oneida Land Cession Treaties of the 1780s," *William and Mary Quarterly*, 47 (October 1990), 533; Anthony Wonderley, "'Good Peter's Narrative of 'Several Transactions Respecting Indian Lands': An Oneida View of Dispossession, 1785–1788," *New York History*, 84 (Summer 2003), 243.

15. Taylor, *Divided Ground*, 136; Francois Marbois, "Journey to the Oneidas, 1784," in Dean R. Snow, Charles T. Gehring, and William A. Starna, eds. *In Mohawk Country; Early Narratives about a Native People* (Syracuse, NY: Syracuse University Press, 1996), 312; Henry S. Manley, *The Treaty of Fort Stanwix* (Rome, NY: Rome Sentinel Company, 1932), 24; Peter S. Onuf, *The Origins of the Federal Republic: Jurisdictional Controversies in the United States, 1775–1787* (Philadelphia: University of Pennsylvania Press, 1983), 103–147.

16. Manley, *Stanwix*, 28.

17. Prucha, *American Indian Treaties*, 42; Banner, *How the Indians Lost Their Land*, 112.

18. Taylor, *Divided Ground*, 156; Manley, *Stanwix*, 27.

19. Fenton, *Great Law and the Longhouse*, 609; Instructions from George Clinton to Peter Ryckman, August 1784, *Public Papers of George Clinton, First Governor of New York*, ed. Hugh Hastings (Albany, NY: James B. Lyon, 1900), 8: 335; Clinton to Lee, Butler, and Wolcott, August 13, 1784, *Papers of George Clinton*, 8: 332–334; Lee and Butler to Clinton, August 19, 1784, *Papers of George Clinton*, 8: 339–340.

20. James Duane to George Clinton, in Franklin B. Hough, ed., *Proceedings of the Commissioners of Indian Affairs, Appointed by Law for the Extinguishment of Indian Titles in the State of New York* (Albany, NY: Joel Munsell, 1861), 22n.

21. George Clinton, Speech to Onondagas, Senecas, Cayugas, and Mohawks, September 5, 1784, *Public Papers of Clinton*, 8: 361–363.

22. Manley, *Stanwix*, 72, 93–95; Fenton, *Great Law*, 619; Calloway, *Pen and Ink Witchcraft*, 100–101.

23. Kappler, comp., *Indian Affairs*, 5–6.

24. Ibid., Taylor, *Divided Ground*, 159–160.

25. Graymont, *Iroquois and the American Revolution*, 273, 276–278.

26. Hough, ed., *Proceedings*, 73, 86–87.

27. Hough, ed., *Proceedings*, 92–93.

28. Hough, ed., *Proceedings*, 102–103, 107; Lehman, "Mystique," 536–538.

29. Taylor, *Divided Ground*, 136–140; Reginald Horsman, *The Frontier in the Formative Years, 1783–1815* (New York: Holt, 1970), 24.

30. "Agreement Between the Commissioners of the Commonwealth of Massachusetts and the Commissioners of the State of New York, 16 December 1786," New York State Archives, Albany, New York; Taylor, *Divided Ground*, 178.

31. The bond is reprinted in Blake McKelvey, "Historical Aspects of the Phelps & Gorham Treaty of July 4–8, 1788," *Rochester History*, 1 (January 1939), 20; Wallace, *Death and Rebirth*, 154; Taylor, *Divided Ground*, 177.

32. Taylor, *Divided Ground*, 178; Abler, *Cornplanter*, 80–82.

33. The "Agreement Between the Commissioners of the Commonwealth of Massachusetts and the Commissioners of the State of New York, 16 December 1786," is housed in the New York State Archives in Albany; Notebook containing Copies of Deeds from the Five Nations to Oliver Phelps and Nathaniel Gorham, New York State Library, Albany, NY, Manuscripts, 11274.

34. Tiro, *People of the Standing Stone*, 77; Wonderley, "Good Peter," 258; Taylor, *Divided Ground*, 173.

35. Tiro, *People of the Standing Stone*, 67–72.

36. Assembly Journal, Eleventh Session, p. 74. *Journal of the Senate of the State of New York, at their Eleventh Session, Begun and Holden at Poughkeepsie in Dutchess County the eleventh day of January, 1788* (Poughkeepsie, NY, 1788), 35, 106, 109, 121; "An Act for Directing the Manner of Proving Deeds and Conveyances to be Recorded," February 26, 1788, *New York Session Laws, Eleventh Session*, Chapter 44, p. 689; *New York Session Laws, Eleventh Session*, Chapter 85, pp. 810–811.

37. Hough, ed., *Proceedings*, 223–224, 228–229.

38. Hough, ed., *Proceedings*, 182–183, 191–192.

39. My understanding of Kirkland's role as an interpreter has been influenced by Karim Tiro's fine article, "James Dean in Iroquoia," *New York History*, 80 (October 1999), 391–422.

40. Michael Leroy Oberg, "Good Neighbors: The Onondagas and the Fort Schuyler Treaty of September 1788," *New York History*, 88 (Fall 2007), 391–418.

41. Oberg, "Good Neighbors," 407–408.
42. Oberg, "Good Neighbors," 411–412. Watson's 1791 journal is housed in the Elkanah Watson Papers, New York State Archives, Albany, Accession Number GB 13294, Box 22.
43. Watson Journal.
44. Oberg, "Good Neighbors," 412.
45. Hough, ed., Proceedings, 235; Lehman, "Iroquois Mystique," 544; Wonderley, "Good Peter," 237–276.
46. Prucha, *American Indian Treaties*, 65–66.

Chapter 3
1. Dowd, *Spirited Resistance*, 91–95.
2. ASPIA, 1: 8–9.
3. Abler, *Cornplanter*, 87; Taylor, *Divided Ground*, 115.
4. Governor of the Western Territories to Henry Knox, July 18, 1788, PCC, in IIM, 39; Taylor, *Divided Ground*, 134.
5. Calloway, *Crown and Calumet*, 13; Jerald A. Combs, *The Jay Treaty: Political Battleground of the Founding Fathers* (Berkeley: University of California Press, 1970), 11.
6. Samuel Flagg Bemis, *Jay's Treaty: A Study in Commerce and Diplomacy* (New Haven: Yale University Press, 1962), 15; Calloway, *Crown and Calumet*, 16–17; Joseph D. Ibbotson, "Samuel Kirkland, the Treaty of 1792, and the Indian Barrier State," *New York History*, 4 (October 1938), 375; Taylor, *Divided Ground*, 114.
7. William A. Starna, "'The United States will Protect You': The Iroquois, New York, and the 1790 Nonintercourse Act," *New York History*, 83 (Winter 2002), 10; Knox to Washington, May 23, 1789, ASPIA 1: 7–8.
8. Banner, *How the Indians Lost Their Land*, 133; Taylor, *Divided Ground*, 247–248; Abler, *Cornplanter*, 78–79; Wallace, *Death and Rebirth*, 171.
9. Francis Paul Prucha, *The Great Father: The American Indian and the United States*, 2 vols. (Lincoln, NE, 1984), 89. See also Jack Campisi and William A. Starna, "On the Road to Canandaigua: The Treaty of 1794," *American Indian Quarterly*, 19 (Autumn 1995), 471.
10. On the trade and intercourse acts generally, see Francis Paul Prucha, *American Indian Policy in the Formative Years: The Indian Trade and Intercourse Acts, 1790–1834* (Cambridge, MA: Harvard University Press, 1962).
11. Ibid.
12. George Washington to Alexander Hamilton, April 4, 1791, in *The Writings of George Washington*, John C. Fitzpatrick, ed. (Washington, DC, 1931–1940), 31: 273–274.

13. George Washington, Third Annual Message to Congress, October 25, 1791, in Francis Paul Prucha, ed., *Documents of United States Indian Policy*, 3rd edition (Lincoln: University of Nebraska Press, 2000), 15–16.

14. Good Peter quoted in Dorothy V. Jones, *License for Empire: Colonialism by Treaty in Early America* (Chicago, IL: University of Chicago Press, 1982), 185; Wonderley, "Good Peter's Narrative," 240, Fenton, *Great Law*, 648.

15. Petition from Cornplanter and Others to the Great Council of the Quaker State of Pennsylvania, March 2, 1790, Historical Society of Pennsylvania, Yi 7313 F4, IIM 40.

16. Taylor, *Divided Ground*, 235–236.

17. Taylor, *Divided Ground*, 236.

18. Copy of a Petition from Robert King for Compensation for his Services, February 5, 1791, HSP, in IIM 40.

19. Taylor, *Divided Ground*, 236; Edward Hake Phillips, "Timothy Pickering at his Best: Indian Commissioner, 1790–1794," *Essex Institute Historical Collections*, 102 (July 1966), 165.

20. Phillips, "Pickering," 166; Gerard Clarfield, *Timothy Pickering and the American Republic* (Pittsburgh, PA: University of Pittsburgh Press, 1980), 117.

21. Paul B. Moyer, "'A Dangerous Combination of Villains': Pennsylvania's Wild Yankees and the Social Context of Agrarian Resistance in Early America," *Pennsylvania History*, 73 (Winter 2006), 37–68.

22. Timothy Pickering to John Pickering, September 7, 1790, Timothy Pickering Papers, Massachusetts Historical Society, Boston, MA, 35: 97; Clarfield, *Pickering*, 117.

23. George Washington to Timothy Pickering, September 4, 1790, TPP.

24. Timothy Pickering to [?] King, September 4, 1790, Timothy Pickering to Seneca Chiefs, September 4, 1790; Timothy Pickering to George Washington, September 5, 1790, all in TPP.

25. B. Seeley and others to Timothy Pickering, September 28, 1790, TPP.

26. Timothy Pickering, Journal, TPP; Clarfield, *Pickering*, 118.

27. Knox quoted in Prucha, *American Indian Treaties*, 89.

28. Dowd, *Spirited Resistance*, 106; Ryan Staude, "Forging the Eagle's Sword: President Washington, the Congress, and the Army," *White House Studies*, 9 (no. 2, 2009), 100; Michael F. Conlin and Robert M. Owens, "Bigger than Little Bighorn: Nomenclature, Memory and the Greatest Native American Victory over the United States," *Ohio Valley History*, 12 (June 2012), 5.

29. Timothy Pickering Journal, December 23, 1790, TPP 61: 42–44, 56–57, 103–103v.

30. "A Further Report of the Proceedings with the Indians, at a Council Held at Tioga, November 1790," TPP 61: 111–114v; Timothy Pickering Journal, 61: 46; and Taylor *Divided Ground*, 244–245.

31. Philips, "Timothy Pickering," 169.

32. Timothy Pickering, Speech to Indians, November 15, 1790, TPP 61: 61–64. IIM.

33. Christopher Densmore, *Red Jacket: Iroquois Diplomat and Orator* (Syracuse, NY: Syracuse University Press, 1999), 31–32; Granville Ganter, "'Make your Minds Perfectly Easy': Sagoyewatha and the Great Law of the Haudenosaunee," *Early American Literature*, 44 (January 2009), 125, 129.

34. Red Jacket speech, November 15, 1790, TPP 61: 61–64. IIM.

35. Red Jacket speech, November 15, 1790, in Granville Ganter, ed., *The Collected Speeches of Sagoyewatha, or Red Jacket* (Syracuse, NY: Syracuse University Press, 2006), 2–4.

36. Council Minutes, TPP 61: 61–64.

37. Red Jacket speech, November 19, 1790, in Ganter, ed., *Collected Speeches*, 5.

38. Red Jacket speech, November 19, 1790, in Ganter, ed., *Collected Speeches*, 7–8.

39. Timothy Pickering speech, November 22, 1790, TPP 61: 92–92v. IIM 40.

40. Timothy Pickering speech, November 22, 1790, TPP 61: 106–106v.

41. Taylor, *Divided Ground*, 246–248; Wallace, *Death and Rebirth*, 163–164; Daniel K. Richter, "Onas, the Long Knife: Pennsylvanians and Indians, 1783–1794," in *Native Americans and the Early Republic*, Frederick E. Hoxie, Ronald Hoffman, and Peter J. Albert, eds. (Charlottesville: University Press of Virginia, 1990), 131–133.

42. Pennsylvania Provincial Council Minutes, October 23, 1790, 16: 504–507, in IIM; Abler, *Cornplanter*, 80.

43. Pennsylvania Provincial Council Minutes, October 30, 1790, 16: 507–508. IIM.

44. Henry Knox to George Clinton, December 2, 1790, in Hough, ed., *Proceedings*, 465–466; Abler, *Cornplanter*, 80–81.

45. Speech of Cornplanter, Great Tree, and Half Town, December 1, 1790, ASPIA 1: 140.

46. Ibid.
47. Ibid.
48. Speech of Cornplanter, Great Tree, and Half Town, December 1, 1790, ASPIA 1: 141.
49. Speech of Cornplanter, Great Tree, and Half Town, December 1, 1790, ASPIA 1: 142.
50. Ibid.
51. Speech of Cornplanter, Great Tree, and Half Town, December 1, 1790, ASPIA 1: 142–143; Speech of Knox to Cornplanter and Others, *Proceedings*, Hough, ed., 468.
52. Speech of Cornplanter, Half Town, and Great Tree, January 10, 1791, Pennsylvania Archives, Series 2, p. 633, IIM.
53. Speech of Cornplanter, Half Town, and Great Tree, January 10, 1791, Pennsylvania Archives, Series 2, p. 634.
54. Speech of Cornplanter, Half Town, and Great Tree, January 10, 1791, Pennsylvania Archives, Series 2, pp. 634–636.
55. George Washington, Reply to Cornplanter's Second Speech, January 19, 1791, ASPIA 1: 144.
56. Speech of Cornplanter, Half-Town, and Great Tree, February 7, 1791, Pennsylvania Archives, Series 2, 637–638, IIM.
57. Message from Cornplanter, March 17, 1791, ASPIA 1: 145.

Chapter 4

1. Timothy Pickering to Samuel Hodgdon, February 28, 1791, TPP 35: 109–110.
2. Henry Knox to George Clinton, April 12, 1791, ASPIA 1: 167.
3. Densmore, *Red Jacket*, 34.
4. Isabel Thompson Kelsay, *Joseph Brant, 1743–1807* (Syracuse, NY: Syracuse University Press, 1984), 444.
5. Speech of the Seneca Young King, May 21, 1791, TPP 61: 220–223v; Red Jacket, Speech of May 15, 1791, in Ganter, ed., *Collected Speeches*, 17–21.
6. Kelsay, *Joseph Brant*, 445–446.
7. George Clinton to Henry Knox, April 27, 1791, ASPIA 1: 167.
8. Henry Knox to George Clinton, May 11, 1791, ASPIA 1: 168.
9. Timothy Pickering to Brothers, Sachems, and Warriors of the Six Nations, April 17, 1791, TPP Volume 60; Timothy Pickering to General Israel Chapin, April 17, 1791, TPP 60: 58–59, IIM.
10. Henry Knox to Timothy Pickering, May 2, 1791, TPP Volume 60, IIM.
11. Ibid.

12. Timothy Pickering to Sachems, Chiefs and Warriors of the Six Nations, May 9, 1791, TPP 60: 65–66; Timothy Pickering to Henry Knox, May 12, 1791, TPP 61: 191–192v, IIM.

13. Joseph Sansom to Parents, July 4, 1791, Quaker Collection, Haverford College Library, IIM.

14. Pickering Journal, Newtown Point Treaty, June 20–29, 1791, TPP 60: 69–77, IIM.

15. Ibid.

16. Ibid., Sansom Journal, IIM.

17. Ibid.

18. Phillips, "Timothy Pickering at His Best," 175; Densmore, *Red Jacket*, 36; Thomas Morris, "Mr. Morris's Recollections of Hamilton," Before 1849, Ontario County Historical Society, Box M–2, 1954.11.

19. Red Jacket, Speech to Pickering at Newtown, July 10, 1791, Ganter, ed., *Collected Speeches*, 24; Morris, "Recollection of Hamilton."

20. Red Jacket, Speech to Pickering at Newtown, July 10, 1791, Ganter, ed., *Collected Speeches*, 23–24.

21. Red Jacket, Speech to Pickering at Newtown, July 10, 1791, Ganter, ed., *Collected Speeches*, 26–27.

22. Timothy Pickering, Speech to the Six Nations, July 13, 1791, TPP 60: 60–67, IIM.

23. Phillips, "Pickering at his Best," 175–177; Timothy Pickering to Cornplanter and New Arrow, July 17, 1791, TOO 60: 62. IIM

24. Dowd, *Spirited Resistance*; Kelsay, *Joseph Brant*, 452.

25. Wallace, *Death and Rebirth*, 160; Staude, "Forging the Eagle's Sword," 97; Conlin and Owens, "Bigger than Little Bighorn," 6.

26. Dowd, *Spirited Resistance*, 106–107; Conlin and Owens, "Bighorn," 10; Christopher Dorsey, "St. Clair's Defeat Revisited: Evolution of Woodland Native American Battlefield Tactics," *Canadian Journal of Native Studies*, 32 (no. 1, 2012), 79–85.

27. Dowd, *Spirited Resistance*, 106–107; Conlin and Owens, "Bighorn," 7; Thomas Mifflin to the President of the United States, December 22, 1791, ASPIA 1: 215; Judah Colt to Oliver Phelps, January 16, 1792; Othniel Taylor to Oliver Phelps, January 15, 1792, both quoted in Herbert Siles, "A Vision of Wealth: Speculators and Settlers in the Genesee Country of New York, 1788–1800" (Ph.D. diss., University of Massachusetts, 1978), 162.

28. Ibbotson, "Indian Barrier State," 376; Colin G. Calloway, *The Shawnees and the War for America* (New York: Penguin, 2007), 94–95.

29. Henry Knox to Cornplanter, January 17, 1792, ASPIA 1: 226; Henry Knox to Samuel Kirkland, December 20, 1791, ASPIA 1: 226.

30. Henry Knox to Samuel Kirkland, December 20, 1791, Kirkland Papers, Burke Library, Hamilton College, IIM; Knox to Kirkland, January 7, 1792, Kirkland Papers, Burke Library, Hamilton College, IIM.

31. Ibbitson, "Kirkland," 382; Taylor, *Divided Ground*, 271; Henry Knox to New Arrow, Cornplanter, Big Log and Others, February 10, 1792, ASPIA 1: 228; Henry Knox to Joseph Brant, February 25, 1792, ASPIA 1: 228.

32. Samuel Kirkland to Henry Knox, February 6, 1792, Kirkland Papers, Hamilton College, IIM.

33. Kelsay, *Joseph Brant*, 458–459.

34. Lehman, "Iroquois Mystique," 523–524; Fenton, *Great Law*, 642.

35. Timothy Pickering to Col. Hamilton, May 8, 1792, TPP 35: 151–151v, IIM; Clarfield, *Timothy Pickering*, 134.

36. Clarfield, *Timothy Pickering*, 134–135; Phillips, "Pickering at his Best," 179.

37. Timothy Pickering to George Washington, March 21, 1792, TPP 62: 11–12v. IIM.

38. Philips, "Pickering at his Best," 179.

39. George Washington to the Chiefs and Representatives of the Five Nations in Philadelphia, March 23, 1792, ASPIA 1: 229; George Washington to the United States Senate, March 26, 1792, ASPIA 1: 225.

40. Abler, ed., *Chainbreaker*, 184; Densmore, *Red Jacket*, 37; Wonderley, "Good Peter's Narrative," 239; Clarfield, *Pickering*, 136. The original medal is housed at the Buffalo and Erie County Historical Society in Buffalo, New York.

41. Red Jacket, Speech to Washington, March 31, 1792, in Ganter, ed., *Collected Speeches*, 34–35.

42. Red Jacket, Speech to Washington, March 31, 1792, in Ganter, ed., *Collected Speeches*, 36.

43. Red Jacket, Speech to Washington, March 31, 1792, in Ganter, ed., *Collected Speeches*, 42.

44. Red Jacket, Speech to Washington, March 31, 1792, in Ganter, ed., *Collected Speeches*, 43.

45. Clarfield, *Timothy Pickering*, 136; Taylor, *Divided Ground*, 273; Henry Knox to Israel Chapin, March 29, 1792, O'Reilly Papers, New York Historical Society, IIM.

46. Henry Knox, Instructions for Israel Chapin, April 25, 1792, Kirkland Papers, Hamilton College, IIM.

47. Clarfield, *Pickering*, 133.
48. Fenton, *Great Law*, 639–641; Kelsay, *Joseph Brant*, 457.
49. Henry Knox to Joseph Brant, June 27, 1792, Northwest Territory Papers, Clements Library, University of Michigan, IIM; Israel Chapin, Jr. to unidentified recipient, June 23, 1792, O'Reilly Papers, New York Historical Society, IIM.
50. Henry Knox to Joseph Brant, June 27, 1792, Northwest Territory Papers, Clements Library, University of Michigan, IIM.
51. Ibid.

Chapter 5

1. Abler, *Cornplanter*, 92.
2. Henry Knox to Hendrick Aupaumut, May 8, 1792, ASPIA 1: 233.
3. Israel Chapin to Henry Knox, June 17, 1792, ASPIA 1: 242.
4. Hendrick Aupaumut to Timothy Pickering, December 11, 1792, TPP 59: 26–27, IIM; Hendrick Aupaumut, Speech in Behalf of the United States to the Western Indians, July 16, 1792, Henry O'Reilly Papers, New York Historical Society, IIM.
5. Timothy Pickering, Speech to the Chiefs of the Five Nations, April 30, 1792, ASPIA 1: 232–233; Chiefs of the Six Nations to Israel Chapin, August 1, 1792, Henry O'Reilly Papers, New York Historical Society, IIM.
6. Abler, *Cornplanter*, 90–91; Fenton, *Great Law and the Longhouse*, 645–646.
7. Wallace, *Death and Rebirth*, 164; Dowd, *Spirited Resistance*, 103.
8. Red Jacket, Speech at the Glaize, 1792, in Ganter, ed., *Collected Speeches*, 46–47.
9. Minutes of the Indian Council at the Glaize, September 30, 1792, Simcoe Papers, Clements Library, University of Michigan, IIM; Calloway, *The Shawnees*, 96–97; Timothy D. Willig, *Restoring the Chain of Friendship: British Policy and the Indians of the Great Lakes, 1783–1815* (Lincoln: University of Nebraska Press, 2008), 41–43.
10. Ganter, ed., *Collected Speeches*, 49; Wallace, *Death and Rebirth*, 164; Abler, *Cornplanter*, 94.
11. Lehman, "The End of the Iroquois Mystique," 524–525; Dowd, *Spirited Resistance*, 103–104.
12. George Washington, Fourth Annual Message, November 6, 1792, In *Messages and Papers of the Presidents*, comp. James P. Richardson (Washington, DC: GPO, 1899), 1: 125–126.
13. Abler, *Cornplanter*, 92–93; Fenton, *Great Law and the Longhouse*, 638.

14. Instructions to Lincoln, Randolph and Pickering, ASPIA, 1: 340.
15. Instructions to Lincoln, Randolph and Pickering, ASPIA, 1: 341.
16. Ibid.
17. Reginald Horsman, "The British Indian Department and the Abortive Treaty of Lower Sandusky, 1793," *Ohio Historical Quarterly*, 70 (July 1961), 192–195.
18. Commissioners' Journal, April 30, 1793, ASPIA 1: 342; Timothy Pickering to Major Craig, May 26, 1793, TPP, 60: 239; Timothy Pickering to Henry Knox, May 27, 1793, TPP, 60: 240.
19. Taylor, *Divided Ground*, 281–282.
20. Willig, *Chain of Friendship*, 48–53.
21. Commissioners' Journal, ASPIA, 1: 346.
22. James Monroe to Thomas Jefferson, June 13, 1793, *The Papers of Thomas Jefferson*, ed. John Catanzares (Princeton, NJ: Princeton University Press, 1995), 26: 275; Thomas Jefferson to James Monroe, June 28, 1793, *The Papers of Thomas Jefferson*, ed. Catanzares, 26: 393; Clarfield, *Timothy Pickering*, 139.
23. Timothy Pickering to Rev. John Clarke, July 10, 1793, TPP, 35: 175–176, IIM; Clarfield, *Timothy Pickering*, 141.
24. Horsman, "British Indian Department," 196–197; Commissioners to Henry Knox, June 20, 1793, ASPIA 1: 348.
25. Commissioners' Speech to Confederated Indian Nations, July 31, 1793, ASPIA 1: 353.
26. Message from the Western Indians to the Commissioners of the United States, August 13, 1793, *Simcoe Papers* 2: 17–20, IIM.
27. Ibid.
28. Clarfield, *Timothy Pickering*, 144.
29. David Paul Nelson, *Anthony Wayne: Soldier of the Early Republic* (Bloomington: Indiana University Press, 1985), 228–243.
30. ASPIA, 1: 477; Copy of Proceedings of Council of Six Nations at Buffalo Creek, Wayne Papers, Historical Society of Pennsylvania, October 8–10, 1793, IIM.
31. Proposed Boundary Line, ca. October 10, 1793, Simcoe Papers, 2: 86, IIM; Campisi and Starna, "On the Road to Canandaigua," 475–476.
32. ASPIA, 1: 478–479.
33. Captain Abeel to Israel Chapin, O'Reilly Papers, NYHS, IIM; ASPIA 1: 480.
34. Anthony Wayne speech to Six Nations, March 26, 1794, *Simcoe Papers*, 2: 195–196.

35. Israel Chapin to Henry Knox, April 29, 1794, ASPIA 1: 480; Clarfield, *Timothy Pickering*, 148; Fenton, *Great Law and the Longhouse*, 645.

36. John Cantine and Simeon DeWitt to Governor George Clinton, ca. November 1793, New York State Legislative Assembly Papers, 40: 142–143, New York State Archives, Albany, NY; Oberg, "Good Neighbors," 390–417.

37. John Cantine and Simeon DeWitt to Governor George Clinton, ca. November 1793, New York State Legislative Assembly Papers, 40: 146–147; Copy of Treaty Between the Onondagas and State of New York, November 18, 1793, New York State Archives, Indian Treaties, 2: 199.

38. Copy of Minutes of a Conference with the Oneidas, Onondagas, and Cayugas at Albany, February 13–15, 1794, Legislative Assembly Papers, 40: 167–190. New York State Archives, Albany, NY.

39. Ibid.

40. Israel Chapin to Henry Knox, June 26, 1794, O'Reilly Papers, NYHS, IIM; Proceedings of a Council held at Buffalo Creek, June 18, 1794, Simcoe Papers, 2: 272–273.

41. Simcoe Papers, 2: 273; ASPIA, 1: 521; Wallace, *Death and Rebirth*, 166–167; Abler, *Cornplanter*, 100.

42. Simcoe Papers, 2: 274; Campisi and Starna, "Road to Canandaigua," 478.

43. Henry Knox to Thomas Mifflin, June 14, 1794, ASPIA, 1: 519; Proceedings of a Council Held at Buffalo Creek, June 18 & July 4, 1794, Simcoe Papers, 2: 275.

44. "John Adlum on the Allegheny: Memoirs for the Year 1794, Part 1," eds. Donald H. Kent and Merle H. Deardorff, *Pennsylvania Magazine of History and Biography*, 84 (July 1960), 303–306.

45. Henry Knox to Thomas Mifflin, June 17, 1794, ASPIA 1: 522; Thomas Mifflin to Henry Knox, July 18, 1794, and July 22, 1794, ASPIA 1: 517–518.

Chapter 6

1. The positions in this debate are ably drawn by Dowd in *Spirited Resistance*.

2. General Wilkinson to Governor Mifflin, May 11, 1794, ASPIA, 1: 505.

3. Lt. Polhemus to General Gibson, June 9, 1794, ASPIA 1: 571.

4. General Gibson to Governor Mifflin, June 20, 1794, ASPIA, 1: 514; A. Ellicott and E. Denny to General Gibson, June 8, 1794, ASPIA, 1: 510; "Extract of a Letter from Captain Denny," June 14, 1794, ASPIA, 1: 514.

5. Petition from Ontario County, May 5, 1794, Legislative Assembly Papers, Correspondence, Petitions and Reports on the Defense of the Frontier, Onondaga Salt Springs, and other Subjects, 1791–1830, New York State Archives, A1827, Frame 9; Henry Knox to George Clinton, May 20, 1794, Legislative Assembly Papers, Correspondence, Petitions and Reports on the Defense of the Frontier, Onondaga Salt Springs, and other Subjects, 1791–1830, New York State Archives, A1827, Frames 25–26.

6. James Roger Sharp, *American Politics in the Early Republic: The New Nation on Trial* (New Haven, CT: Yale University Press, 1993), 69–91; Jeffrey L. Pasley, *The First Presidential Contest: 1796 and the Founding of American Democracy* (Lawrence: University Press of Kansas, 2013), 102.

7. Kelsay, *Joseph Brant*, 469.

8. Nelson, *Anthony Wayne*, 252–253.

9. Nelson, *Anthony Wayne*, 254, 257–258, 261.

10. Israel Chapin, Speech to Six Nations, August 15, 1794, Henry O'Reilly Papers, NYHS, IIM; Timothy Pickering to Israel Chapin, August 16, 1794, Henry O'Reilly Papers, NYHS, IIM.

11. Israel Chapin to Henry Knox, August 12, 1794, O'Reilly Papers, NYHS.

12. Dowd, *Spirited Resistance*, 113; Calloway, *Crown and Calumet*, 195.

13. Dowd, *Spirited Resistance*, 113.

14. Dowd, *Spirited Resistance*, 111–112.

15. Fenton, *Great Law and the Longhouse*, 660; Thomas Morris to unknown, September 20, 1794, NYSL, Mss. 11203, IIM.

16. Fenton, *Great Law and the Longhouse*, 660; William N. Fenton, "The Journal James Emlen Kept on a Trip to Canandaigua, New York," *Ethnohistory*, 12 (Autumn 1965), 285; Karim M. Tiro, "'We Wish to do you Good': The Quaker Mission to the Oneida Nation, 1790–1840," *Journal of the Early Republic*, 26 (Fall 2006), 356–357; Frederick B. Tolles, "Nonviolent Contact: The Quakers and the Indians," *Proceedings of the American Philosophical Society*, 107 (April 1963), 98–99.

17. Fenton, ed., "Emlen Journal," 285–287; Journal of William Savery, in *A Journal of the Life, Travels and Religious Labors of William Savery, Late of Philadelphia*, comp. Jonathan Evans (London: Charles Gilpin, 1844), 55–56.

18. Fenton, ed., "Emlen Journal," 288–289.

19. Fenton, ed., "Emlen Journal," 291–292.

20. Thomas Morris to unknown, September 20, 1794, NYSL, Mss. 11203; Timothy Pickering to Henry Knox, September 20, 1794, TPP, 60: 201; Timothy Pickering to Henry Knox, October 8, 1794, TPP, 60: 203a; Clarfield, *Timothy Pickering*, 149.

21. Timothy J. Shannon, *Iroquois Diplomacy on the Early American Frontier* (New York: Penguin, 2008), 207–208.

22. Savery Journal, 57; Timothy Pickering to Henry Knox, September 27, 1794, TPP 60: 202.

23. Fenton, ed., "Emlen Journal," 289–290.

24. Fenton, ed., "Emlen Journal," 290–291; Savery Journal, 57; David Bacon's Journal of the Treaty of Canandaigua, Haverford College Library, Quaker Collection, IIM.

25. Fenton, ed., "Emlen Journal," 291; Savery Journal, 59.

26. Herbert A. Wisbey, *Pioneer Prophetess: Jemima Wilkinson, the Publick Universal Friend*, (Ithaca, NY: Cornell University Press, 1964), 111–119; Edwin B. Bronner, "Quakers Labor with Jemima Wilkinson, 1794," *Quaker History*, 58 (Spring 1969), 42; Stanley J. Thayne, "Walking on Water: Nineteenth Century Prophets and a Legend of Religious Imposture," *Journal of Mormon History*, 36 (Spring 2010), 168.

27. Savery Journal, 58–59; Fenton, ed., "Emlen Journal," 293–294.

28. Fenton, ed., "Emlen Journal," 296–297.

29. Fenton, ed., "Emlen Journal," 297–298.

30. Timothy Pickering, Document about Treaty of Canandaigua, TPP 60: 217; Fenton, *Great Law and the Longhouse*, 669.

31. Pickering, Document about Treaty of Canandaigua, TPP 60: 219.

32. Pickering, Document about Treaty of Canandaigua, TPP 60: 220.

33. Fenton, ed., "Emlen Journal," 299–300; Savery Journal, 61.

34. Pickering, Document about Treaty of Canandaigua, TPP 60: 224–226.

35. Pickering, Document about Treaty of Canandaigua, TPP 60: 226–227.

36. Ibid.; Savery Journal, 62–63.

37. Savery Journal, 64; Fenton, "Emlen Journal," 301; Fenton, *Great Law and the Longhouse*, 669.

38. Savery Journal, 64–65.

39. Fenton, *Great Law and the Longhouse*, 630. For Iroquois population figures, see the estimates made by Pickering and housed in the Jasper Parrish Papers at Vassar College, and included in the IIM.

Chapter 7

1. Savery Journal, 65.
2. Fenton, *Great Law and the Longhouse*, 631–632.
3. Fenton, *Great Law and the Longhouse*, 675; Taylor, *Divided Ground*, 290; Densmore, *Red Jacket*, 43; Richter, "Onas, The Long Knife," 159.
4. Savery Journal, 65–66; Fenton, ed., "Emlen Journal," 302.
5. Savery Journal, 66; Fenton, ed., "Emlen Journal," 302–303.
6. Savery Journal, 67; Fenton, ed., "Emlen Journal," 303–304.
7. Fenton, ed., "Emlen Journal," 304; Savery Journal, 67–68.
8. Fenton, ed., "Emlen Journal," 304–305; Savery Journal, 67–68.
9. Savery Journal, 67–68; David Bacon's Journal of the Treaty of Canandaigua, Haverford College Library, Quaker Collection September 15–November 21, 1794, IIM; E. W. Vanderhoof, *Historical Sketches of New York* (Buffalo, NY: The Matthews-Northrup Works, 1907), 114; Phillips, "Timothy Pickering at his Best," 196.
10. Bacon Journal, IIM; Fenton, ed., "Emlen Journal," 305; Savery Journal, 69.
11. Fenton, ed., "Emlen Journal," 305–306.
12. Ibid.
13. Fenton, ed., "Emlen Journal," 307–308.
14. Fenton, ed., "Emlen Journal," 308; Bacon Journal, IIM.
15. Savery Journal, 71; Fenton, ed., "Emlen Journal," 308; Bacon Journal, IIM.
16. Savery Journal, 71–72; Fenton, ed., "Emlen Journal," 308–309.
17. John Graves Simcoe to Alexander McKee, November 1794, Simcoe Papers, IIM; Timothy Pickering, Document about Treaty of Canandaigua, TPP 60: 234–236, IIM.
18. Timothy Pickering, Document about Treaty of Canandaigua, TPP 60: 236–241, IIM; Fenton, ed., "Emlen Journal," 309–310.
19. Fenton, ed., "Emlen Journal," 310; Henry O'Beale to Joseph Brant, October 25, 1794, Simcoe Papers, 3: 154; Timothy Pickering to Henry Knox, October 28, 1794, TPP 60: 206a.
20. Savery Journal, 74; Fenton, ed., "Emlen Journal," 312–313.
21. Fenton, ed., "Emlen Journal," 312–313; Savery Journal, 74–75.
22. Savery Journal, 76.
23. Ibid.
24. Ibid.
25. Fenton, ed., "Emlen Journal," 314–315.
26. Bacon Journal, IIM; Savery Journal, 79–80.
27. Savery Journal, 80–81.

28. Savery Journal, 81.
29. Savery Journal, 81–82.
30. Savery Journal, 82–83.
31. Savery Journal, 83.
32. Savery Journal, 84.
33. Savery Journal, 84–85.
34. Savery Journal, 85–86.
35. Savery Journal, 86.
36. Savery Journal, 87–88.
37. Savery Journal, 88.
38. Savery Journal, 89.
39. Savery Journal, 89–90.
40. Savery Journal, 90–91; Timothy Pickering to Henry Knox, November 7, 1794, TPP 60: 206–206a; Fenton, *Great Law and the Longhouse*, 695–696.
41. Savery Journal, 91.
42. Savery Journal, 91–92; David Bacon Journal, IIM.
43. Savery Journal, 93–94.
44. Savery Journal, 94–96; David Bacon Journal, IIM; Fenton, *Great Law and the Longhouse*, 700.
45. Fenton, *Great Law and the Longhouse*, 701.
46. David Bacon Journal, IIM; Savery Journal, 96; Timothy Pickering to Henry Knox, November 12, 1794, TPP 60: 208–209.
47. Savery Journal, 97–98; David Bacon Journal, IIM.
48. Kappler, *Treaties*, 2: 37–39; Phillips, "Timothy Pickering at his Best," 199.

Chapter 8
1. Kappler, comp., *Treaties*, 34; Senate Executive Journal, 3rd Congress, January 2 and 9, 1795, pp. 168, 170.
2. Timothy Pickering, Report on Frontier Affairs, January 1795, ASPIA 1: 547.
3. Kappler, comp., *Treaties*, 35; Fenton, *Great Law and the Longhouse*, 625.
4. Kappler, comp., *Treaties*, 35; Timothy Pickering to Henry Knox, November 12, 1794, TPP 60: 209.
5. Kappler, comp., *Treaties*, 35.
6. Kappler, comp., *Treaties*, 36.
7. Ibid.
8. Ibid.

9. Alexander De Conde, *Entangling Alliances: Politics and Diplomacy under George Washington* (Durham, NC: Duke University Press, 1958), 105–111. On impressment, see Denver Brunsman, "Subjects v. Citizens: Impressment and Identity in the Anglo-American Atlantic," *Journal of the Early Republic*, 30 (Winter 2010), 537–586.

10. The text of Jay's Treaty is available at Yale University Law School's Avalon Project website. See http://www.yale.edu/lawweb/avalon/avalon.htm.

11. Ibid.

12. The Treaty of Ghent is available at Yale University Law School's Avalon Project website. See http://www.yale.edu/lawweb/avalon/avalon.htm; See also Mary E. Fleming Mathur, "The Jay Treaty and Boundary Line," *Indian Historian*, 3 (1970), 37.

13. Clinton Rickard, *Fighting Tuscarora: The Autobiography of Chief Clinton Rickard*, ed. Barbara Graymont (Syracuse, NY: Syracuse University Press, 1973), 68–89.

14. Sharp, *American Politics in the Early Republic*, 117.

15. Richard C. Knopf, ed., *Anthony Wayne, A Name in Arms: Solider, Diplomat, Defender of Expansion Westward of a Nation: The Wayne-Knox-Pickering-McHenry Correspondence* (Pittsburgh, PA: University of Pittsburgh Press, 1960), 393–403.

16. *Indian Affairs*, 39–40; Calloway, *The Shawnees*, 106–108.

17. Timothy Pickering to the Six Nations, January 22, 1795, National Archives of Canada, Superintendent General's Office, 1791–1828, available at "Papers of the War Department, 1784–1800" (www.wardepartmentpapers.org), accessed March 8, 2014; Timothy Pickering to Israel Chapin, Jr., April 6, 1795, Henry O'Reilly Papers, NYHS, IIM.

18. Fenton, *Great Law and the Longhouse*, 631; Robert W. Venables, "Some Observations on the Treaty of Canandaigua," in *Treaty of Canandaigua*, eds. Jemison and Schein, 91; and Daniel K. Richter, "The States, The United States, and the Canandaigua Treaty," in *Treaty of Canandaigua*, eds. Jemison and Schein, 81–82.

19. Timothy Pickering to Israel Chapin, Jr., June 29, 1795, O'Reilly Papers, NYHS, IIM.

20. Israel Chapin, Jr., to Timothy Pickering, July 31, 1795, O'Reilly Papers, NYHS, IIM.

21. Ibid.; and Laurence M. Hauptman, *Conspiracy of Interests: Iroquois Dispossession and the Rise of New York State* (Syracuse, NY: Syracuse University Press, 1997), 80–81.

22. James Stirling Young, *The Washington Community, 1800–1828* (New York, 1966), 29; Leonard D. White, *The Federalists: A Study in Administrative History, 1789–1801* (New York, 1948), 256.

23. Francis Paul Prucha, *American Indian Policy in the Formative Years: The Indian Trade and Intercourse Acts, 1790–1834* (Cambridge, MA: Harvard University Press, 1962), 48, 186.

24. On the Onondaga cessions, see Oberg, "Good Neighbors"; Lehman, "The End of the Iroquois Mystique," 523–547; Hauptman, *Conspiracy of Interests*; and Tiro, *People of the Standing Stone.*

25. Charles E. Brooks, *Frontier Settlement and the Market Revolution: The Holland Land Purchase* (Ithaca, NY: Cornell University Press, 1996), 13–14; Wallace, *Death and Rebirth,* 179–180.

26. Wallace, *Death and Rebirth,* 179–183; Taylor, *Divided Ground,* 313–316; Hauptman, *Conspiracy of Interests,* 91–92; Norman B. Wilkinson, "Robert Morris and the Treaty of Big Tree," *Mississippi Valley Historical Review,* 40 (September 1953), 257–278.

27. Kappler, comp., *Treaties,* 1028.

28. Oliver Forward to James Barbour, September 2, 1826, LR OIA, Seneca Agency, frames 21–22. The size of the cession was closer to 44% of the Senecas' remaining lands.

29. Hauptman, *Conspiracy of Interests,* 81–82, 84, 86, 89. See also the Opinion of the Indian Claims Commission, Docket 342-A, 368-A, October 24, 1963, ICC Materials, Paul G. Reilly Collection, Buffalo State College, Buffalo, New York, Box 27, Document 81, pp. 12–13. Depositions collected by R. W. Livingston at Buffalo, and supportive of the federal government's position that the Senecas received no threats and were not coerced, can be found in the Reilly Collection, Box 47, Document 3.

Chapter 9

1. On Oneida removal, Michael Leroy Oberg, *Professional Indian: The American Odyssey of Eleazer Williams* (Philadelphia: University of Pennsylvania Press, 2015), 49–157

2. Matthew Dennis, *Seneca Possessed: Indians, Witchcraft, and Power in the Early American Republic* (Philadelphia: University of Pennsylvania Press, 2010), 204.

3. The most important study remains Wallace, *Death and Rebirth.*

4. Morgan, *League of the Iroquois,* 223.

5. Morgan, *League of the Iroquois,* 240.

6. Dowd, *Spirited Resistance*, 126–127; Wallace, *Death and Rebirth*, 239–262.

7. Morgan, *League of the Iroquois*, 171–172; Diane Brodatz Rothenberg, "Friends Like These: An Ethnohistorical Analysis of the Interaction between Allegany Senecas and Quakers, 1798–1823" (Ph.D. dissertation, City University of New York, 1976), 175.

8. Minute Book, Philadelphia Yearly Meeting of the Society of Friends, Indian Committee Records, Volume 1, 1795–1818 (Haverford College Library, Haverford, PA), p. 8; David Swatzler, *A Friend among the Senecas: The Quaker Mission to Cornplanter's People* (Mechanicsburg, PA: Stackpole Books, 2000), 13; Abler, *Cornplanter*, 179–180; Lois Barton, *A Quaker Promise Kept: Philadelphia Friends' Work with Allegany Senecas, 1795–1860* (Eugene, OR: Spencer Butte Press, 1990), 1; Anthony F. C. Wallace, ed., "Halliday Jackson's Journal to the Seneca Indians, 1798–1800," *Pennsylvania History*, 19 (April 1952), 128, 132.

9. Minute Book, PYMIC, 1: 16; Conference Minutes, February 28, 1810, PYMIC, Conferences with Indians, 1792–1815, Haverford College.

10. Timothy Pickering to Jasper Parrish, February 15, 1796, Letters to PYMIC, Haverford College; Dennis, *Seneca Possessed*, 119.

11. Dennis, *Seneca Possessed*, 151, 154.

12. Dennis, *Seneca Possessed*, 146–147; Rothenberg, "Friends," 178; Minute Book, PYMIC, 1: 108–109; Committee Members to Cornplanter, February 18, 1801, Minute Book, PYMIC, 1: 141–142; Visit of Gerard Hopkins to Buffalo (1804) in "Narratives of Early Mission Work on the Niagara Frontier and Buffalo Creek," ed. Frank H. Severance, *Collections of the Buffalo and Erie County Historical Society*, 6 (1903), 221; Committee Report, August 21, 1807, Minute Book, PYMIC, 1: 246–247; PYMIC Reports, "For English Friends."

13. Dennis, *Seneca Possessed*, 150–151, 162–163; Joseph Elkinton to PYMIC, March 5, 1821, Letters to PYMIC.

14. Dennis, *Seneca Possessed*, 165; Rothenberg, "Friends," 211, 214.

15. Rothenberg, "Friends," 194–195, 203; Annual Report, PYMIC, April 13, 1826, PYMIC, 2: 197.

16. Rothenberg, "Friends," 198–199; Speech of Senecas Living at Cattaraugus, Historical Society of Pennsylvania, Separate Box, September 25, 1809, IIM.

17. PYMIC, Annual Report for 1818, 2: 54; Statement on Sawmills, M234, R584, LR-OIA-NY, frame 83; Rothenberg, "Friends," 209.

18. Charles E. Congdon, *Allegany Oxbow: A History of Allegany State Park and the Allegany Reserve of the Seneca Nation* (Little Valley, NY:

Straight Publishing Company, 1967), 36–37; Rothenberg, "Friends," 206–207, 185–186; Swatzler, *Friends*, 239–240.

19. Rothenberg, "Friends," 187–188, 208; Swatzler, *Friends*, 241; Dennis, *Seneca Possessed*, 164–165.

20. The story is told best in Hauptman, *Conspiracy of Interests*, 176–190.

21. *Further Proceedings of the Joint Committee Appointed by the Society of Friends, Constituting The Yearly Meetings of Genesee, New York, and Philadelphia, for Promoting the Civilization and Improving the Condition of the Seneca Nation of Indians* (Baltimore, MD: W. Woody and Sons, 1850), 33.

22. New York Session Laws, 68th Session, Chapter 150, enacted May 8, 1845; *Further Proceedings*, 33; Thomas S. Abler, "Factional Dispute and Party Conflict in the Political System of the Seneca Nation (1845–1895): An Ethnohistorical Analysis" (Ph.D. dissertation, University of Toronto, 1969), 103–104; New York Session Laws, 70th Session, Chapter 365, enacted November 15, 1847; *The Statutes at Large and Treaties of the United States*, Volume IX (Boston, MA: Little, Brown and Company, 1862), Chapter LXVI, p. 203; ARCIA, 1846, p. 400.

23. *Further Proceedings*, 19, 70; Conable, "Steady Enemy," 343; Abler, "Factional Dispute," 108–111.

24. Zechariah Jimerson to A. H. H. [Stuart], November 23, 1850, M234 R 587, LR-OIA-NY; Committee of Safety, SNI, to President of the United States, December 20, 1851, M234 R588, LR-OIA-NY; Ely Parker to George H. Manypenny, July 18, 1853, M234 R588, LR-OIA-NY.

25. Seneca Nation of Indians, Council Minutes, March 9, 1878, p. 254; January 9, 1878, pp. 196–197, Seneca Nation of Indians Clerk's Office, Salamanca, NY (hereafter SNI Council Minutes).

26. SNI Council Minutes, February 23, 1876, and March 18–19, 1876, pp. 163–179; December 21, 1881, pp. 195–196; January 4, 1893, p. 4. The law appears in the New York Session Laws, 115th Session, Chapter 679 (1892), pp. 1573–1601.

27. SNI Council Minutes, January 6, 1881, pp. 25–26; SNI Council Minutes, June 2, 1858, p. 266; E. R. Ames to Commissioner of Indian Affairs, July 23, 1869, October 5, 1869, December 28, 1869, and May 22, 1872, in M234 R591, LR-OIA-NY, and Daniel Shaw to Francis A. Walker, May 22, 1872, in M234, R591, LR-OIA-NY.

28. SNI Council Minutes, April 21, 1863; January 14, 1878, pp. 210–211; January 19, 1878, p. 220; March 13, 1883, p. 486; Kassuth Bishop and William Nephew to Carl Schurz, May 6, 1879, M234 R596, LR-OIA-NY.

29. Kappler, comp., *Treaties*, 508.

30. For an example of the sort of census material compiled by federal authorities, see that dated May 3, 1877, in M234 R593, LR-OIA-NY, frames 184–186; SNI Council Minutes, June 16, 1858, p. 279, June 26, 1862, pp. 248–249; D. W. Pierce to Daniel Sherman, December 26, 1876, M234 R594, LR-OIA-NY, frames 399–400; Daniel Sherman to John Q. Smith, January 2, 1877, M234, R. 594, LR-OIA-NY, frame 393.

31. SNI Council Minutes, February 28, 1877, pp. 290–291; March 16, 1877, pp. 315–316.

32. SNI Council Minutes, April 15, 1889, pp. 158–159.

33. Joelle Rostkowski, "The Redman's Appeal for Justice: Deskaheh and the League of Nations," in *Indians and Europe: An Interdisciplinary Collection of Essays*, ed., Christian F. Feest (Lincoln: University of Nebraska Press, 1999), 438.

34. Laurence M. Hauptman, "The Idealist and the Realist: Chief Deskaheh, George Decker, and the Six Nations Struggle to Get to the World Court, 1921–1925," in *Seven Generations of Iroquois Leadership: The Six Nations Since 1800* (Syracuse, NY: Syracuse University Press, 2008), 124–142.

35. Laurence M. Hauptman, *The Iroquois Struggle for Survival: World War II to Red Power* (Syracuse, NY: Syracuse University Press, 1986), 205–207; Rickard, *Fighting Tuscarora*, 65.

36. Reid, *Kahnawake*, 149–150.

37. Hauptman, "Alice Lee Jemison: Seneca Journalist as Activist," in *Seven Generations*, 74–79.

38. Ibid.

39. "Chiefs of Iroquois Tribes Vote to Join War; Call on Six Nations Fight Against the Axis," *New York Times*, June 13, 1942.

Conclusion

1. Keith R. Burich, "'No Place to Go': The Thomas Indian School and the 'Forgotten' Indian Children of New York," *Wicazo Sa Review*, 22 (Fall 2007), 93–110.

2. On Kinzua, see Joy A. Bilharz, *The Allegany Senecas and the Kinzua Dam: Forced Relocation Through Two Generations* (Lincoln: University of Nebraska Press, 1998); Paul A. Rosier, "Dam-Building and Treaty-Breaking: The Kinzua Dam Controversy, 1953–1958," *Pennsylvania Magazine of History and Biography*, 119 (October 1995).

3. N. Bruce Duthu, *American Indians and the Law* (New York: Penguin, 2008), 73–75.

APPENDIX: THE TREATY OF CANANDAIGUA

....

A Treaty between the United States of America, and the Tribes of Indians called the Six Nations.

The President of the United States having determined to hold a conference with the Six Nations of Indians, for the purpose of removing from their minds all causes of complaint, and establishing a firm and permanent friendship with them; and Timothy Pickering being appointed sole agent for that purpose; and the agent having met and conferred with the Sachems, Chiefs and Warriors of the Six Nations, in a general council: Now, in order to accomplish the good design of this conference, the parties have agreed on the following articles; which, when ratified by the President, with the advice and consent of the Senate of the United States, shall be binding on them and the Six Nations.

ARTICLE 1
Peace and friendship are hereby firmly established, and shall be perpetual, between the United States and the Six Nations.

ARTICLE 2
The United States acknowledge the lands reserved to the Oneida, Onondaga and Cayuga Nations, in their respective treaties with the state of New-York, and called their reservations, to be their property; and the United States will never claim the same, nor disturb them or either of the Six Nations, nor their Indian friends residing thereon and united with them, in the free use and enjoyment thereof: but the said reservations shall remain

191

theirs, until they choose to sell the same to the people of the United States, who have the right to purchase.

ARTICLE 3

The land of the Seneka nation is bounded as follows: Beginning on Lake Ontario, at the north-west corner of the land they sold to Oliver Phelps, the line runs westerly along the lake, as far as O-yŏng-wong-yeh Creek, at Johnson's Landing-place, about four miles eastward from the fort of Niagara; then southerly up that creek to its main fork, then straight to the main fork of Stedman's creek, which empties into the river Niagara, above fort Schlosser, and then onward, from that fork, continuing the same straight course, to that river; (this line, from the mouth of O-yŏng-wong-yeh Creek to the river Niagara, above fort Schlosser, being the eastern boundary of a strip of land, extending from the same line to Niagara river, which the Seneka nation ceded to the King of Great-Britain, at a treaty held about thirty years ago, with Sir William Johnson); then the line runs along the river Niagara to Lake Erie; then along Lake Erie to the north-east corner of a triangular piece of land which the United States conveyed to the state of Pennsylvania, as by the President's patent, dated the third day of March, 1792; then due south to the northern boundary of that state; then due east to the south-west corner of the land sold by the Seneka nation to Oliver Phelps; and then north and northerly, along Phelps's line, to the place of beginning on Lake Ontario. Now, the United States acknowledge all the land within the aforementioned boundaries, to be the property of the Seneka nation; and the United States will never claim the same, nor disturb the Seneka nation, nor any of the Six Nations, or of their Indian friends residing thereon and united with them, in the free use and enjoyment thereof: but it shall remain theirs, until they choose to sell the same to the people of the United States, who have the right to purchase.

ARTICLE 4

The United States having thus described and acknowledged what lands belong to the Oneidas, Onondagas, Cayugas and Senekas, and engaged never to claim the same, nor to disturb them, or any of the Six Nations, or their Indian friends residing thereon and united with them, in the free use and enjoyment thereof: Now, the Six Nations, and each of them, hereby engage that they will never claim any other lands within the boundaries of the United States; nor ever disturb the people of the United States in the free use and enjoyment thereof.

ARTICLE 5

The Seneka nation, all others of the Six Nations concurring, cede to the United States the right of making a wagon road from Fort Schlosser to Lake Erie, as far south as Buffaloe Creek; and the people of the United States shall have the free and undisturbed use of this road, for the purposes of travelling and transportation. And the Six Nations, and each of them, will forever allow to the people of the United States, a free passage through their lands, and the free use of the harbors and rivers adjoining and within their respective tracts of land, for the passing and securing of vessels and boats, and liberty to land their cargoes where necessary for their safety.

ARTICLE 6

In consideration of the peace and friendship hereby established, and of the engagements entered into by the Six Nations; and because the United States desire, with humanity and kindness, to contribute to their comfortable support; and to render the peace and friendship hereby established, strong and perpetual; the United States now deliver to the Six Nations, and the Indians of the other nations residing among and united with them, a quantity of goods of the value of ten thousand dollars. And for the same considerations, and with a view to promote the future welfare of the Six Nations, and of their Indian friends aforesaid, the United States will add the sum of three thousand dollars to the one thousand five hundred dollars, heretofore allowed them by an article ratified by the President, on the twenty-third day of April, 1792; making in the whole, four thousand five hundred dollars; which shall be expended yearly forever, in purchasing clothing, domestic animals, implements of husbandry, and other utensils suited to their circumstances, and in compensating useful artificers, who shall reside with or near them, and be employed for their benefit. The immediate application of the whole annual allowance now stipulated, to be made by the superintendent appointed by the President for the affairs of the Six Nations, and their Indian friends aforesaid.

ARTICLE 7

Lest the firm peace and friendship now established should be interrupted by the misconduct of individuals, the United States and Six Nations agree, that for injuries done by individuals on either side, no private revenge or retaliation shall take place; but, instead thereof, complaint shall be made by the party injured, to the other: By the Six Nations or any of them, to the President of the United States, or the Superintendent by him appointed:

and by the Superintendent, or other person appointed by the President, to the principal chiefs of the Six Nations, or of the nation to which the offender belongs: and such prudent measures shall then be pursued as shall be necessary to preserve our peace and friendship unbroken; until the legislature (or great council) of the United States shall make other equitable provision for the purpose.

NOTE. It is clearly understood by the parties to this treaty, that the annuity stipulated in the sixth article, is to be applied to the benefit of such of the Six Nations and of their Indian friends united with them as aforesaid, as do or shall reside within the boundaries of the United States: For the United States do not interfere with nations, tribes or families, of Indians elsewhere resident.

In witness whereof, the said Timothy Pickering, and the sachems and war chiefs of the said Six Nations, have hereto set their hands and seals.

Done at Konondaigua, in the State of New York, the eleventh day of November, in the year one thousand seven hundred and ninety-four.

[Signatures and Marks]

First Column from the Left
Witnesses:
Israel Chapin
William Shepard, Jr.
James Smedley
John Wickham
Augustus Porter
James K. Garnsey
William Ewing
Interpreters
Israel Chapin, Jr.
Horatio Jones
Joseph Smith
Jasper Parish
Henry Abeele

Second Column from the Left
Timothy Pickering
Onoyeahnee, his x mark

Konneatorteeooh, his x mark, or Handsome Lake
Tokenhyouhau, his x mark, alias Captain Key
Oneshauee, his x mark
Hendrick Aupaumut
David Neesoonhuk, his x mark
Kanatsoyh, alias Nicholas Kusik,
Sohhonteoquent, his x mark

Third Column from the Left
Ooduhtsait, his x mark
Konoohqung, his x mark
Tossonggaulolus, his x mark
John Skenendoa, his x mark
Oneatorleeooh, his x mark
Kussauwatau, his x mark
Eyootenyootauook, his x mark
Kohnyeaugong, his x mark, alias Jake Stroud
Shaguiesa, his x mark
Teeroos, his x mark, alias Captain Prantup
Sooshaoowau, his x mark
Henry Young Brant, his x mark

Fourth Column from the Left
Sonhyoowauna, his x mark, or Big Sky
Onaahhah, his x mark
Hotoshahenh, his x mark
Kaukondanaiya, his x mark
Nondiyauka, his x mark
Kossishtowau, his x mark
Oojaugenta, his x mark, or Fish Carrier
Toheonggo, his x mark
Ootaguasso, his x mark
Joonondauwaonch, his x mark
Kiyauhaonh, his x mark
Ootaujeaugenh, his x mark, or Broken Axe
Tauhoondos, his x mark, or Open the Way

Fifth Column from the Left
Twaukewasha, his x mark
Sequidongquee, his x mark, alias Little Beard

Kodjeote, his x mark, or Half Town
Kenjauaugus, his x mark, or Stinking Fish
Soonohquaukau, his x mark
Twenniyana, his x mark
Jishkaaga, his x mark, or Green Grasshopper, alias Little Billy
Tuggehshotta, his x mark
Tehongyagauna, his x mark
Tehongyoowush, his x mark
Konneyoowesot, his x mark
Tioohquottakauna, his x mark, or Woods on Fire
Taoundaudeesh, his x mark

Sixth Column from the Left
Honayawus, his x mark, alias Farmer's Brother
Soggooyawauthau, his x mark, alias Red Jacket
Konyootiayoo, his x mark
Sauhtakaongyees, his x mark, or Two Skies of a length
Ounnashattakau, his x mark
Kaungyanehquee, his x mark
Sooayoowau, his x mark
Kaujeagaonh, his x mark, or Heap of Dogs
Soonoohshoowau, his x mark
Thaoowaunias, his x mark
Soonongjoowau, his x mark
Kiantwhauka, his x mark, alias Cornplanter
Kaunehshonggoo, his x mark

INDEX

·······················

A

Adams, John Quincy, 143
Adlum, John, 96
Agents, Indian: Chapin's responsibilities
  as, 77–78
Akwesasne: founding of, 16
  gaming at, 161–162
Albany (NY), 19
  Seneca treaty at (1802), 142–143
Alcohol, 14, 107
  at Canandaigua council, 128–129
  Handsome Lake religion, 145–146
Algonquians, Canadian, 8
Algonquians, New England, 16–17
Allegany Reservation, flooding
  of, 161
Allegheny River, 32, 122–123
Allotment, policy of, 153–154
American Revolution, 25–26, 36
Andros, Sir Edmond, 16
Annuities, in Canandaigua
  treaty, 134
Aupaumut, Hendrick, 84, 88
  accompanies Kirkland, 73
  at Canandaigua council, 130
  at Miami conference, 82
  at Newtown, 68

B

Bacon, David: at Canandaigua
  council, 102
  homesickness of, 119
  Oneidas visited by, 107–108
  Wilkinson described by, 118
Bacon's Rebellion, 17
Beech Tree (Oneida), 68
Berry, Gilbert, 107
Big Bear Creek, Senecas murdered at, 62
Big Tree (Seneca): death of, 91–92, 94
  in Philadelphia, 57–62
  visits Wayne, 80
Big Tree, Treaty of (1797), 141–142
Black Cap (Onondaga), 38–40
Black Rock, 142
Blue Jacket (Shawnee), 53, 100
  St. Clair's defeat, 71
Boarding schools, 161
Bradford, William, 139
Brant, Henry Young (Mohawk), signs
  Canandaigua treaty, 130
Brant, Joseph (Mohawk), 120, 121,
  130, 156
  American overtures toward, 66
  appearance of, 20
  assists Phelps and Gorham, 35

197